SOVIET CONQUEST

Berlin 1945

Translated by

Tony Le Tissier

Featuring the memoirs of
Marshal Katukov, Marshal Babadshanian,
Marshal Chartshenko, General Poplavski,
Lieutenant-Colonel Mironov and General Dragunski

Pen & Sword
MILITARY

First published in Great Britain in 2014 by
PEN & SWORD MILITARY
an imprint of
Pen & Sword Books Ltd
47 Church Street
Barnsley
South Yorkshire
S70 2AS

ISBN 978-1-47382-110-1

A CIP catalogue record for this book is available from the British Library.

Typeset by Concept, Huddersfield, West Yorkshire.
Printed and bound in England by CPI Group (UK) Ltd, Croydon CR0 4YY.

Pen & Sword Books Ltd incorporates the imprints of Pen & Sword Archaeology,
Atlas, Aviation, Battleground, Discovery, Family History, History, Maritime,
Military, Naval, Politics, Railways, Select, Social History, Transport, True Crime,
and Claymore Press, Frontline Books, Leo Cooper, Praetorian Press,
Remember When, Seaforth Publishing and Wharncliffe.

For a complete list of Pen & Sword titles please contact
PEN & SWORD BOOKS LIMITED
47 Church Street, Barnsley, South Yorkshire, S70 2AS, England
E-mail: enquiries@pen-and-sword.co.uk
Website: www.pen-and-sword.co.uk

Contents

List of Maps and Illustrations

List of Plates

Introduction

The Second World War ended in Europe as a triumph for the Allies, but especially for the Soviets with their taking of Berlin. Of course things had not gone as smoothly as the Soviets would have liked and, as always, involved massive casualties. One would have expected a flood of Soviet literature about the Second World War, but Stalin steered away from this course by banning the publication of personal accounts and having an official Soviet history compiled by a team of historians promoting Stalin's own status as the supreme commander-in-chief. Then in 1972 Marshal Chuikov's book was published as a critical attack on Marshal Zhukov's handling of the battle for Berlin.

In fact Zhukov had blundered early in the initial stages of the battle for Berlin. When Stalin had taunted him with his lack of success in contrast to his rival Marshal Koniev's crossing of the Neisse River to the south, Zhukov's reaction had been to order his tank armies into the Seelow Heights battle, contrary to the original plan of reserving them for the breakthrough to Berlin once these forward German positions had been destroyed. The result was complete confusion on the cramped battlefield as the tanks belatedly tried to intervene; instead of the anticipated one-day breakthrough battle, it took Zhukov's 1st Byelorussian Front four whole days and enormous numbers of casualties to complete this first stage. The follow through to Berlin consequently involved considerable readjustment to the plan of battle as the exhausted infantry struggled to keep up with the advancing armour.

Meanwhile, unknown to Zhukov, Stalin had permitted Koniev to intrude on the Berlin battlefield with his 3rd and 4th Guards Tank Armies. Stalin further banned the Red Air Force from informing Zhukov of Koniev's participation, while the latter urged his forces to beat his rival into Berlin.

Nevertheless it was the 2nd Guards Tank Army of Zhukov's Front that first broke into the eastern suburbs of Berlin on the morning of 21 April, closely followed that evening by the scouts of the 3rd Guards

Tank Army. Next day Koniev ordered the 3rd Guards Tank Army to prepare to assault across the Teltow Canal, which formed part of the city's southern boundary, on the morning of the 24th, adding considerable artillery and air support to the operation. Allegedly Zhukov did not learn of the presence of Koniev's troops until the evening of that day, when he had officers sent to confirm who and what was involved and what their objectives were.

Once both Fronts were engaged within the city, Stalin was obliged to draw and adjust their boundaries as the fighting continued. However, when Koniev launched a massive attack on the morning of the 28th, with the aim of occupying the Tiergarten, it was soon discovered that his troops were firing into the rear of Chuikov's troops, occupying an area already taken. It was Koniev's turn to be humiliated. Mortified, he left the 3rd Guards Tank Army to continue the battle on a modified line of advance, while Zhukov went on to capture the prestigious goal of the Reichstag.

The fall of Berlin brought Zhukov his third gold star as a Hero of the Soviet Union, an honour Stalin could not deny him. Zhukov represented the Soviet Union at the surrender ceremony conducted at Karlshorst on 8 May, with his co-signatory Air Chief Marshal Sir Arthur Tedder of the UK and witnesses General Carl Spaatz of the US Strategic Air Force and General Jean de Lattre de Tassigny of the 1st French Army. The reviewing officer at the victory parade on Red Square should have been Stalin as commander-in-chief, but Zhukov later learned that Stalin had been unable to control the magnificent horse selected for the role, so Zhukov was given the task.

Later in the year Stalin's henchman, Viktor Abakumov, appeared in the Soviet Zone of Germany and started arresting members of Zhukov's staff – a distinctive sign of Stalin's lack of favour for his deputy. Shortly afterwards Stalin accused Zhukov, in his absence, of claiming the credit for Red Army victories during the war and belittling the role of the Stavka, the Soviet high command.

In March 1946 Zhukov was recalled to Moscow and appointed Commander-in-Chief of the Ground Forces, but promptly came into conflict with Bulganin, the First Deputy Commissar for Defence, who blocked Zhukov's access to Stalin. From then on, Zhukov was gradually stripped of all his offices and appointments. When Stalin died in March 1953, his successor, Nikita Khrushchev, reinstated Zhukov as Minister of Defence and in 1956 had Zhukov awarded his fourth star as Hero of the Soviet Union on his 60th birthday, but a year later relieved him of all his duties with the accusation of being inclined to adventurism in the Soviet Union's foreign policy and overall lacking in the Party spirit.

Deprived of his position as a member of the Presidium and the Central Committee and as Minister of Defence, Zhukov withdrew to the dacha outside Moscow that Stalin had given him for life during the war. *Pravda* then published an article by Marshal Koniev that amounted to a scathing attack on Zhukov's role both during the war and as Minister of Defence. In March 1958 Zhukov was further humiliated by his contrived retirement as a Marshal of the Soviet Union; this was an unprecedented step, for marshals were normally transferred to the Group of Inspectors, whose occasional duties justified the continuation of their active duty perquisites, such as an aide-de-camp and a chauffeur-driven car. Zhukov was now fair game for his old antagonists, and in March 1964 Marshal Chuikov attacked Zhukov for not going on to take Berlin in February 1945, his book *The End of the Third Reich* being the first of the senior commanders' memoirs allowed to be published after the war.

In 1965, under the Brezhnev regime, Zhukov was invited to attend a celebration of the twentieth anniversary of the victory over Germany, at which he received a great ovation. The next day he joined his old colleagues in reviewing the victory parade from the top of Lenin's mausoleum.

Stalin's clampdown on personal accounts of experiences in the Second World War continued long after his death in 1953, and it was only in 1967 that that of Marshal Chuikov became to be the first to be published, even then intended as a snub to Zhukov, whose attempts to publish his own account had been repeatedly turned down.

Other accounts, including Zhukov's at last in 1974, then followed, adding some light to the otherwise strictly Communist Party conformist theme.

Despite the length of this introduction, which I believe to be necessary for the overall comprehension of the reader, this book has been produced with a view to providing some interesting details and a wider view of the final battle for Berlin in 1945. It consists of the translations of six personal accounts taken from the East German editions of the original Soviet publications, omitting those of Marshals Chuikov, Koniev and Zhukov, whose autobiographies have long been available in the English language.

Chapter 1

Spearhead

By Marshal of Tank Troops
Michael Yefimovitch Katukov

When Marshal Zhukov prepared his 1st Byelorussian Front for the battle of Berlin, Katukov was the colonel-general commanding the 1st Guards Tank Army. He already had considerable experience of armoured warfare, having been involved in the defence of Moscow, the battle of Kursk and the consequent clearance of the Ukraine, Poland and Eastern Pomerania.

* * *

Our army received new vehicles before the storming of Berlin. Apart from that the 11th Tank Corps under General Yushtchuk was attached to us, so that at the beginning of the Berlin operation we had over 854 fit for action. We had not had such a large number of tanks and self-propelled guns throughout the whole war.

As always when preparing for an important operation, the commanders of the brigades conducted daily exercises with officers and soldiers so that above all the cooperation between tanks and self-propelled guns with the infantry, artillery and engineers in attacks on individual strongpoints as well as in street fighting worked well. In this our previous experience was useful.

I worked on exact instructions for the commitment of assault detachments and groups in the streets of Berlin. Great help came from the topographers at Front Headquarters, who made several scale models of the city, of which we obtained one. All members of the assault team – tank troops, infantry and gunners – practised on this model. They pursued every step of their future progress in the streets of the German capital and detected the places where danger especially threatened. Additionally we concentrated on the radio communications and other factors of the forthcoming fighting in the suburbs and centre of Berlin.

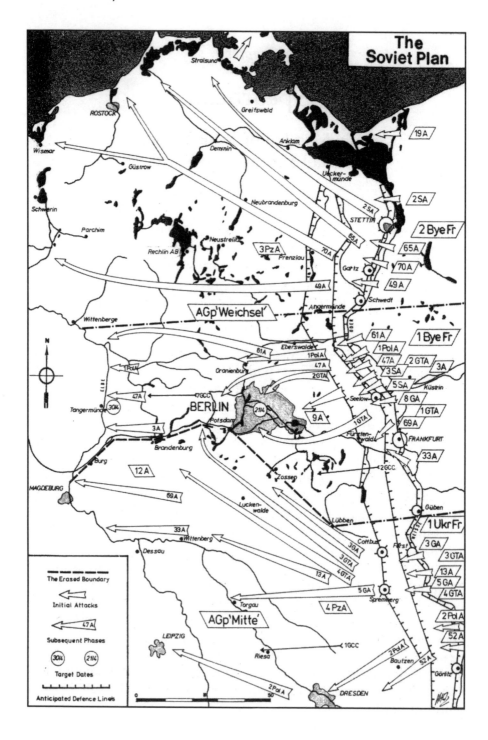

The most burdened in the preparations for the Berlin operation were the army's political organs, which above all had to deal with the new comrades. At meetings in all the detachments, veterans spoke to the young soldiers about the army's outstanding traditions. We organised political education in the units, meetings for young soldiers with experienced fighters, masters of their skills. Political workers organised performances and speeches on Lenin's 75th birthday.

On the 5th April the army's commander-in-chief's Front staff, the members of the Council of War, the artillery commanders as well as the corps commanders, met for a detailed report on the enemy and to allocate specific tasks to each unit.

While we were fighting in Pomerania, the Anglo-American troops had pushed east without forcing the sixty German divisions opposing them to resist. Although the western front of Fascist Germany had collapsed, the Fascists had not transferred a single division from the Soviet–German front. On the contrary, as our reconnaissance at the end of March/beginning of April had established, they had even transferred nine divisions from the western front to the east, so that now 214 German divisions were in action on the Soviet–German front.

For the defence of Berlin – connected with the Army Groups *Weichsel* and *Mitte* – were altogether 48 infantry, 4 Panzer and 10 motorised divisions, as well as a large number of independent brigades, regiments and various reinforcement elements. Altogether defending the approaches to Berlin and the capital were about 1,000,000 men with some 10,000 guns and mortars, 1,500 tanks and self-propelled guns and 2,200 aircraft. The last battles would be severe.

Our troops facing Berlin had over 6,200 tanks and self-propelled guns, over 42,000 guns and mortars with calibres of 76 millimetres and over, and also more than 2.5 million men. 270 guns per kilometre were concentrated on the main line of attack.

A war game on maps and a model of Berlin made it clear to us that the terrain with its partly swampy rivers, brooks, canals and lakes would not only tie down the attacking troops but would wear them out.

There was yet another difficulty for the tank troops, for behind the swampy Oder depression rose the Seelow Heights, as well as a deeply cut railway line running from north to south, yet another serious obstacle.

The enemy had made this area suitable for the coming fighting with great expenditure on numerous concrete pillboxes or earth and wooden bunkers. The whole area and the city itself formed a thorough defensive zone. The enemy's first defensive positions lay between the Oder and the Seelow Heights, against which we would have to attack the Seelow Heights with our main forces.

A glimpse at the model and the maps showed that in this terrain the variants of a deep breakthrough like those between the Vistula and the Oder could not be repeated. The conditions for a wide tank manoeuvre were lacking. We could only advance step by step to break through the enemy defences with desperate fighting. But the victories our troops had had in previous battles had given us much confidence. No one doubted that we would sweep aside all the fortifications on the way to Berlin.

At the conference that followed the war game Marshal Zhukov decorated me with my second star of 'Hero of the Soviet Union' for my participation in the Vistula–Oder Operation. At the Front Headquarters I discovered that Gussakovski had also become a 'Hero of the Soviet Union' for the second time. Colonel Semliakov and Lieutenant-Colonel Mussatov were awarded the same title for the first time for undertaking the thrust on Gotenhafen with their troops, thus ensuring the success of the 2nd Byelorussian Front's operation.

In accordance with a directive of the Front's Council of War of the 12th April we had to advance to the Küstrin bridgehead on the far side of the Oder and prepare ourselves for insertion into a breach made by Colonel-General Chuikov's 8th Guards Army. North of us Bogdanov's 2nd Guards Tank Army would attack in the area Kalenzig–Küstrin. The 5th Shock Army had first to break through the defences for them.

The Front Headquarters' plan foresaw us using the breakthrough as soon as the 8th Guards Army reached the line Seelow–Dolgelin–Alt Mahlisch, developing the attack in a westerly direction and reaching the eastern suburbs of Berlin on the second day of the operation. Further, a thrust by the army to the southwest was planned to go round the German capital from the south and take its southern and south-westerly suburbs.

The total depth of the Front's operation was about 160 kilometres; for the 1st and 2nd Guards Tank Armies at most 80 to 90 kilometres each, with the taking of the southern and south-westerly suburbs their goal. The average speed of advance should be 35 to 37 kilometres a day.

According to the Front directive, the main task of the tank armies was clearly the battle for Berlin. With it the possibility of manoeuvre, especially for our army, was limited from the start. From our previous experience all attempts to use tanks in operational depth in built-up areas, particularly large ones, were a lost cause.

After the war many historians concerned themselves with the question whether the high command of the 1st Byelorussian Front had handled things correctly, as it sent the two tank armies against the still-not-tied-down defences in the Seelow Heights area and then finally obliged them to fight in the streets of Berlin.

Yes, an unusual role fell to both the tank armies in the battle for Berlin. They were also unable to separate themselves from the infantry and attain their operational depth. But does that mean that the tank armies were not used properly? One can only assess the selected decision of the high command of the 1st Byelorussian Front correctly if one takes into consideration the conditions and the strategic aim.

According to the decision of the governing heads of the Allied Powers at the conference at Yalta, Berlin belonged to the Red Army's operational area. But already in April 1945 our high command had learnt from the brisk activity of reactionary circles in the USA and Great Britain that they planned to forestall us and let Anglo-American troops take Berlin.

The Soviet Union on its side feared the conclusion of a separate agreement by the Allies with the Fascist government, which would be contrary to unconditional surrender and would result in an unacceptable post-war situation in Europe. And as documents that were published after the war show, these fears were real. Thus the Soviet government decided to expedite the taking of Berlin to prevent a forced separate agreement.

The attention of our headquarters in the planning of the Berlin operation focused on speed and fierceness of attack to prevent the Fascist high command from manoeuvring its forces. The troops committed against Berlin had the high historical task of putting an end to this last bastion of Fascism. Under these historical conditions the commitment of the 1st and 2nd Guards Tank Armies in the battle of Berlin by the 1st Byelorussian Front was not only proper but also historically justified.

* * *

Zhukov's attack on the Seelow Heights proved to be an unusually poor performance by a man with so many victories to his credit, being little short of a disaster. There were serious defects in the planning, with the unrehearsed use of searchlights in action (intended to increase the hours of daylight to work in), and the failure to identify the strength of the German defences. The worst fault, however, and the point most criticised by Chuikov in the first military account to be approved for publication over ten years later, was the premature introduction of his two tank armies when he was brought under pressure by Stalin for failing to meet his immediate objectives. The battle cost him the equivalent of a tank army in armour and an admitted 33,000 killed. Not only did this battle leave his armies exhausted, it made necessary a hasty revision of his plans for the taking of Berlin.

Zhukov's slow progress had enabled Koniev to get his own two tank armies to Potsdam, with the southern suburbs of Berlin ahead of them, a fact that an angry Zhukov found incredible. Koniev then left the rest of his army group to his chief of staff to manage while he concentrated on the heavily reinforced 3rd Guards Tank Army's thrust for the Reichstag, the acknowledged victor's prize. He was only thwarted in his aim by Chuikov having a shorter route to take, so being able to cross the inter-Front boundary in his path. In this deadly game Stalin kept both his marshals unaware of the other's actions, so it was only when Koniev's troops discovered they were attacking Chuikov's rear that he broke off the action, humiliated in his turn.

*   *   *

According to the order of the Front high command, the 1st Guards Tank Army was to advance during the night of the 16th April into the Alt Mahlisch–Dolgelin–Seelow sector of the bridgehead in which the 8th Guards Army was located.

For one last time I visited the camouflaged units and elements of our army in the woods on the right bank of the Oder with Popiel and Shalin. At short notice our sappers had set up a proper settlement here with little wooden barracks. The political workers had assembled the troops in clearings for political instruction. Mechanics were checking the readiness of the tanks for battle.

Finally I checked over Shalin's plan for the crossing of the troops and their deployment on the west bank. Then I drove with Nikitin across to the bridgehead. The torn-up road was strewn with poplars. Explosions were still going on. Starlings, startled by the noise, flew screaming over the tops of the trees. Roadside ditches and shell craters stood full of water. Although the hard rules of war seemed to have overcome everything, nature continued its own, independent life that demanded its rights in its own territory.

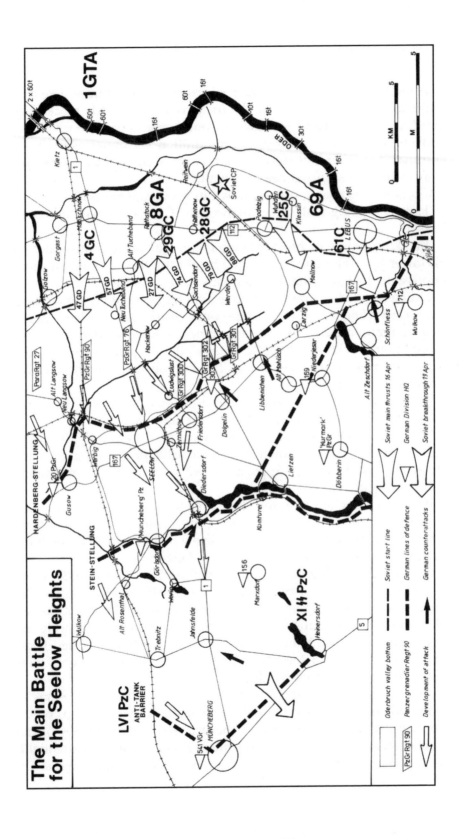

The Main Battle
for the Seelow Heights

In the bridgehead on the Oder swarmed a great throng like that some time ago on the Vistula. The roads were completely blocked by the 8th Guards Army. Everywhere one came across trenches and bunkers. Equipment or boxes of ammunition lay under every bush. Fortunately our aircraft ruled the air. A massive blow by Fascist aircraft would have caused heavy casualties.

Chuikov was pacing up and down in his command post.

'How is it going with the breakthrough? Can you make it in time?' I asked.

'Breakthrough here, breakthrough there.' The army commander bit his lower lip. 'Taking these damned heights on the move is just about impossible. Just see what the Germans have constructed.'

Chuikov rolled out on the table several large aerial photographs of the Seelow Heights, on which one could clearly see the dense net of rifle, communication and anti-tank trenches. Rows of dark spots we could identify without difficulty as tank pits, steep slopes and places. Especially numerous were the gullies cutting through the Heights from east to west.

'Yes, it won't be easy to take these heights,' I agreed. 'Until the infantry reach the crest, the tanks can do nothing.'

'It's particularly difficult,' Chuikov went on concernedly, 'we can't see the positions from down here. Our artillery can't conduct any aimed fire. And hitting the positions with only anti-aircraft gunfire will be difficult.'

It had been obvious to us for a long time that these last battles would be difficult, and the talk with the Army commander-in-chief reinforced me in this opinion. The enemy knew that the fate of Berlin hung from the beginning on the battle on the Oder.

On the night leading to the 16th April the army crossed under cover of darkness to the west bank and pressed itself literally into its allocated sector of the bridgehead. In accordance with Marshal Zhukov's plan, the attack was due to begin at night. The Front commander-in-chief had decided to blind the enemy with searchlights. I had taken part in an exercise a few days before when the searchlights were tested. It was an impressive display.

At 0500 hours on the 16th April the ear-splitting explosions of thousands of guns began the last decisive attack by our troops on the German capital. The droning in the heavens of the engines of our bombers was ceaseless. After the artillery preparation, 140 searchlights were switched on. The Oder valley lay under a bluish light. The painful din of thousands of exploding shells and aircraft bombs was so dense that even the strong anti-aircraft searchlights could not get through.

Chuikov's infantry went into the attack. They took the first positions across no-man's-land quickly, but as the divisions approached the second strip the heavy fire caused their progress to slow down. The breakthrough did not succeed.

Chuikov ordered another artillery preparation. Like arrows the shots of the *Katiushas* joined in, the wave of fire rolling over the heights. Immediately afterwards the infantry and tanks attacked, our bombers and fighters joining in.

The attackers came under heavy fire from the heights. Only towards Dolgelin were the infantry able to force their way into the second line of defence. But the enemy deployed a fresh motorised division, the *Kurkmark*, out of his reserves and pushed our infantry back into the valley.

Everywhere the enemy was conducting a bitter resistance. As our air reconnaissance established, he was bringing his second echelon into the battle. Apart from this, two motorised divisions were approaching the Seelow Heights on our main line of attack, and two further divisions were on the march from the Schwedt area.

'It's hardly believable. The enemy is sending reserves into action during the fight for the second line of defence,' commented Shalin on the situation. 'There, look.' He passed me a leaflet. It was an appeal by the commander of an SS tank corps to his soldiers. It said that the 'beloved Führer' had declared on the 12th April that Germany now had, as never before, a real chance to stop the advance of the Red Army, that Germany had vast amounts of artillery and tanks at its disposal. All requirements had been met for the coming battle of Titans on the Oder that would bring about a change in the war.

A call over the radio telephone line interrupted our talk. I recognised the well-known voice of the Front commander. He gave the surprising order that before the enemy resistance had been completely broken, the 1st Guards Tank Army was to enter the battle and complete the breakthrough of the tactical defence zone with the 8th Guards Army.

I was not enchanted with the idea of setting our vehicles against the still unsuppressed nests of fire, although I saw that the marshal could not decide otherwise under the circumstances. After nine hours of ceaseless attacks Chuikov had only been able to penetrate a few sections of the second line of defence. The whole of the Front's attack operation was threatening to collapse. Apart from this it would be to our advantage if the enemy brought his reserves from Berlin up into the open ground where one could defeat them more easily on the Seelow Heights than in the city's streets.

I immediately ordered all three corps to deploy in the bridgehead. I sent the 11th Tank Corps under General Yushtchuk to the right wing, in the centre [was] the 11th Guards Tank Corps under Colonel Babadshanian, and on the left wing General Dremov's 8th Mechanised Guards Corps. However, the manoeuvrability of the tanks was so limited by the narrowness of the bridgehead, the numerous ditches and minefields, that it was not possible to get the army's main forces into action simultaneously.

From my observation post I could see Babadshanian's tanks manoeuvring between shell holes and ditches before they could attack. As they could not overcome the steep slopes of the Seelow Heights, they had to seek the narrow ways through under especially heavy fire.

The remainder of the day brought no happy news. With great difficulty and heavy losses the tank troops had bitten into the defences, but were unable to push forward from positions occupied by the infantry. The rifle divisions operating closely with the tank corps also had a hard time of it.

I was working with my staff in a narrow rifle trench. The saturated ground splashed under my feet. Apart from Shalin, I met Sobolev, the chief scout.

'How's it going for the enemy?' I asked.

'They are defending themselves like the devil. One division is holding on the average a 5 kilometre wide sector. Thus a battalion has only 800 metres of front.'

'That's quite a lot. Formerly the Fascists usually defended sectors of 15 kilometres. And how many reserves have you established?'

'Until now eight divisions, of which five are motorised and one armoured. Apart from that there are about 200 *Volkssturm* battalions in Berlin, many anti-aircraft gun elements and various special units.'

With good cover they were actually in a position to conduct a serious defence. But how could we avoid unnecessary losses? This question occupied the whole of my time.

Shalin unfolded an aerial photograph and a large-scale map. It seemed to me that the ground north of Seelow was more suitable for tanks and that the defence there was less than that on the Heights.

'Certainly,' agreed Shalin. 'To attack a sector like the present one makes less sense.'

'One must give the units on the right flank more artillery and air support, and break through in that direction. If that works we can commit the whole army.'

It was only at the end of the 17th April that Babadshanian reported that his brigades had completed the breakthrough of the second line of defence with the cooperation of the infantry, and had pushed on. Over the radio I ordered Dremov to leave behind a brigade as security, but to send his main forces through the breach created by Babadshanian and to support him in the development of the success. I also sent Boiko's 64th Guards Tank Brigade into the same breach with two self-propelled artillery regiments and other units.

But the enemy deployed fresh forces into the threatened area from the left flank. Babadshanian fell into a difficult situation, as he now had to repel counterattacks on his left flank on top of meeting frontal assaults. I reinforced Boiko's brigade with artillery as well as a mortar unit, and charged him with repelling the attacks on his left wing with infantry and tanks. I was certain that this energetic and resourceful commander would fulfil his task. In fact he reliably secured Babadshanian's flanks and caused the enemy attack to fail.

The 11th Guards Tank Corps commanded by General Yushtchuk was able to advance somewhat faster, its units being able to penetrate 10 kilometres into this area against a considerably weaker defence. In the same area General Berzarin's 5th Shock Army was able to advance about 10 kilometres further north.

On the 18th April the fighting for the Seelow Heights reached its crisis. The enemy kept throwing in new divisions, *Volkssturm* units and tank-hunting commandos of the Hitler Youth. Anti-aircraft gun batteries on the tanks' line of advance caused considerable difficulties. With the enemy literally climbing out of his deep trenches, having silenced his concrete firing positions as well as fixed tank turrets and dug-in tanks, our tank troops advanced at the most only 4 kilometres per day on the 17th and 18th April.

I had General Krupski, commander of the air corps, in my command post constantly with me. As soon as a commander reported that in this or that map square he had come across a strong defensive position, I immediately informed the general. He then had his pilots fly to the hotly disputed point. These air strikes were effective. That our troops were able to break through the defences on the Seelow Heights in one or two days was without doubt Krupski's airmen's greatest service. Together with the ground troops, they smashed breaches in the mighty defensive system.

Meanwhile the units of the 1st Guards Tank Army pushed forward unstoppably in close cooperation with General Chuikov. Babadshanian's corps going around Seelow from the north helped the infantry to clear the enemy out of the town on the evening of the 17th April. Our headquarters then deployed to the edge of the town. The main and side streets were blocked with vehicles, tanks and self-propelled artillery. The enemy artillery still shelled the town and there were air battles, but Seelow was in our hands. As Babadshanian reported, there was some hard fighting at Müncheberg, halfway between Seelow and Berlin. The SS people fought despairingly, the town changing hands three times. Members of the motorcycle battalion commanded by Lieutenant Baikov captured thirty-eight intact aircraft on the airfield near Müncheberg.

During the course of the first four days of the attack the 1st and 2nd Guards Tank Armies were engaged primarily in the immediate support of the infantry. Today, now that all the details of the fighting for the Seelow Heights are known, one knows that the Front command made a series of errors, particularly in the underestimation of the strength of the Seelow Heights' two defensive strips. During the course of our attack we detected that the enemy had put his main effort into the defence of the Seelow Heights. Because of this the Fascist high command had withdrawn a large part of its forces and resources from the forward strips in this area. Consequently, the Front's troops, instead of thrusting forward, had to work their way slowly through the defensive positions.

At the same time our thrust forward was complicated because the left flank remained open as our troops got nearer to Berlin. To our left, moreover, was the strong enemy group at Frankfurt an der Oder. Shalin had reported having received from the reconnaissance the alarming report that the Fascists had concentrated about 100,000 men near Frankfurt, thus having considerable forces for an attack on our flanks.

We had vainly hoped that the advancing troops of the 1st Ukrainian Front would hit the Frankfurt group further left of the 1st Byelorussian Front. However, they had not yet reached the area, so Dremov had to split his forces. While his brigades pressed forward as before on Berlin's outer defensive ring, they constantly had to fight off attacks

from the flanks. The enemy fought so bitterly that the elements that
we had committed to the development of the thrust on Berlin had to
be deployed on the left flank and brought into the battle. In doing so
the forces of the 1st Guards Tank Army were weakened because of the
11th Guards Tank Corps having to support the 5th Shock Army after
the breakthrough.

The counterattack eased off. If this continued, an appreciable thrust
by the Mechanised Corps could not be counted on. Something must
have happened. I briefed Zhukov on the situation by telephone and
asked him to send us any kind of troops to cover our left flank and
release Dremov's corps. Zhukov did not reply immediately. Apparently he was looking for a solution: 'There is a cavalry corps in my
reserves. I will give the order immediately. The cavalry will come to
you. And another thing: Guard your flanks firmly on your advance.
Otherwise it will go badly not only for your army but for the rest of the
Front's troops.'

The cavalry corps did not keep us waiting long. A little later it
relieved the flanks of the engaged brigades of the Mechanised Corps
and markedly improved their situation. The troops of the 1st Ukrainian
Front were approaching the outer defensive ring of Berlin with us, so
that we were able to make contact with the advancing 3rd Guards
Tank Army of General Rybalko.

On the evening of the 20th April Army Headquarters received the
following telephone message from the Front Commander:

Katukov, Popiel!
To the 1st Guards Tank Army falls the historic task of being the
first into Berlin and hoisting the banner of victory. I task you
personally with its fulfilment. Send the best brigade from each
corps to Berlin and give them the task of breaking through the city
boundary at the latest by 0400 hours on the 21st April.
                                        Zhukov, Telegin.

As ordered, I entrusted the best brigades of our army, the 1st and the
44th, with this task. The way to the German capital led through woods
on the one road flanked by a chain of lakes. In the burning woods the
smoke made breathing and visibility difficult. Everywhere lurked
carefully camouflaged guns and hidden soldiers with *Panzerfausts*.
Marching infantry at the head of the brigades destroyed these
obstacles, finally opening the way to Berlin for the tanks.

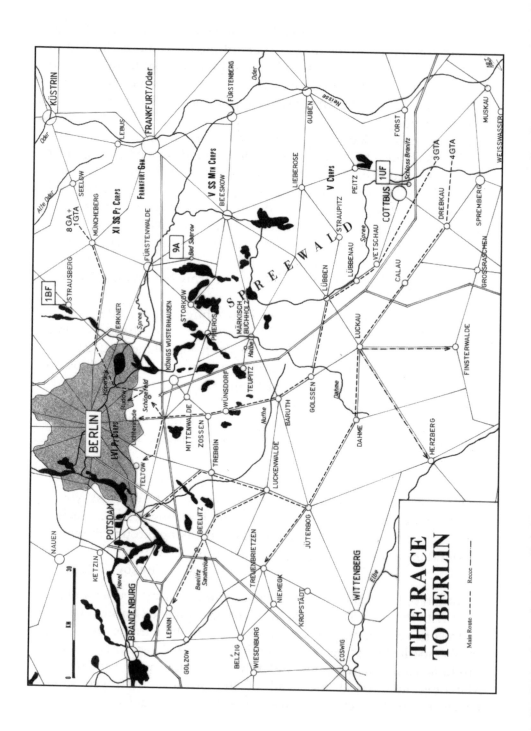

THE RACE
TO BERLIN

Main Route ---- Recce ----

In the night leading to the 21st April the brigades covered 25 kilometres via Erkner and opened the battle for the outer defensive ring of the German capital. Babadshanian's corps went round Karlshorst, while Dremov thrust into Köpenick with Chuikov's infantry. Simultaneously Bogdanov's tank-men and Bersarin's infantry broke through the northern suburbs.

During the fighting for Erkner, Babadshanian reported by telephone: 'I have some Japanese here, Comrade Commander-in-Chief.'

'What kind of Japanese, then? Where do they come from?' I asked, not understanding.

'They are apparently diplomats from the Japanese Embassy in Berlin.'

'Bring them here.'

One hour later the whole diplomatic mission appeared at my command post, repeatedly bowing and smiling. From their appearance they were uncertain whether we would receive them in a friendly manner. Added to this was the anxiety that they had felt in crossing the front line. One diplomat, a man of medium size, declared in painful Russian that they were members of the Japanese Embassy and had decided to seek protection and assistance from the Russian high command.

'We want to go back to our home country,' he concluded.

Although I was not inclined to be helpful to representatives of a country allied to our enemy, I saw that to avoid diplomatic complications I was obliged to provide a means of transport for these refugees and send them on to the Front Headquarters.

During the fighting in Berlin later I experienced a further 'diplomatic' incident. Gussakovski's brigade had broken through cellars and passages to a building from which German machine-gunners were firing. The tank-men came across cases of Brambach mineral water in the cellars of these buildings. Hot and thirsty from the fighting, they emptied several bottles. As it later transpired, this mineral water belonged to the embassy of a neutral state, whose employees had nothing better to do than write us a formal letter of protest. I could not understand these diplomats that would not even allow our soldiers some bottles of mineral water while they were risking their lives in the battle against the Fascists.

The fighting flared up on the German capital's outer defensive ring. We had to overcome a whole system of fire nests, bunkers, obstacles, barricades and booby traps in a storm of fire. We passed minefields and barricades in an area in which the enemy had prepared every building for defence.

Our sappers had it particularly difficult. As the Fascists had destroyed all the bridges in their retreat, we were obliged to construct crossing facilities over numerous rivers, lakes and canals.

But nothing could shatter the attacking spirit of our soldiers. All attempts by the Fascists to scare them remained unsuccessful, as also did this leaflet: 'You are not far from Berlin, but you will never enter our capital. Berlin has 600,000 buildings and every one of them is a fortress that will become your grave.' But the wind scattered the leaflets and, as every day passed under the mighty blows from our troops, the alleged claim that Berlin was unobtainable was further reduced.

How many Soviet soldiers had dreamed that the war would end in Berlin, and for how many was this dream unfulfilled! But now the Reich capital was within reach. The distances on the kilometre stones and the signposts became ever less. At a crossroads I read, hastily written in chalk, 'To the Reichstag 15 km.' But what kilometres!

In Berlin there were over 500 strongpoints in various buildings. They covered themselves mutually with fire and were connected by passages to points of resistance, defensive positions, strips and sectors. We virtually had to take a fortress with 300,000 defenders. Elite Fascist units and a Hitler fanatic element of the population were defending the city. Berlin then embodied for us Fascism in all its bestiality. Our soldiers and officers were only animated by one wish: to put an end to this once and for all, that which had inflicted so much pain on our people.

As was reported to me, many of the lightly wounded were secretly creeping away from the field hospitals in order to participate in the last of the fighting. I understood them only too well. Who did not want to participate in the storm on the German capital?

I worked my way up to Köpenick with an operational team late at night. The enemy was shelling this part of the city ceaselessly to prevent a concentration by our troops. Before us lay the last water obstacle: the Spree River. Would the scouts be able to take the bridge in time? On the 23rd April Dremov's command post was in the cellar of a half bombed-out house right on the bank of the Spree. The corps commander looked tired. He reported that the bridge had been blown. A newly formed special detachment had forced the river in order to cover the sappers constructing a crossing point.

'Now we want to shell the opposite bank.' he went on. 'The Fascists over there are unbelievably stubborn, firing with everything they have got. One can hardly lift one's nose, those devils are so persistent – presumably SS.'

Dremov went to the field telephone and exchanged a few words with a gunner. Shortly afterwards the explosions increased. I went up to one of the cellar windows. On the opposite bank walls were collapsing in clouds of dust. There were fires everywhere and a thick cloud of smoke was climbing into the sky. The explosions left Dremov unmoved. He displayed no feelings but fought soberly and without risks. For him the war was an everyday matter and even the unbelievable performance of his Guardsmen he reported as if it was the most normal thing in the world.

Covered in dust and breathless, a lieutenant burst into the cellar. Uncertain as to whom he should report, he looked from Dremov to me.

'Comrade Commander-in-Chief,' he said finally, 'allow me ...?'

'OK. Go on.'

'The 19th Mechanised Guards Brigade has forced the Spree.'

Dremov and I looked at each other.

'Where and at what point?' I asked.

'Over the railway bridge a bit north of Adlershof.'

That was good news. I immediately ordered part of the corps to set off for the railway bridge, the remainder to cross by the bridge that the sappers had built. In this way almost all the units of the 1st Guards Tank Army could cross the Spree and reach the Schöneweide–Adlershof area.

'The bridge will be ready in two or three hours and we can get over,' assured Dremov.

During the night of the 24th April the 1st Guards Tank and 8th Guards Armies crossed the Spree, reached the Adlershof–Bohnsdorf area and occupied favourable positions for their further attack on the city centre from the southeast. Then we could make contact with the 1st Ukrainian Front's 3rd Guards Tank Army.

So began the street fighting in Berlin. As mentioned, we had previously attacked in Chuikov's army's sector. He had been put in overall charge by Zhukov. As the situation within the city was now different, I asked the Marshal to allocate the 1st Guards Tank Army its own line of attack. Zhukov agreed, but ordered that I hand over the 64th Independent Guards Tank Brigade and the heavy self-propelled

artillery to the 8th Guards Army. They remained with the 8th Guards
Army until the capitulation of Berlin.

Our attack axis led to Wilhelmstrasse, running parallel to the
Tiergarten, not far from the Reichs Chancellery and the Reichstag.

A great obstacle for us were the *Panzerfaust* men shooting our tanks
into flames from their secure hiding places in the sewers and cellars.
But the Fascists had not reckoned on these weapons being turned
against their originators. During the East Pomeranian operation we
had captured 4,500 *Panzerfausts*, of which about 1,500 had been used
on exercise in the preparation for Operation Berlin. The troops learned
how to use them in assault teams. We had kept back the remaining
3,000 *Panzerfausts* for the fighting in Berlin. Now we put these weapons
to use successfully in the streets of Berlin. While machine-pistol
soldiers could not be smoked out of buildings themselves, the Red
Army soldiers worked on the enemy with their *Panzerfausts* and set the
buildings on fire with several shots. Then our guardsmen attacked.

The majority of the important enemy strongpoints were found in
big, old buildings whose masonry withstood the tank guns and artillery. When I asked Marshal Zhukov for stronger artillery to deal with
these apparently indestructible buildings, he sent me a detachment of
305 millimetre guns. In former times these were known as the 12-inch
siege artillery.

When these vast guns went into action the situation improved
immediately. One or two 305 millimetre shells were sufficient to
destroy an old building and bury the occupants under the rubble.

Berlin was bitterly defended. Every building received us with a hail
of fire. Not only the tank-men and the infantry had it difficult, but also
the staff officers in their command posts, while the corps and brigade
commanders following their troops on foot were attacked time and
time again. Again and again Fascists appeared out of side streets, even
in apparently cleared streets, armed with submachine-guns and
Panzerfausts. Quite often they came under the fire of German artillery
or were attacked from the air.

On the 23rd April I received the order from Marshal Zhukov to form
a special team for the taking of the Adlershof and Tempelhof airfields.
As our reconnaissance had reported, the private aircraft of the Fascist
high command and the Nazi party, including also Hitler's aircraft,
were located here ready for flight. To take Adlershof did not appear
too difficult, as it was about 4 kilometres from the front line on our line
of attack. It was more difficult to work our way forward to Tempelhof

airfield as it was practically in the centre of the city, only a few kilo-metres from the Reichs Chancellery.

Dremov, whom I consulted, suggested I delegate Major Grafov's independent reconnaissance battalion to take Adlershof. The battal-ion commander had recently distinguished himself in the fighting at Erkner and had been recommended for decoration as a Hero of the Soviet Union. I knew the major as a bold soldier and approved Dremov's suggestion.

The most difficult part of the task, the breakthrough to Tempelhof and the conquest of the airfield, was voluntarily taken over by the 23-year-old major and battalion commander V.A. Zhukov, a veteran of the 1st Guards Tank Brigade, who had repeatedly participated in reconnaissance raids and proved himself a resourceful commander. The reconnaissance teams would destroy aircraft found on the ground and hold the position until the main forces arrived. We reckoned that in the confusion of battle and under cover of darkness the tank soldiers and riflemen would be able to get there unnoticed, at least for part of the way. The scouts then studied the city map.

At about 0100 hours our sappers, protected by heavy artillery fire, erected a crossing point over the Spree. The first to cross was Grafov's battalion. An hour later the scouts reached their goal safe and sound, surprised Adlershof airfield and destroyed seventy aircraft. When the battalion then came under enemy fire and was engaged by superior forces, Temnik's and Anfimov's brigades came to their help.

The situation was more difficult for Major Zhukov. He led his men to the Teltow Canal, crossed it fighting and reached the airfield from the southern side. Meanwhile Grafov had also got close to the airfield. Once both battalions had united on the airfield, the enemy had also become aware and sent tanks and motorised infantry against them. For two whole days the reconnaissance teams repelled numerous attacks by overwhelming forces on the airfield until our troops came to their rescue. Zhukov lost his life in this action.

We tore the enemy out of one suburb after another. At 1030 hours on the 24th April the following radio message was received from the commander of the motorcycle regiment, Mussatov: 'Have reached the suburb of Teltow. Have met Rybalko's tank troops. Mussatov.'

I hastened to pass on this pleasing news to the Front commander-in-chief.

'Are you sure?' he said.

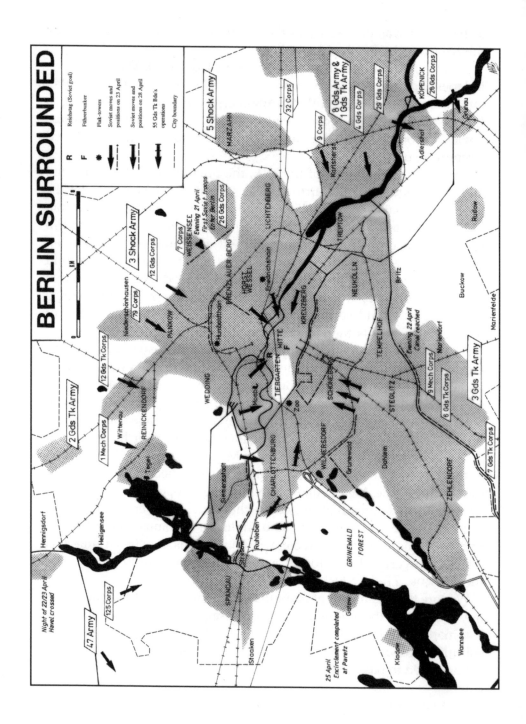

'I have even received a radio message from our regimental commander.'

'Check the information immediately on the spot.'

I despatched several staff officers to the given area. They not only confirmed Mussatov's message but brought back further good news. Advance detachments of General Leliushenko's 4th Guards Tank Army had already approached Potsdam and were in contact with our 47th Army and 2nd Guards Tank Army. Thus both Fronts, the 1st Byelorussian and the 1st Ukrainian, were closing the ring around the German capital. Apart from this, the main forces of the Frankfurt group – the 9th German Army and the 4th German Panzer Army – were now cut off from Berlin and surrounded in the woods southeast of the city. Another few days and Berlin would fall. No one doubted that the capitulation of the German capital would end the war.

Primarily, however, the Fascist leadership was trying to fight its way out of being surrounded. Dremov's men were involved in heavy fighting at the Anhalter railway station. At his command post the news reached me of the severe wounding of the commander of the 1st Guards Brigade, Colonel Temnik, who died next day in an army hospital.

Usually the sappers and infantry cleared the way for the tanks. Attempts to commit the tanks without cover merely led to high losses from artillery fire and *Panzerfaust* men. As the brigades only had a limited number of infantry for their protection, the tank soldiers had to clear the way themselves. In narrow streets, however, only two tanks could advance at the same time. The first opened fire, being covered by the second. Thus metre by metre our Guardsmen smashed a breach in the dense enemy defences.

As the ranks of our infantry and sappers had suffered so much, Temnik assembled the members of his staff and ordered them to arm themselves with machine-pistols. He put himself at the head of the assault team he had formed. For a whole hour the brigade commander fought like a common soldier. No sooner had a housing quarter been cleared of the enemy than a mine exploded. Wounded by a splinter in his lower body, Temnik was taken to hospital, but all aid proved unsuccessful. We buried Temnik in the vicinity of the Reichstag building where today the memorial for the Soviet soldiers who died in the last battle stands.

I had seen many comrades die during the Great Fatherland War, and suffered deeply from every new loss. One does not get accustomed to death. Who can forget all those who are no longer with us?

Towards noon on the 25th April the Berlin group, consisting of six divisions of the 9th German Army, an SS-guards brigade, several police units, ten artillery divisions, an anti-aircraft division, a self-propelled artillery brigade, three tank-hunting brigades, six anti-tank artillery brigades as well as several *Volkssturm* battalions, was completely surrounded. All these units and troop elements were supported by the inhabitants.

Our troops involved in the capital – the 47th Army, 3rd and 5th Shock Armies, 8th Guards Army, part of the 28th Army and the 1st, 2nd, 3rd and 4th Guards Tank Armies – considerably outnumbered the enemy in strength. To every reasonably thinking statesman it would have been obvious that further resistance was futile and would only lead to further unnecessary casualties and destruction. But Hitler sought fanatically to extend the Reich's fight to the death.

Our soldiers and commanders knew that the war was coming to an end. Everyone wanted to survive, to witness the end of the war. But also in these hours no Guardsman took care to spare his life. Without regard for the death lurking step by step in the street fighting, they all fought on determinedly obstinate and bold.

On the morning of the 27th April, as I was on my way to the 11th Guards Tank Corps command post, the writer Michail Bragin appeared. 'Take me to the command post with you?' he asked after a short chat.

'For a writer it is senseless driving there where things are hot,' I said, trying to talk him out of it. But as he remained stubborn about accompanying me, I finally agreed. The way was not so far, but there could not have been more damned a street. From everywhere shells, mortars and bullets roared and whistled over our heads. Nevertheless we eventually got to our destination. Among the staff of the 11th Guards Tank Corps, which was located in the cellar of a former office building, we met the chief of staff, Colonel Vedenitshev, a veteran of the 1st Guards Tank Army. I had experienced so many dangerous situations together with him. Before we could greet each other, dust fell on our heads. German aircraft had attacked the building.

'Damn it, leave me in peace!' swore Vedenitshev. 'Every ten minutes three or four aircraft fly over and bomb just this building. They have surely heard that our staff is in the cellar. We must find another place to stay straight away.'

Several minutes later the duty officer reported that five men had been killed in the attack and two guns of the anti-aircraft artillery had been damaged. Straight afterwards there was another hefty explosion. The shock was so great that the cellar shook and we were thrown to the ground. Filing cabinets, shelves and dust fell on us. We could only free ourselves with difficulty. We looked at one another and brushed the dust off each other. Fortunately it seemed no one was hurt. But our faces were so black that our teeth shone unnaturally white. A bomb had broken through the thick masonry and had exploded in a neighbouring cellar. We would probably not have got off so lightly had not the filing cabinets protected us. We now discussed why the enemy was constantly bombarding this building so precisely. His determination seemed suspicious.

'There must be an aiming point here somewhere,' said Vedenitshev. 'The Germans know there are headquarters here. Order the building to be searched.'

Several soldiers set off immediately to search every corner of the extensive cellars. Behind an out of the way partition they eventually found a German civilian with a radio. From his interrogation we discovered that he was the deputy director of this establishment and a member of the Nazi Party. He had been directing the aircraft here from his hiding place by radio.

Vedenitshev unfolded a map of Berlin. Red arrows pointed to important railway junctions. The 29th Guards Rifle Corps was fighting with the 11th Guards Corps in a quarter bordering this area.

'Here,' Vedenitshev pointed to the map, 'the remains of the *Müncheberg* Panzer Division are defending themselves. Apart from them there are also *Volkssturm* people engaged.'

Vedenitshev had to interrupt his speech when, as smart as ever, noisily and impetuously, every inch of compressed energy, Babadshanian burst in.

'How is it, Arno? It seems to be somewhat hot here!'

'That is not the point, Comrade Commander-in-Chief. All hell is let loose. The Fascists are behaving frantically today. They have counterattacked five times. And what have they not offered. Youths, still half children, and old men! Things are bad for Hitler!'

'We'll talk about Hitler later. How does it look with you?'

'All attacks have been repelled. We are advancing. But the barriers and barricades in the streets give us much to do. Neither tanks nor guns can get through. The sappers cannot get to the barriers because of the firing. But Chuikov's men have given us some practical assistance by smoking out the vermin with flamethrowers.'

Despite all these difficulties, the 11th Guards Tank Corps, together with the 29th Guards Rifle Corps, took the railway junction, and the corps staff moved up closer to the leading troops.

In these days the Fascists fought not only on the ground and in the air but especially underground. Although we knew there was an underground railway in the city, in the heat of battle we either forgot or simply underestimated the military significance of the underground connections. These, however, gave the Fascists excellent manoeuvrability. By means of the U-Bahn they were able to conduct attacks on troops that had already thrust into the centre of the city.

Consequently we controlled more strongly than before the city areas already cleared of the enemy. For this we used the self-propelled artillery brigade under Semliakov, who had won the title Hero of the Soviet Union at Gotenhafen. The members of his brigade, which also belonged to the reserve, patrolled the streets, kept order and forestalled treacherous enemy machinations.

There were goods trains standing on the captured railway lines. Our patrolling soldiers soon discovered what they were carrying. The inhabitants were taking sacks of flour from the wagons. To prevent looting, Semliakov ordered the trains to be guarded so that the flour could be distributed among the Berliners later.

Slowly but surely the Red Army troops were closing in on the city centre. On the 27th April only a kilometre separated the 8th Guards Army and our army from the Tiergarten, the final goal of our attack. The fighting now blazed up in the part of the city in which the most important authorities of Fascist Germany, the city's defence headquarters and Hitler's bunker, could be found. The enemy forces now occupied an area 3 to 5 kilometres wide and 16 kilometres long, lying under ceaseless attacks from our artillery and aircraft. In addition, the enemy had lost both his aerodromes – Adlershof and Tempelhof. However, the reserve landing strip on the Charlottenburger Chaussee found itself under the special control of our 16th Air Army.

Although the situation for the Berlin garrison was hopeless, the Fascists continued to hit out with the courage of despair.

In the heat of the fighting it was impossible to record all the acts of bravery by the soldiers and officers of the 1st Guards Tank Army. Only later, as I went through the political advisers' reports from the brigades and units, did I get the full picture of the moving stories of many tank-men, riflemen and gunners who had won eternal fame by their deeds. These reports resurrected the fighting in Berlin in all its

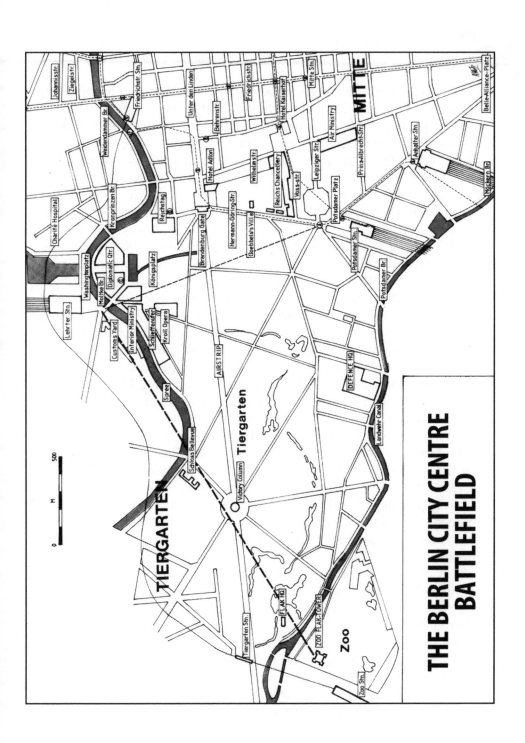

THE BERLIN CITY CENTRE BATTLEFIELD

details. Many pages dealt with the clever handling of our riflemen opening the way for the tanks through the labyrinth of destroyed streets.

The machine-gun team under Sergeant Kolesnikov had fought with exemplary courage. The sole survivor of this team, Private Kudriashov, reported: 'Towards midday on the 29th April the Germans assembled in a building at most 50 metres from us. Apparently they thought that the right wing of our rifle battalion was exposed and wanted to fall on our rear. We sat back in ambush and lay in wait until the Fascists advanced. When they were about 30 metres from us we opened fire. The Fascists ran about and left numerous dead in front of our position.

'Thinking of the Guards' rule of changing position as soon as the enemy have identified you, we took the machine-gun to another part of the building. The Fascists prepared to attack again, first throwing a grenade into the building, but we remained silent. Then, as the Fascists came across to our side, we fired everything in the belt, many Germans thus losing their lives. As Kolesnikov and the ammunition carrier had fallen in this fighting, I jammed myself behind the machine-gun and fired until the ammunition ran out. Still the Germans came on towards our position. I had only six hand grenades. Suddenly I saw how our wounded commander got up, stuck a hand grenade in his pocket, left cover and went towards the Fascists. They thought that the Soviet soldiers were surrendering, so held their fire for a second. Lying behind the silent machine-gun I saw Kolesnikov, carefully putting one leg before the other, his hand pressed to his breast, and going on towards the enemy. Several seconds later three Fascists came round a corner to cut him off. My heart threatened to stop. At the same moment there was an explosion. Before the Fascists could come to grab the wounded commander they flew into the air. Kolesnikov also died this way.'

This already historical political office report moved me deeply. Again and again I came across further pages of incidents showing the devotion of our soldiers towards the Party, the Soviet people and their Guards' banners.

The following lines are dedicated to Sergeant Prishimov, a brave man who deserves a place next to heroes like Lavrinenko, Samochin, Burda and Podgorbunski. Used to completing the most difficult and responsible tasks, he carried out reconnaissances and brought back prisoners. As an armoured unit was approaching a railway station, he fell into the enemy drumfire. The tank-men stopped and fired. But they had to go on, not wanting to be shot up themselves. Guards Sergeant Prishimov went off with his own men to find out where the enemy artillery was firing from. As they were working their way forward along the rails, he saw an enemy tank that seemed to be directing the fire. Unnoticed, the sergeant was able to enter the tank and kill the crew. Then he turned the gun around and fired at a nearby enemy fire nest. Our tank-men used the situation to push forward into the railway station and took it almost without casualties.

But let us return to the fighting in the centre of Berlin. During the last days of April the Fascist high command feverishly tried to relieve the city. Three groups tried to fight their way through to the capital and help the besieged garrison: from the north, General Steiner; from the west, General Wenck; and from the south-east the Frankfurt–Guben group. But all three were defeated or destroyed.

Already on the 25th April the 1st Ukrainian Front's 5th Guards Army under General Shadov and the 1st American Army had met up, thus splitting the territory of Fascist Germany and its forces in two. The Berlin garrison's situation was catastrophic.

What involved my tank soldiers was the complete clearing of the Anhalter railway station on the 28th April by Babadshanian's corps in cooperation with the 5th Shock Army's 9th Rifle Corps.

Dremov's corps together with units of the 8th Guards Army thrust in a south-westerly direction towards the 3rd Shock Army, which had reached the grounds of the Reichstag.

On the evening of the same day a call from Front Headquarters warned me about shooting at the Reichstag, which elements under Colonel-General Kusnetzov had already reached. We were sorry not to have had the honour of raising the victory banner over the Reichstag, but at the same time rejoiced over every step taken by our comrades that brought us closer to victory.

On the 29th April I gave Dremov the task of taking the Zoological Gardens in cooperation with elements of the 8th Guards Army. Babadshanian had the Potsdamer Platz railway station and the Reichs Chancellery to take. Both corps were to combine with elements of Kusnetzov's and Bogdanov's armies. From the upper storey of a half-destroyed building, where my command post was located, one could already see the Brandenburg Gate, where we would meet up with our fighting colleagues. Wide areas of the city were visible from this command post, which took several hours to tidy up. However, as thick smoke generally covered the whole area, we had to move our command post closer to the Zoological Gardens.

Shalin, Nikitin and General Frolov, chief of our army's artillery, got no rest. While Frolov constantly had to allocate new targets to his artillery, Shalin and Nikitin had their hands full issuing orders and instructions.

On the 29th April, when the army headquarters moved closer to the Zoological Gardens, I received a report from the 19th Mechanised Guards Brigade fighting in Urbanstrasse, which ran towards the Zoological Gardens. As one of the brigade's battalions pressed forward towards the entrance of the Zoological Gardens, the enemy laid down a mighty barrage on their route. The chief of artillery had the buildings in which the Fascists were concealed shelled, but the Fascists continued to maintain a determined resistance. Other measures were required.

As always, the reconnaissance had the first word. Guards Sergeant-Major Nikanorov, with the scouts Ivanov, Apanasiukov and Dobrovolski, offered to get into the building, whose occupants were giving the storm troops far too much to do. Covered by the ruins, the scouts forced their way into the building, fell on the occupants and silenced their strongpoint. Now the battalion's tanks were able to proceed another 100 to 200 metres along Urbanstrasse.

Nikanorov, who had just cleared the building of Fascists and then informed the riflemen, came across a tank from whose hatches smoke and flames were emerging. As the crew of the T-34 appeared to be dead, Nikanorov wanted at least to save the tank. But the vehicle lay under fire from submachine-gunners hidden nearby. Nikanorov ordered Apansiukov and Dobrovolski to engage the enemy with fire and provide him with a diversion. The plan succeeded. Engaged in the lively exchange of fire, the Fascists took their eyes off the tank. Ivanov climbed aboard, extinguished the fire and checked the condition of the machine. The tank was only slightly damaged, the engine and controls being intact. The clever sergeant got into the driving seat and drove the tank out of the zone of fire.

I ordered my radioman to connect me with Babadshanian. Colonel Vedenitshev reported back and informed me that Babadshanian had decided to advance not only along the streets but also through the U-Bahn tunnels. The storm troops were involved in heavy fighting with every individual building. However, Babadshanian had to give up his idea as Hitler had ordered the floodgates of the Landwehr Canal to be opened to flood the U-Bahn.

Because of the high losses, I sent Babadshanian the last of my reserves, the headquarters guard company, to his aid. I found it difficult giving up these battle-experienced men, but the war was still claiming its victims.

Behind the Zoological Gardens, around which was a 2-metre-high wall, lay the Tiergarten, in which were concrete bunkers and specially built massive buildings. All the streets around the Zoological Gardens were blocked by barricades lying within range of the artillery and machine-guns. The garrison comprised about 5,000 men. We were to destroy these last defensive installations with the Guards of the 39th Rifle Division.

Our sappers worked on the wall and blew it in several places, while covered by strong artillery fire and a curtain of smoke. The infantry, tanks and artillery assembled behind the ruins and barricades. Several guns opened fire simultaneously. Smoke and dust rose above the Zoological Gardens. In the vast din the sound of the engines of the bombers flying over the Zoo to drop their bombs could not be heard.

Upon the signal to attack, the riflemen and sappers stormed the gaps and occupied the aquarium. As they were unable to take the concrete bunker that the enemy were defending fanatically, we brought in 152mm howitzers that took on the bunker with direct fire at a range of 200 to 300 metres, but still without success. Even these large calibre shells were unable to penetrate the thick walls.

Only when the divisional commander, Colonel Martshenko, ordered the demolition of the entrance doors was it possible to penetrate the bunker. On the 1st May the whole of the Zoological Gardens were in our hands. Later it became known that the command post and communications centre of the commander of the Berlin Defensive Area, General Weidling, were located in one of the bunkers. The general had had to move to another command post.

In this fighting the rifle and tank-men commanded by Majors Shestakov and Gavriliuk particularly distinguished themselves.

On the night leading to the 1st May I visited the command post of our fighting colleague, General Chuikov. Once we had sorted out our business, the chief of the German Army's General Staff, General Krebs, sought to pass 'an especially important message' to the Soviet high command. As we later discovered, Krebs brought the news of Hitler's suicide to our high command with a list of names of the new German government, as well as an appeal by Goebbels and Bormann to the Soviet high command for a temporary ceasefire in Berlin in order to enable the arrangement of peace talks between Germany and the USSR.

When our high command was informed of the Fascist leadership's intentions, we immediately increased the storm on Berlin. At 1800 hours on the 1st May the guns thundered once more. Together with Chuikov's infantry, the 1st Guards Tank Brigade went into a last attack on the Tiergarten. Opposite them fought the 3rd Shock Army under General Kusnetzov and the 2nd Guards Tank Army under General Bogdanov. On the evening of that same day the forward elements of these four armies destroyed the last resisting units. The Tiergarten was littered with burnt trees and destroyed vehicles and ploughed up with trenches, bomb and shell craters.

Soldiers and officers fell into one another's arms. Only a few kilometres had separated both armies, but with what high losses they had had to win.

The fate of the Berlin garrison was sealed. At 0200 hours on the 2nd May General Weidling appeared at Chuikov's command post, where Goebbel's deputy, Fritsche, had been brought that same morning. Both declared themselves prepared to issue the following order for the capitulation of the troops in Berlin:

> On the 30th April the Führer, to whom we had all sworn an oath of allegiance, forsook us by committing suicide. Faithful to the Führer, you German soldiers were prepared to continue the battle for Berlin, even though your ammunition was running out and the general situation made further resistance senseless.
>
> I now order all resistance to cease immediately. Every hour you go on fighting adds to the terrible suffering of the Berlin population and our wounded. In agreement with the high command of the Soviet Forces, I call on you to stop fighting forthwith.
>
>
>
> Weidling
> General of Artillery
> Former Commander
> Berlin Defence Area
>
>

Over all the loudspeakers the German army was ordered to cease fire immediately.

The city was on fire. Clouds of smoke rose up into the spring sky. Here and there machine-guns still rattled. Again and again the loudspeakers broadcast the orders in Russian and German to cease fire.

Officers of Chuikov's and Weidling's staffs drove slowly through the streets and passed the order of the former commander of the Berlin Defence Area.

German soldiers crawled out of cellars, underground passageways and U-Bahn tunnels. Tattered, unshaven, in filthy uniforms, they went through the weapon collecting points in single file. What a sad end to an army that four years previously had marched victoriously through so many European countries.

The final point of the gigantic Berlin operation had been reached. The enemy had capitulated at 1500 hours on the 2nd May 1945. That same day I had a surprise encounter with General Weidling that recalled many thoughts to me. Near the Reichstag a column of prisoners was drawing past the smoking rubble. At their head walked several generals. A colonel-general took a long look at our tank. Perhaps the tank reminded him of something? After a short hesitation he continued on his way with lowered eyes.

'Who is that general?' I asked Sobolev, who was standing near me.

'Weidling. Colonel-General Weidling.'

This name I had already recalled. Weidling had begun his military career on the Soviet–German front as a first lieutenant. He was one of the commanders of the Fascist hordes that had tried to break through on the Volokolamsker Chaussee to Moscow. There he had learned of the strength and courage of the soldiers of our 1st Guards Tank Brigade. Perhaps he already knew then that the famous German fighting slogan 'surround, close in, destroy' was useless. Weidling encountered the 1st Guards Tank Army for the second time at the Kursk Bend. Apparently his *Tigers* and *Ferdinands* tried to ram our defences on the Oboianer Chaussee. Now they lay near Kursk as rusty heaps of scrap metal.

What the slogan 'surround, close in, destroy' really meant, Weidling discovered in the summer of 1944, when, already a general and commander-in-chief of the 9th German Army, he was with his troops in the Bobruisk cauldron. Our tanks cut through his army's communications, his staff became prisoners and he himself escaped by a miracle.

Near Berlin occurred the third decisive encounter of the 1st Guards Tank Army with the German 9th Army's XVIth Panzer Corps. Beaten back by us, its commander withdrew to Berlin with the remains of his troops. Now he too was in the column of prisoners of war. With him went the whole of the Fascist Wehrmacht.

That evening I drove with Shalin and Nikitin through the still-smoking city. Unimaginable scenes in the streets. Everywhere hugging, kissing, laughing and singing. Berlin had fallen. Here and again the cracking of shots. The soldiers were firing their victory salutes. Soldiers were dancing next to their tanks. For four long, bloody years the people had had to wait for this hour. Now the hour of victory had arrived. A red flag waved over the Reichstag.

At a crossroads Shalin suddenly grasped my arm: 'Look there!' Corpses were hanging from a lamppost.

'*Volkssturm*,' explained Shalin. 'Gestapo victims. They wanted to end the senseless fighting, so they were hanged as a warning.'

At this time a question was being repeatedly asked: 'What's happened to Hitler?' The suggestion that he had committed suicide was not convincing. One thought was that his companions had got this rumour going to obliterate his traces. The desire to capture Hitler and publicly try him was in everyone's mind.

Naturally Hitler's remains were also discussed by us. Nikitin suggested that we visit the Führerbunker at the Reichs Chancellery.

'Where is Hitler? Show us him!' we asked of the commandant of the Reichs Chancellery, Colonel Shevzov.

'He's gone, the swine. He was here but he's gone. Only a charred corpse is left,' he replied.

We went down some steep steps into the bunker. Stale air hit us. We entered a long corridor, turned left and then right and finally stood in front of a massive door, similar to that of a treasury.

'This is where he lived,' said Shevzov and stood aside to let us through. We inspected Hitler's reception room, his bedroom, his dining room and his bathroom. Shevzov told us that immediately above Hitler's quarters lay massive iron plates for protection against bomb and shell attacks.

All these years we had sworn to enter the Fascist cave and now we stood in our goal. It really was a cave, the description of a living bunker was out of place.

In a neighbouring room was the corpse of a man in a general's uniform. 'The chief of the army staff, General of Infantry Krebs,' explained Schevzov. It was the same man that had brought to the bunker the news that the Soviet Supreme Command was sticking to the unconditional surrender and refusing all dealings with the Fascists. This information led to several suicides in the bunker.

We thanked Shevzov for his trouble and left the Reichs Chancellery.

The street fighting in Berlin was finished. The formations and units of the army paraded in front of the Reichstag. According to orders we had to leave the city and redeploy in a new area.

In Berlin peaceful life returned while in other sectors the Soviet–German war still raged. Our troops continued to fight against the armies of Schörner, Manteufel and other Fascist generals, in all over 1.5 million men. Daily came reports of German units surrendering en masse to our western allies, but others continued to fight determinedly against us.

On the morning of the 3rd May our fighting companions, those who had lost their lives in the last fighting in Berlin, were buried. Silent and bare-headed, the Guardsmen thought about their comrades. They were buried at the Brandenburg Gate and in Treptow Park, covered in spring flowers and garlands.

Chapter 2

Main Striking Force

By High Marshal of Tank Troops
Amasasp Chatshaturovitch Babadshanian

Babadshanian commanded the 11th Guards Tank Corps of the 1st Guards Tank Army with the rank of major general.

* * *

The headquarters of the 1st Byelorussian Front was sited on the edge of the little town of Birnbaum. On the 5th April 1945 were assembled there the commander-in-chief, the members of the War Councils and chief of staff of the armies as well as the commanders of the tank and mechanised corps. Marshal of the Soviet Union Zhukov was escorted by the Member of the War Council of the Front, Telegin, and the Chief of Staff, Malinin.

Zhukov informed us that he had just come from the Supreme Commander in Chief. The situation had developed in such a way that he had to summon us urgently, as the Berlin operation had to commence earlier than planned.

The marshal was quiet for a minute and then explained the reasons for this to us. Since our Allies had dealt with the German group quickly, they were now planning an attack on Leipzig and Dresden, and we must accept that they wanted to reach Berlin before us. This all went under the pretext that they wanted to help us. Our headquarters had also discovered that two parachute divisions were being hastily prepared for an attack on Berlin. That suited the Fascists. While they conducted fierce resistance against us even in the smallest villages, they surrendered whole cities to the western Allies on the western front.

'That forces the Supreme Headquarters to hurry,' resumed Zhukov. 'The exact details of the offensive you will learn later. Now it is necessary to explain the task.'

A curtain was removed, revealing a map on which the enemy defensive sectors were shown exactly. They extended at distances of from 10 to 15 kilometres from the Oder River to the Seelow Heights.

A second curtain slipped aside. Before us hung a relief map of Berlin. Streets, buildings, fortifications, barriers, fixed firing positions, even the destroyed city districts were shown. The important objectives were numbered.

'Direct your attention, please, to Object Number 105.' The Field Marshal pointed with his stick to a large square. 'That is the Reichstag. Who will be the first to reach it? Katukov? Chuikov? Perhaps also Bogdanov or Berzarin?' Without waiting for a reply, he went on: 'And that is Number 106, the Reichs Chancellery.'

In this way he presented the future objectives to us.

Chaos reigned in Berlin. The leading circles of Fascist Germany were disintegrating. Out of anxiety for their crimes to be accounted for they turned to total mobilisation. Old men, invalids and young lads were to save them from their certain downfall. Simultaneously the Fascist leadership sought a political way out by negotiating with the Allies for an honourable peace. But it was all in vain; the Fascist rulers could no longer save anything.

On the Oder and Neisse Rivers were concentrated the 1st and 2nd Byelorussian and the 1st Ukrainian Fronts. In this concentration were four tank armies, numerous independent tank and mechanised corps, as well as a vast number of guns and aircraft. We were stronger than ever before.

But the task awaiting us was not an easy one. In the Berlin direction, especially where he expected our main thrust, the enemy had organised a strong defence in depth. All the lines of defence had been occupied by their troops in time. Apart from this it was hilly terrain with numerous rivers, streams, canals, lakes and villages, all ideal for defence purposes.

During the conference with Marshal Zhukov we were entrusted with the basic idea for the coming operation.

The main thrust was to be conducted from the Küstrin bridgehead with five infantry and two tank armies. The infantry armies would break through the tactical defensive zones and take suitable preparatory measures for the introduction of the tank armies. Working on the flanks of the main thrust, the tank armies would thus have the necessary room for manoeuvre and for the decisive thrust into the enemy's rear. The infantry armies would lighten the future development of the attack. The tank thrusts would go round the north and south of Berlin and, with the 1st Ukrainian Front, close the ring around the city in the Potsdam–Brandenburg area.

Unfortunately this did not involve our 1st Guards Tank Army. During the discussions on the 5th April the commander of the 2nd Guards Tank Army, General Bogdanov, had persistently sought to point out that his army required more freedom of movement for a wide-sweeping circumvention of Berlin in the north. Marshal Zhukov had remarked: 'Do you want to fight for Berlin or spend the whole time rolling to the north?'

Should the 2nd Guards Tank Army nevertheless have been able to make such an extensive and above all effective by-pass operation, the 1st Guards Tank Army would not have needed to have conducted any similar manoeuvre. Why? I will come back to this later.

On the evening of the 15th April the 1st Guards Tank Army left its concentration area and rolled under cover of darkness to the Oder. High above us droned the engines of enemy bombers. Here and there searchlights tore through the darkness.

Towards midnight our leading elements reached the Oder crossing points. Isolated shots coming from the bank showed that the enemy was nervous and was expecting our attack at any moment.

And then it happened! The night was lit up by signal rockets and muzzle flashes. The earth resounded and rocked. Howitzers crashed, shots from the *Katyushas* whistled overhead. Our mighty artillery and air preparation had begun. Holding their breath, the soldiers and officers listened to the din. Many of them had already experienced the bombardments of Moscow, Stalingrad and Kursk, but what was happening now put everything in the shade.

On the 16th April the 1st Byelorussian Front went into the attack from the bridgehead, breaking through the first defensive strip, and shortly afterwards reached the second one before the Seelow Heights. Here the troops were brought to a halt by the strong, concisely organised fire.

The Seelow Heights governed the whole Oder depression and were a serious obstacle on the way to Berlin. The 8th Guards Army – infantry, artillery and allocated armour – became jammed in front of the Heights and were unable to go further.

Already at the conference of the 5th April several generals had drawn the Front commander's attention to the fact that the main enemy defensive position ran along the Seelow Heights, so the artillery fire and air attacks should be concentrated on these Heights. Unfortunately this advice was not taken.

'When I now, after a long time, think back over the plans for Operation Berlin,' wrote Zhukov, 'I come to the conclusion that the smashing of the enemy's Berlin group and the taking of the city of Berlin could have gone differently.'

The Front commander could see for himself, from his command post next to that of the 8th Guards Army, that our own forces were not in a position to break through the enemy defences in their whole tactical depth. As further delay put the success of the whole operation in question, he had the 1st Guards Tank Army enter the 8th Guards Army's sector.

In the night leading to the 18th April, as the second defensive strip was breached and our troops pursued the attack, General G.I. Gerko appeared at my command post. He told me that I was to drive back immediately with him to Seelow to participate in a consultation with War Council Member Telegin.

'Right now?'

'Straight away!'

I reported my thoughts about leaving the troops during the attack, but found no listener. General Gerko only shook his shoulders and indicated, orders are orders.

We struggled along a badly damaged road to Seelow. There did not seem to be one stone left on another in the place. After a long search we came across a still undamaged building in which the consultation was to take place.

The weak illumination from some dim trench lights fell on the faces of the assembly. Telegin's appearance gave the impression of strength, but he could not hide his dejection. I had known him since 1942. Even in complicated situations, Telegin remained for me an example of partiality and strong principles. His correctly stressed appearance reminded me always of the commissar of Tschapaiev's division. And now this depression. Doubtless, he must have also heard something about the delay in front of the Seelow Heights.

Most of the assembly came from the tank troops. That looked almost as if they were responsible for the fact that their tanks had not had the necessary manoeuvrability in depth, I thought.

It was well past midnight when we received permission to return to our units. Silently we drove back as before to my command post. The head of the corps' operations department, Colonel Lebediev, briefed us on the situation.

Slowly morning dawned. I was dead tired. I had been unable to close my eyes for almost three days. Lebediev advised me to take a nap, at least half an hour. It was already dawn. Daylight brought the growling of artillery, the clanking tracks of tanks going into the attack with the 8th Guards Army. The terrain made the massive tank attack more difficult. But what else could we do? Manoeuvring between lakes and strongpoints, our tanks and the infantry advanced.

Already during the first days of the Berlin operation the 1st Guards Tank Army had suffered considerable casualties. The fact that the introduction of tanks into the tactical zone of the enemy defences is seldom effective and always unwanted had once more been confirmed here. And it made no difference if Marshal Zhukov in his memoirs emphasised the prominent role of the 1st Byelorussian Front's 1st Guards Tank Army.

Significantly more effective was the commitment of the 3rd and 4th Guards Tank Armies of Generals Rybalko and Leliushenko. In a brilliant manoeuvre these two armies attached to the 1st Ukrainian Front had covered great distances in the shortest time, thrust towards Berlin and enclosed the city from the south and south-west.

After some bitter fighting for the Seelow Heights, our troops reached the third line of defence in the Müncheberg–Diedersdorf sector.

With some of my corps' officers I drove to the command post of General Schemenkov's 29th Guards Rifle Corps to get agreement on the further operations. His staff had set themselves up in a manorial farm.* We went through several big rooms and came to the library. Books with expensive bindings occupied the shelves. A grey-haired lieutenant-colonel told us that this library was invaluable and he had come here from Leningrad especially to prevent them being destroyed.

We went through still more rooms and finally ended in the room in which the rifle corps' staff operated. Immediately after our greeting, Schemenkov disclosed to me that he could not attack at 0800 as ordered and had put back the attack time to 0900 hours.

'But it must be reported to Chuikov!'

But Schemenkov ignored my objection.

'What do you mean, delayed?' Chuikov exploded.

* This was the big manor farm in the village of Diedersdorf, about 5 kilometres beyond Seelow on the Berlin highway.

How the conversation continued, I am unable to say, as Katukov took me to one side and whispered: 'There is nothing more for you to do here. Go back to your people as quickly as possible. The order must be fulfilled exactly as scheduled.'

Yes, orders are orders and the operative–tactical creativity of a commander cannot be opposed. That is the nature of the art of warfare.

I returned head over heels to my corps, gave the necessary orders and shortly afterwards the tanks opened fire. It did not take long before the defence line was broken and our tanks and the 29th Guards Rifle Corps stormed through. Colonel Gussakovski's 44th Guards Tank Brigade and Colonel Fiodorvich's 27th Guards Motorised Rifle Brigade developed the attack and reached the Berlin autobahn ring.

On the 20th April a telegram arrived. 'To Katukov, Popiel! The 1st Guards Tank Army has the historic task of being the first into Berlin and to hoist the banner of victory. The organisation and execution I will take over myself. Send the best brigade of every corps to Berlin and give them the task by at the latest 0400 hours on the 21st April, cost what it might, to break through the city perimeter. I await the immediate report so that Stalin can be informed of the event and that the information can be published by the press. Zhukov. Telegin.'

We read this telegram with mixed feelings. On one side we were happy and proud about the honourable task, but on the other side we were peeved that our tank army was to be committed like a normal formation. We had no idea yet what awaited a tank army in street fighting.

But the feeling of pride won the upper hand. With the elements of the 29th Guards Rifle Corps, we had already penetrated the suburbs of Berlin on the 21st April.

The tanks thrust forward. Our longed-for goal came ever closer. But the nearer we got, the more bitter the fighting became. Our tanks were unable to fully use their fighting capacity in the narrow streets. Although we were used to dealing with incendiaries, we came up against a no less dangerous enemy: the *Panzerfaust*.

The Hitler clique undertook desperate efforts to avoid their downfall. One 'hold on' slogan followed another. Those who retreated without orders could expect death. Until then I had believed that these words applied only to the members of the Fascist armed forces who dared not throw away their weapons. But later, when I read the memoirs of former Fascist officers, I realised how much the consciousness of the population had been poisoned.

'We were soldiers,' wrote Guderian, 'to defend our Fatherland and to bring up our youths as upstanding and fighting men, and we were happily so. Soldiering was for us a high duty born out of the love of our people and our country.'

In order to 'defend their fatherland' they had to occupy Austria and Czechoslovakia, Poland, Greece, Yugoslavia, Norway and Denmark? Were there not enough of these for Guderian to overdo the hypocrisy? Do you see anything of the love of their people as they sent millions of people to the ovens of Auschwitz and Maidanak? The end was getting nearer and all further resistance was futile, but blind obedience and fanaticism had no limits. On the walls of buildings gleamed large boasting slogans like: 'Berlin remains German!' One of us had added in crayon, 'But without Fascists!'

Berlin was surrounded. From the north moved in the 2nd Guards Tank Army and the 3rd Shock Army, from the east the 11th Independent Tank Corps and the 5th Shock Army. In the west elements of the 47th Army and the 9th Guards Tank Corps took Nauen and on the 24th April connected with the 4th Guards Tank Army of the 1st Ukrainian Front breaking in from the south. In the south-east were fighting the 8th Guards Army and 1st Guards Tank Army, as well as the 3rd Guards Tank Army and the 28th Army of the 1st Ukrainian Front, which were already in the city.

So there lay Berlin before us. Our first objective was not its architectural beauty, although quite near must be the university at which Marx and Engels had studied and where Albert Einstein had been a professor. In Berlin masses of people drunk with victory had celebrated the taking of Prague, Warsaw, the Hague, Brussels and Paris. This is where Fascism had grown. But there was also another Berlin, in which Karl Liebknecht and Rosa Luxemburg had founded the German Communist Party, a Berlin where at the Reichstag tribune Ernst Thälmann had warned of the dangers of Fascism.

The West German historian Jürgen Thorwald wrote in his book *The End on the Oder*:

On the morning of the 21st April, as Marshal Zhukov's breakthrough to Berlin became irrevocable and refugees from the east appeared on the streets of Berlin, Goebbels lost control for the first time.

The sirens sounded the tank alarm once more as Goebbels' fellow workers assembled for an eleven-hour conference in the cinema at the Goebbels Villa. Goebbels' usually sunburnt face was dead white. He understood for the first time that the end was near. His unbearable inner tension erupted in passionate hatred. The German people, he shouted, the German people, what can one do with a people whose men will no longer fight when their wives are being raped. All the National Socialist plans, all its thoughts and aims were so big and so precious for this people. The German people had become too cowardly to involve themselves. In the east they ran away. In the west they hindered the soldiers from fighting and greeted the enemy with white flags. The German people have deserved the fate that now awaits them.

There was fighting everywhere in Berlin. Our soldiers drove the enemy out of the cellars and buildings from the ground to the roofs. The tanks slowly crept through the streets, the sappers finding the de-mining of the routes not easy.

Our corps staff were accommodated in a lovely building, at the urging of Colonel Vedenitshev, who had a weakness for art and architecture. When General Katukov sought us out I invited him to enter our apartments. However, he rejected my hospitality, turned his back on the building and stood back a few paces. 'I'll not put a foot in that building. And I recommend you to clear out of this palace as soon as possible. This place simply reeks of mines.'

While Vedenitshev was seeing to the immediate removal of the staff, I stood with Katukov in the grassed area in front of the building listening to the roar of the engines of aircraft taking off from the Tiergarten for the west. 'Hitler and his chums are decamping,' I said out loud.

'That is not impossible,' agreed Michael Yefimovitch Katukov.

Towards the morning the palace blew up. General Katukov had been quite right.

Danger threatened every step in the street fighting. If we shut the enemy up in one building, he escaped by underground passages and appeared again in another building. He also used the extensive drainage system for manoeuvring underground.

Firing was going on everywhere. Leaflets in the Russian language were meant to raise fear in our soldiers: 'In Berlin there are 600,000 buildings. Each one will be turned into a fortress and will be your grave.' But our soldiers did not allow themselves to be frightened by them. They had come here to put an end to Fascism and to liberate the German people.

Neither the water supply nor the electricity worked in the destroyed city. Women and children were huddled in the cellars. In order to rescue them we sent in special troops. They carried the people out of the rubble and administered first aid. Where the enemy had mined apartments, numerous Soviet soldiers were killed in these rescue operations. Our soldiers helped the women and their children out of the dangerous areas and shared their rations with them.

The little Berliners came to our field kitchens without the least fear, thrust out cups and spoons and begged for food. *Kuschatch* – food – was the first Russian word they learnt. Our cook filled the bowl of a little lad to the brim. 'Danke schön,' said the little one but made no indication of leaving.

'What do you want then?' asked the cook in Russian. 'Shall I make some more?'

'For Mama,' explained the little one, dipped a finger in his bowl, licked it and vanished as quickly as his little legs could carry him. 'He'll certainly come again,' said the cook happily.

Sergeant Darinkov's submachine-gunners saved about twenty women and children from danger of death from the upper storeys of a burning building. Perhaps these were the wives and children of those men that had been firing at us with *Panzerfausts*? We Soviet citizens were drawn in the spirit of humanitarianism and discriminated precisely between the Germans and the Fascists. Every time I returned to Berlin later, I visited the Soviet Memorial in Treptow Park. The Soviet soldier with the sword and the child in his arms has become the symbol of members of the Red Army.

Berlin stood in flames. A giant cloud of black smoke hung over the city. Thousands of guns were firing and bombers were dropping their loads on the city, but the Fascists were still not prepared to surrender.

Let us recall: on the 12th October 1941 the German high command had informed the commander-in-chief of Army Group *Mitte*: 'The Führer has newly decided not to accept the surrender of Moscow, even should the enemy offer it.' What was now being played out were the results of this 'logical' conclusion. Should thousands, hundreds of thousands die, the main thing was that the Hitler clique would save themselves. 'If we have to slam the door shut behind us,' Goebbels had cried, 'then the whole world will tremble.'

On the evening of the 27th April members of the 27th Motorised Brigade and the 40th Guards Tank Brigade captured several trains. In some of the wagons they found boxes of chocolate. It occurred to no one to keep the booty. The soldiers distributed the chocolate to the starving children. To show the little ones that there was no need to be frightened, the Soviet soldiers broke off a piece from every bar and ate it. It was strictly forbidden to eat captured foodstuffs, but who was thinking about that at the moment.

After several hours I was informed that traces of poisoning had appeared among some soldiers. In view of the previous experience in Gotenhafen, I quickly ordered the train to be set alight. Later it transpired that the men had simply eaten too much chocolate.

On the night leading to the 30th April a German major appeared with his interpreter in the bunker I was occupying with my operational team. The major said that he had been empowered by his commander to inform me that he would surrender with his 900 men if we guaranteed their lives. I assured him that the Red Army would guarantee the safety of everyone who laid down his arms.

'I have already told him that,' explained the interpreter in the clearest Russian. To the question of where he had learnt the language so well, the soldier explained that he was German but born and bred in Odessa. As a teacher he had not been evacuated in time and so had been taken into the Wehrmacht by the Germans.

'I have explained to the commander that the Soviet men will not shoot any prisoners, and assured him that is in accordance with our customs. During my enforced service in the Wehrmacht I have had time to think over many things.'

We believed him, as what he said was truly meant. Life in the Soviet Union had left deep traces in the consciousness of this man.

The enclosing ring around Berlin drew ever tighter. Especially affected were the *Müncheberg* Battle Group, the 11th Motorised SS Division and other units defending the Tiergarten with the Reichstag, Gestapo Headquarters and the Reichs Chancellery.

On the night leading to the 24th April the 44th and 45th Guards Tank Brigades opened fire on the Reichs Chancellery. Not one of us had any idea what was happening in there at that time. As the sun went down our troops made a determined attack on the Tiergarten and the Reichs Chancellery. As we later learned, Hitler had committed suicide. As his successor he had named Grand Admiral Dönitz, who intended pursuing the war until the end.

Soldiers of the 3rd Shock Army had raised the victory banner over the Reichstag on the evening of the 30th April. The last attack began in the night leading to the 2nd May. In the morning the 1st Guards Tank

Army thrust into the Tiergarten and connected with units of the 2nd Guards Tank Army and the Polish troops taking part in the storming of Berlin. The tank soldiers had been fighting for sixteen days in conditions unusual to them against a deeply echeloned defence equipped with anti-tank weapons, leaving heavy losses behind them in the bitter street-fighting. These losses hit us especially hard as we knew how much all had looked forward to the hour of victory.

Under our heavy blows the German troops began striking their weapons on the morning of the 2nd May. Some 7,700 men surrendered to our 1st Guards Tank Army. They came out of cellars and U-Bahn tunnels, from cellars and attics; dirty, ragged, hollow-eyed, with their heads lowered.

Berlin had capitulated.

Chapter 3

Special Duties

By Marshal of Engineers
Victor Kondratievitch Chartshenko

Born in the Ukraine in 1911, Chartshenko left in 1929 for Leningrad (now St Petersburg once more), where he was eventually assigned to a large electronics factory in the Vyborg District, soon being elected secretary of the Komsomol group in his building and following a political career leading to his election to membership of the Communist Party. Following the Japanese invasion of Mongolia, it was suggested he attend the F.E. Dzierziynski Military Technical Academy, where he was accepted as a student in October 1932. Among those he met there was Michail Fadeievitch Joffe, under whom he was later to serve in the Red Army. Chartshenko graduated in December 1940 and was persuaded by Joffe to join him in his electrified fencing project at the academy.

At the end of 1941 Stalin ordered the formation of the first independent engineer brigades for the establishing and overcoming of obstacles of all kinds, particularly minefields. The 33rd Independent Engineer Brigade was established at Kaluga under Lieutenant-Colonel Axiutshiz, with Joffe as his deputy and Chartshenko as chief of staff.

In May 1944 several motorised engineer brigades were formed out of the original brigade, each consisting of three motorised engineer battalions, an electric fencing battalion and a company for special mining tasks. At the same time the independent engineer battalions serving with the Fronts and armies were amalgamated into brigades at army level. Special assault engineer brigades were formed for breaking through enemy defences, and the number of engineer pontoon bridging brigades increased.

At the beginning of 1945 the components of the 33rd Independent Engineer Brigade were assigned within the 1st Byelorussian Front as follows: 1st and 7th Battalions to the 5th Shock Army, 2nd and 3rd Battalions to the 61st Army, and 4th and 5th Battalions to the 47th Army, with the 6th and 8th Battalions in reserve.

Launching their attack on 14 January, leading elements of the 1st Byelo-russian Front reached the Oder River near Küstrin on the 31st and established a bridgehead on the west bank, but much of the area east of the river had yet to be cleared. In fact the Soviet plans for the destruction of the German forces in Prussia were still tying down Marshal Rokossovski's 2nd Byelorussian Front there. When the Germans assembled a large force to clear Pomerania, the area east of the Oder, from the north, Stalin had to order the 1st Byelorussian Front to drop Zhukov's plans for the immediate taking of Berlin and wheel north to clear the area that Marshal Rokossovski would occupy for the com-bined Soviet assault on the city in due course. Zhukov launched his attack on 1 March and achieved his objective within three weeks. He then left holding detachments on the east bank of the Oder until Rokossovski could take over, while he started preparing for the main assault on Berlin, but the key location of Küstrin did not fall to the Russians until 29 March.

*   *   *

The Küstrin Bridgehead

Our 1st and 7th Battalions had been in the Küstrin area with elements of the 5th Shock Army since the beginning of February 1945. During the first days of February the enemy had blown up the ice on the Oder River above the bridgeheads, thereby artificially removing access across the ice. The situation in the bridgeheads became drastic, our troops being cut off from their supply depots. Only seldom did we receive radio messages from the bridgeheads. One clearly detected that the radio operators of the isolated battalions wanted to preserve their batteries. Most were: 'All in order. Mines wanted urgently.'

Following a talk with the brigade commander, I decided to drive to the bridgehead. We got through to a small village on the east bank of the Oder. My driver, Volodia Koslov, found it easily. Suddenly several shells exploded quite close. We stopped next to a traffic controller.

'Where is that coming from?' asked Koslov.

'From Küstrin,' answered the girl. The enemy controlled a bridge-head on the east bank of the Oder with the town of Küstrin and its fortress. Several attempts to remove it had failed so far.

It was not quite so simple to get to our bridgehead. At the beginning of February we had thrown several pontoon and shallow bridges of various carrying capacities over the Oder but, as a result of the arti-ficially speeded up thawing of the ice and encroaching spring flood-ing, they had been swept away despite all the sappers' efforts. There was nothing for us to do except bring all loads across to the other bank by boats and ferries. Long queues formed at the crossing points. Finally, after a long wait and a short but heated dispute with the commander of the crossing point, we obtained a place on the ferry.

The river at this point was about 300 metres wide. Ice floes floated in the blue-grey water. With them in the flow on the river floated stakes with torn barbed wire and dead bodies. Silently we removed our headwear.

The staff of the 7th Battalion had set themselves up in the cellar of a half-destroyed building in Kienitz. In the vaulted room, lit only by a flickering light coming from a makeshift funnel made out of shell cases, I was received by Major Ogurzov, the deputy battalion commander. He had joined the army immediately after graduating at the Leningrad Water Transport School of Engineering in December 1940. The war had caught him by surprise on the western border. He had fought his way out with our troops to Kiev and further back to the Don and Volga. Ogurzov had belonged to the brigade since it had been formed. The major was an experienced, strong-willed man.

'You are surely frozen through, Comrade Colonel. Do you want to warm yourself up a bit?' asked Ogurzov, and held out the field flask. 'I know how difficult the way is.'

'Thank you, later. Where is Issaiev?'

'He is sleeping nearby. Issaiev was up the whole night in the front line controlling the survey of the newly laid mines. Finally we will have to clear them again one day. Shall I wake him?'

'Let him sleep. Tell me how things are with you.'

'Who's there?' sounded a strong bass voice from behind the rain curtain covering the entrance. Issaiev had woken up. A moment later he came in adjusting the collar of his shirt as he did so. We saluted each other.

'You want to know what we are doing? We are laying mines in front of the position.' The battalion commander spoke in short, clipped sentences. 'Then we beat back all attacks. If we only had more mines. All in all we still have 200 in stock.'

I also visited Folov's 1st Battalion, where everything was also taking its normal course, but 200 to 300 mines were requested.

On the bridgehead I met the commander of the operational group, Lieutenant-Colonel Golub. He had considerable concerns. 'General Fursa has ordered mines to be laid in the river to protect the crossing points. However, we only have the SRM type – they react to the pressure of the stream and cause the mine to detonate.'

A difficult situation. The enemy was trying to destroy our crossing point by all means available. This had failed by air as our fighters and anti-aircraft guns had beaten back all attacks. Now the enemy was using floating mines and sundry assault groups.

Under these conditions the demand of the 5th Shock Army's chief engineer, General Fursa, was completely understandable but technically impossible. I had to go and discuss the situation with him. As always we were quickly unanimous and decided to protect the crossing points with several steel cables stretched across the river upstream to catch the floating mines or cause them to explode. Special teams were to repair torn cables and prevent frogmen breaking through to the crossing points. But the Fascists gave us no peace. One day I was offered an unusual spectacle. A *Heinkel 111* dived out of the clouds and aimed for a pontoon bridge over which a stream of soldiers was crossing. After a short delay the 37mm anti-aircraft guns opened fire. Suddenly the bomber went into a dive and bored into the collapsed soft bank 800 metres from the crossing point. A mighty column of fire rose into the sky. Several seconds later the hot blast of the explosion hit us and swept several men off the bridge, but the traffic continued.

Later we discovered that the enemy had tried to use flying bombs (*Mistels*) against our crossing points. A crewless *He 111* was suspended under a *Focke-Wolfe 190* and stuffed full of explosives. Shortly before reaching the target, the fighter released the bomber, which was radio-controlled and flew independently to its target. Theoretically this system worked faultlessly, but in practice no hits were made on our bridges. Apparently the 'helmsman' lost his nerve in the face of our anti-aircraft gunfire and the expected attack by fighters. The enemy tried once more near Küstrin, but also without success.

From the bridgehead I was able to return to the brigade headquarters without any big adventures. Even the two *Focke-Wulf 190s* that dived down on our ferry could not change anything. Their bombs exploded well away from us and we were merely splashed by a few drops of water.

While our sapper battalions were blocking the way for German tanks with their mines, and those near Stargard and on the Oder conducted counterattacks, the 8th Guards Special Mine Laying Battalion had been carrying out tasks of a special kind. Ships and boats of the Dnepr Red Banner Flotilla had to be moved from the Vistula to the Oder, going from Bydgoszcz by canal to the Varta and on to the Oder.

Our guardsmen had to clear the canal route for the flotilla to get through. The deputy commander of the 8th Battalion, Major Boltov, was entrusted with this task, with his deputy, Captain Melamed. Attached to them were Captain Budko's 2nd Company and a naval diving team from the Fleet.

The clearing of the route began in Bydgoszcz. The canal's lock gates were still in order, the enemy apparently no longer bothering to destroy them in his retreat, but several bridges had been blown in the town itself. In order to impede the restoration work, the enemy had driven vehicles, locomotives and wagons onto the bridges before blowing them. The rubble now lay at the bottom of the canal that our sappers had to make navigable again.

The schedule timing was difficult, which is why General Joffe in his orders had told them not to spare the explosives. Naturally it would have been easiest to clear the canal with heavy explosives. We had captured enough Trotyl, but we could only use it at some distance from the built-up areas as the shock waves would have caused too much damage. The work in Bydgoszcz took several days to achieve, the destroyed bridges having to be blown with appropriately small charges. The rubble was then secured to long cables and hauled off the bottom of the canal by winches and tractors.

Once the route had been cleared, our sappers returned to the Varta. Near Deutsche Krone they discovered a *T-34* at the bottom of a lock. Local people said that its crew had tried to cross the canal over the footbridge, but the bridge was unaccustomed to such a weight and collapsed under the tank. How could we get past the *T-34*? We lacked the means of lifting it, and using explosives might damage the locks. Fortunately there was a tank repair workshop battalion nearby that collected and repaired damaged equipment. Boltov began his talk with the commander of this battalion by going straight to the point. 'We have a fully intact *T-34* for you.'

The captain was immediately excited. 'Where is it?'

'At the bottom of the lock!'

But this did not put the captain off. Next day he turned up with a towing vehicle and recovered the tank.

Shortly afterwards the divers were called away and our sappers had to continue on their own. The base of the canal was protected against the explosive charges with a home-made apparatus consisting of a steel hawser with weights towed by two boats.

At the beginning of March the Varta had spilled wide over its banks, the fast current forming many whirlpools. Nevertheless the sappers went on clearing the channel. On the 13th March the boat containing Major Boltov and his sappers was driven by the strong current on to a destroyed bridge, hitting it. The men fell into the ice-cold water. Comrades in the rescue and mining detachment under the deputy battalion commander for political work, Major Beumelstein, hurried to their help. In doing this the major himself fell into the water and had to take an icy bath.

Immediately behind the clearing team came the ships and boats of the Dnepr Red Banner Flotilla. They continued on to the Spree River and took part in the battle for Berlin. The armoured gunboats achieved considerable success, being armed with multi-barrelled weapons. They later enabled our troops to make a quick forced crossing of the Spree. The boats were also used for reconnaissance and transporting men and equipment. Our Guards Engineers also played a part in the sailors' achievements.

Once the water route to the Oder had been cleared, our 8th Battalion was given a completely new task. The sappers had to make floating mines to go down the Oder into the Oder Harbour. The task of constructing these floating mines was given to Captain Melamed and several sappers.

Captain Melamed set up a research station on a little lake where he blew up captured steel pontoons, as next he had to establish the approximate weight load suitable for speedboats and other small craft. After several attempts the men decided upon a weight of 10 kilograms of Trotyl. The explosions thus produced were sufficient to severely damage the boats.

Meanwhile the battalion's field workshop was fully occupied. Various floating mines with wooden casings were built there. Some were equipped with FTD apparatus with which the mine could be fired by radio, others had clockwork or chemical fuses. Apart from this, the mines had contact fuses that immediately detonated when the end of a wooden pole hit the ship's side.

The prepared mines were carefully released into the water under cover of darkness from a destroyed bridge. A gentle push and the mine slipped off noiselessly into the stream. They were still safe, as the electrical fuses had not yet been set. Only after a certain time, when the mines were sufficiently distant from the bank, were these engaged. Our sappers constructed the various safety devices, most being electro-chemical. After a certain time the acid ate away a copper wire, thereby closing the contact to feather-weight pressure, the ignition only being activated when the fuse was disturbed. Sometimes the mine was only activated when a pin was pulled out by a line.

One night I watched the floating mines being launched. They were released at intervals of two to three minutes. It was pitch black. Only to our right were there flares going up near Stettin occasionally. Now and then the searchlight of a German warship tore through the darkness. Time passed slowly. A good hour had gone since the launching of the first mine. It could not have reached its target.

Suddenly the darkness was lightened by a glaring light. 'Damn it!' swore Lieutenant Colonel Pergament. 'The wind drove the mine on to our own bank.' He had hardly finished his sentence when another explosion followed. A little later two further mines went up on the river bank. 'We are out of luck; the wind is blowing from the west.'

Then came a long interval. It was almost dawn when there were two explosions out there in the harbour. That could have been German ships.

We obtained better results with winds coming from the east or the south. Then the mines were carried quickly into the harbour and our observation posts registered their explosions.

Naturally it was difficult to estimate enemy losses from our mines. But we established from our observation posts that the enemy lost three ships and a loaded barge, a mine-sweeper was badly damaged and two bridges destroyed. Far more important than these losses was the uncertainty our floating mines caused among the German sailors. The shipping traffic in the harbour was destroyed.

Unfortunately we sometimes had to wait several days for favourable winds. During one of these imposed breaks Colonel Leontiev, the deputy brigade commander for technical equipment, visited the battalion. He suggested Lieutenant-Colonel Pergament should occupy himself seriously with 'Sapper Artillery'. During the offensive our troops had captured artillery ammunition of all kinds of calibres that could not be used by our artillery, so our sappers decided to organise their own sapper artillery.

At this juncture Major Boltov, who had cleared the canals with Captain Budko's company, returned.

'Right, comrades, get busy with the captured shells,' proposed Leontiev. The colonel issued general instructions. Construction and fitting went to the officers, NCOs and sappers of the company. The best ideas came from the platoon commander, Lieutenant Alexandrov.

On the west bank of the Oder the enemy had gone over to the defensive. For the first barrage 200 captured shells of between 150 and 211 millimetres were assembled; explosive, splinter, shrapnel, fire and smoke shells. The sappers had dug launching ramps out of the earth and laid each shell on a plank 4 to 6 centimetres wide and about 50 centimetres long. On the plank they fastened an Ammotol explosive charge, over which a second plank held the base of the shell. Instead of the head fuse, a 75 gram Trotyl was inserted in the shell body. Every shell had two electronic fuses. The first, with immediate ignition, sat in the Ammotol explosive body, the second, with a delay of 3 to 5 seconds, in the hole in the shell head. Two batches each of 100 shells were prepared in this way.

Towards midnight the enemy began expanding his defences on the west bank. We heard voices, the blows of axes and the rattling of metal. Towards 0200 hours, when the work on the west bank was in full flow, the command to fire was given.

Flames blazed up on a width of about 500 metres. 200 shells of varyingly set explosive timings flew in the enemy direction. Some exploded over the water, but most burst over the enemy trenches, a fire storm falling on the west bank. Flashes of explosions, crashes, smoke and dust! The losses could only be assessed with difficulty but were certainly significant.

In contrast we could reckon our losses exactly. Our specialists were so engaged with their task that they had not reckoned with the weight of the propelling charges of almost 1.5 kilograms. That was 300 kilograms for 200 loads. The detonation shock waves damaged several positions on our bank and severed telephone cables. Also the rifle company commander's position collapsed in which Lieutenant Alexandrov was located with the firing controls. Fortunately all got out with minor bruises.

On the 12th March the 5th Shock Army had taken the town and fortress of Küstrin after a short but devastating artillery preparation. Ten days later it attacked out of the Kienitz bridgehead north of Küstrin, as did the 8th Guards Army from a bridgehead south of the town. After some bitter fighting they joined up west of Küstrin, confining the remains of the enemy garrison to the suburbs and Oder Island.

The enemy quickly sent in fresh forces and tried several times to release those trapped. On the 26th and 28th March they attacked at intervals of two to four hours. The enemy counterattacks were conducted in narrow strips with forces of up to a battalion reinforced by ten to thirty tanks, but all attacks could be beaten back. Two battalions covered the tank-vulnerable directions with mine barriers, mobile blocking battalions being prepared in time. Thanks to the well organised reconnaissance and stable radio connections, the enemy tanks kept running up against our mobile blocking units. On the 26th and 28th March the enemy lost twenty-six tanks and about 200 men to the mines laid by the 1st Battalion.

On the evening of the 28th March the surrounded group was destroyed. From the large bridgehead thus formed, our troops would soon set out to storm the capital of Fascist Germany.

During the first days of April the destruction of the German groups in East Prussia was completed. The 1st Byelorussian Front was no longer threatened from the north. The 2nd Byelorussian Front destroyed the enemy near Gotenhafen and Danzig and began redeploying to the lower reaches of the Oder. The 47th and 61st Armies moved to the area south of Schwedt and went over to the defence. Our 2nd, 3rd, 4th and 5th Motorised Guards Engineer Battalions that were included in the ranks of these armies went temporarily into reserve.

The enemy engaged in bitter attacks against the 1st Byelorussian Front's bridgeheads. His desperate assaults broke on the staunchness of our soldiers. A contribution to this was made by the combatants of the 1st and 7th Motorised Guards Engineer Battalions commanded by Lieutenant-Colonels Frolov and Issaiev. The enemy lost forty tanks and more than 300 soldiers to the mines laid by them.

The temporary pause could not fool anyone. It was obvious that we would soon be striking out with the last and decisive blow. Our goal was Berlin.

In the woods were the thickly packed tanks and vehicles of the 2nd Guards Tank Army, mainly moving at night. Nevertheless such a mighty concentration of troops could not be kept secret from enemy reconnaissance.

That day the staff held a conference with the battalion commanders. Colonel Sokolov unfolded a large map made up of several pieces stuck together. On its left side was shown Berlin, the city that we had been marching towards for four long years. Numerous defensive rings were shown around Berlin.

'Our troops have to break through a massive defence. Its general depth, including the fortifications in Berlin, is about 120 kilometres. Here on the Oder', Colonel Sokolov indicated the river with his pointer, 'begins the up to 10 kilometre deep main defensive lines, which consist of two or three positions with fully constructed rifle trenches. Numerous barbed wire obstacles have been erected before the front line and deep minefields laid. All barriers and obstacles are covered by numerous fire points.

'The second line of defence lies 10 to 12 kilometres behind it, is up to 5 kilometres deep and includes at most three fully constructed lines of trenches. The strongest sector of the second line of defence is at the Seelow Heights. The third line of defence was built 20 to 40 kilometres beyond the Oder and consists of up to two lines of trenches. All villages have been carefully prepared for defence.

'Then come the Berlin defences. They consist of three defensive zones: the outer barrier zone, the outermost defensive ring and the inner defensive zone. Apart from this the Berlin defence is divided into eight sectors, in the centre of which lies the special sector "Z". In this sector is the Reichstag.

'The outer defensive one begins 25 to 40 kilometres from the city centre and consists of strong-points with numerous barricades and street barriers. The outer defensive zone extends along the city boundary and consists of 3 to 5 lines of trenches for a depth of about 5 kilometres. The inner defensive ring follows the S-Bahn ring. The strongest fortified is sector "Z", where every building is a small fortress. Now we know what to expect,' ended Colonel Sokolov.

The stability of the enemy defence was significantly enhanced by the terrain. Even from a fleeting glimpse of the map one could make out the natural obstacles in the attacking strips: lakes, rivers, canals, woods and villages, whose massive buildings could be used for the defence. All this presented serious difficulties and demanded a careful preparation from us, military craftsmanship and great courage.

'Yes, it won't be easy,' remarked a battalion commander quietly.

No loud words were spoken at this conference. No one doubted our victory. We had been convinced of this before Moscow, and in the difficult days of the retreat to the Volga, utterly convinced of a successful outcome to the war. But we also knew that not all present here would survive to that happy day.

In the discussion above all we talked about how we could best use the remaining time before the beginning of the attack in training for

THE KÜSTRIN BATTLEFIELD

① 31 Jan – Penetration by 6 Soviet tanks.
② 8 Mar – Neustadt occupied by 5 SA.
③ 9 Mar – Soviet landing fails.
④ 11 Mar – Kietz falls to 8 GA.
⑤ 22 Mar – Soviet bridgeheads unite.
⑥ 27 Mar – Bienenhof falls to 8 GA.
⑦ 28 Mar – Kietz Gate breached by 8 GA.
⑧ 29 Mar – Altstadt occupied by 8 GA.
⑨ 30 Mar – Volkssturm surrender 0500 hrs.

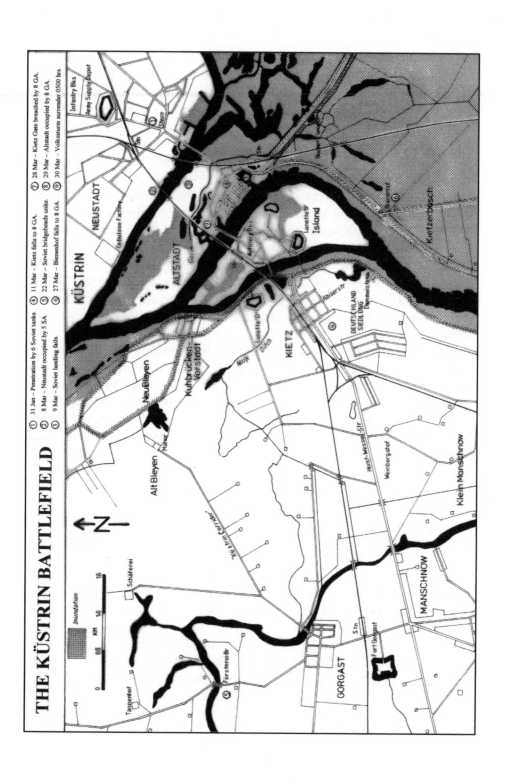

battle. The basic tasks for the brigade were clear. Firstly, gaps had to be made in the minefields in front of the enemy defences to ensure the passage of the second echelon and the tank army. Subsequently came the secure handling of the tank troops in depth. We knew these tasks well enough. On the other hand we were disturbed by the thoughts that our sappers would have to cooperate with the storm troops in the fighting in built-up areas. Such fighting had only been experienced by the 4th and 6th Battalions so far. All others would have to enter new territory. Consequently the officers of these two battalions were given the task of supporting the training and passing on their experiences.

Our troops near Küstrin received further reinforcements, ammunition, fuel and food. In order to handle this, the Front's sappers erected several new bridges. For this construction work our 17th Battalion under Major Stessel was brought in. The task that the 5th Shock Army's Chief Engineer, Major-General Fursa, had set was particularly significant. The sappers had to erect a flat water bridge with a weight capacity of 60 tons. This carrying capacity could only be for one reason: that the bridge was intended for the crossing of the heavy *IS* tank, the strongest fighting vehicle of the Second World War. However, as a rule this tank was only deployed on the main line of attack.

We had also General Fursa's earlier orders to fulfil. At the front every task was important and answerable, and those received from him especially so. The general set high demands, was punctual to the minute, was an expert engineer and controlled everything himself. He often helped out at the front, always had a ready joke, and was always ready to help. Despite his not immediately impressive way of speaking, he was much liked by everyone.

Usually the Oder was about 250 metres wide but, due to the flooding in April 1945, we had to build a bridge almost 400 metres long. The conditions were complicated. The bridgehead at this point was no deeper than 2 kilometres and the enemy could overlook it from the heights on the west bank. Before the construction of the bridge could begin, Major Stessel made a reconnaissance of the actual building site and all its approaches with the battalion's officers. The various parts of the bridge would be assembled in a little wood about 2 kilometres from the Oder. The crews of the diesel-driven pile-drivers prepared their equipment and practised the rapid assembly of ferries on the Warthe.

Construction began at dawn as the chemical warfare troops laid a thick smokescreen. Senior Lieutenant Melkumov's sappers quickly assembled two ferries. Noiselessly they launched them from the river bank and they glided across the dark surface of the water. Everything was quiet on the enemy side. Then the diesel-driven pile-drivers roared as they hammered in the piles, the noise rumbling over the river. A few minutes later two shells exploded a good 200 metres from the working platforms. The enemy artillery had opened fire. But the sappers kept on working indefatigably. They were used to being under fire. They were more concerned about the piles, driving them only one and a quarter metres into the river bed instead of the usual one and a half metres.

'What should we do?' Stessel wanted to know from me.

But as I also did not know the answer, we decided to immediately inform the brigade staff. Three quarters of an hour later came the reply: 'According to the Front Staff's technical department the river bed is firm enough for a depth of one metre to be sufficient. Sokolov.'

The enemy kept on firing. We had dead and wounded, but the work went on. The place of someone falling out was immediately taken by another. Stessel's men were used to all kinds of tasks. At the slightest failure of a pile-driver Sergeant Majors Krasnoshtchek and Permiakov were there and sorted it out.

General Proschliakov had ordered that the state of construction be reported to him hourly. It was already apparent how important the construction of the bridge was to the Front Staff. The work continued even at night. As the morning dawned the last planks were inserted. This work had been led by Captain Shirov. Several times Stessel had demanded: 'Vassia, lie down for at least an hour. You have already been the whole day on your feet!' But Shirov remained on the bridge. Nobody would leave his post voluntarily.

Exactly twenty-four hours after the work had begun the bridge was complete. Slowly a self-propelled *ISU-152* gun inched over the bridge. Would the sappers's efforts pass the test? The bridge sank a little under the weight of the gun. The men turned ice cold at the sight. It was the same with me. The gun rolled slowly forward. It worked! Once several tanks and self-propelled guns had crossed the bridge it had sunk 60 to 70 centimetres deeper. How far would it have sunk after hundreds of heavy tanks had rolled over it? But everything went well, the bridge held!

Through the self-sacrificing engagement of the sappers there were already twenty-five bridges across the Oder by the beginning of April. Guardsmen of the 17th Mechanised Battalion had participated in building three of them. Apart from this there were forty ferries with carrying capacities ranging from 3 to 60 tons.

Our 2nd, 4th, 5th and 7th Battalions were at the Küstrin bridgehead on the 16th April and were under the command of the 3rd and 5th Shock Armies. The members of these battalions had cleared the concentration areas and the approach routes of mines during March and early April. Parallel to this was the engineering reconnaissance, as well as the structural reconnaissance by the battalions, led by the reconnaissance teams from each company. The battalion commanders Koslov, Eiber and Issaiev spent many hours in the front lines observing the enemy defences. From time to time our sappers even went behind the enemy lines with the army scouts, reconnoitring the defensive mine layout behind the front lines and the terrain in the lines of attack.

In the woods north of Küstrin on the east bank lay the 3rd and 6th Battalions allocated to the 2nd Guards Tank Army. They had their hands full with the simultaneous testing of the river banks and the de-mining of the army's concentration area and its approach route to the bridgehead.

In reserve were the 1st Battalion, the 6th Battalion for electrical barriers and the 8th Battalion for special de-mining tasks, who were preparing themselves for mine clearance in Berlin and its suburbs.

On the night leading to the 13th April paths through their own minefields were cleared for the 3rd and 5th Shock Armies. By midnight four to six paths for every rifle battalion and two to three paths for every tank company had been cleared. Altogether 340 paths were cleared in the 1st Byelorussian Front's area, the sappers having cleared and deactivated 72,000 mines.

The night leading to the 16th April was stressful. Time seemed to stand still. Then, exactly at 0550 hours, the earth shook. Thousands of guns and mortars showered the enemy with a hail of fire. This hurricane of fire fell on the Seelow Heights for 70 minutes while 800 long-range aircraft bombarded the enemy's second line of defence. Then 140 mighty searchlights lit up and blinded the enemy. The artillery moved their fire deeper into the defence. Two or three minutes later the infantry and tanks thrust forward. As it became light, the air was filled with the droning of aircraft engines.

Towards 0700 hours the first line of the main line of defences was breached almost along the whole front, but the resistance increased.

Every metre had to be fiercely fought for. It was only on the morning of the 18th April that the second line of defence was breached.

As the attack began, the elements of our brigade in the rifle corps battle groups cleared the main lines of advance and de-mined them. Each battalion kept back a company at the commander's disposal for expanding the gaps in the previous front line.

Our 3rd Battalion dealt with the Guards tank units. On the morning of the 14th April Lieutenant-Colonel Gassenko had received orders from General Joffe to concentrate his battalion in the Genschmar area by the 15th April, where it would then come under the operative command of the 9th Guards Tank Corps.

The battalion moved out of the bridgehead that night. The vehicles moved with their headlights masked. All equipment not specifically required was left behind with the Rear Services. Finally a deep penetration into the enemy hinterland lay before them. Near Alt-Schaumburg the column passed over a flat water bridge that had been constructed by the engineers while under artillery and air attack. Individual planks had been destroyed several times, but could be quickly replaced. The bridge reflected this: it was awry and crooked with ups and downs between the pillars. Here and there the planks of the decking had been replaced by solid poles, whose uncut ends stuck out widely over the water. The sappers had not had it easy here.

On the approach to the bridge all the lights were switched off and the vehicles drove carefully over the bridge. In the darkness there seemed to be no end to its 400 metres.

The bridgehead bore traces everywhere of bitter fighting. On the 14th and 15th April our units had forcibly cleared it and pushed the enemy back 2 to 4 kilometres. The land won that way was regularly studded with mines.

The commander of the 9th Guards Tank Corps, General Vedeneiev, explained the task to Gassenko. 'Above all the corps' concentration area must be checked and cleared of mines. Here and here.' The general pointed to the map. 'Secondly, check the two routes from the concentration area to the enemy's front line and clear all mines to a width of 100 metres. The corps operates in two echelons. In the first echelon a tank brigade advances on each route, in the second echelon a tank brigade on the right-hand and the motorised infantry on the left-hand route. After the corps has driven into the breach there are two routes for the brigades to advance along to be reconnoitred and de-mined.'

By the morning of the 16th April the routes were ready and carefully checked. Towards midday the first tank officers met Gassenko to make themselves familiar with the routes and by 1630 hours the tanks were rolling westwards.

For the reconnaissance and clearing of the routes a sapper company was officially allocated to each of the brigades. The third company remained in the corps commander's reserve.

The sapper scouts worked with the battle reconnaissance troops sent forward by the tank units. Should they come across mines, the sappers would sign them and make a way through for the tanks and armoured cars. By radio the tank troops informed the leader marching with the sapper platoon in the vanguard about the obstacles. If need be the company commander could send the two remaining platoons in support. Thus it was ensured that the route would be cleared before the arrival of the brigade's main forces. The platoon with which the vanguard dealt had to be changed every two or three days because of the losses and severe strain on the nerves.

Lieutenant-Colonel Gassenko and the reserve company stayed with the tank corps headquarters. Communication with the companies was by radio and despatch rider.

These methods showed their value best in the introduction of the tanks into the breach. The enemy had generally not laid any mines previously in the depth of his defence, but first laid them during the fighting, mainly under pressure of time, openly and only scantily camouflaged. Mines found like this were disarmed or blown relatively easily by our men.

During the breakthrough of the enemy defences in the Wriezen–Altfriedland sector, the 9th Guards Tank Corps pushed on in order to go round Berlin from the north. Our Guards Engineers also advanced with the tank troops. On the night leading to the 20th April the 1st Company of the 2nd Battalion found itself at the head of the 65th Tank Brigade. Shortly before dawn vehicles with infantry hanging on drew into a wood next to the sappers. In the half-darkness and still moving forward, no one was interested in who was driving at the back of the column.

As it grew light in the east the column stopped. The leading battalion had become engaged in the fight for a village. In this stressed situation the company commander, Captain Schimarovski, noticed that some vehicles were following his unit with their headlights on. He ordered his sergeant-major to immediately get them switched off and get things in order.

A soldier hurried to the rear. But before he reached the vehicles he was shot from the first vehicle. At the same moment the other vehicles opened fire on our column. Germans!

The tank-men turned the turrets of their *T-34s* and fired. Our sappers also fired. Within a short time the enemy column was defeated. Twenty-six vehicles and dozens of soldiers and officers were squashed flat by the tank tracks; the remainder fled into the wood leaving eight guns behind.

Mines at the Brandenburg Gate
On the morning of the 21st April a cheerful atmosphere reigned at brigade headquarters. Our troops had broken through the outer defence zone and were now fighting on the Berlin city boundary.

The first were elements of General Bessarin's 5th Shock Army storming the Fascist capital from the east. In their ranks were our 2nd and 7th Guards Engineer Battalions. Lieutenant-Colonel Assonov's operational group coordinated the management of the battalions.

Berlin had been reached! How long had we yearned for this day, now it was here at last! But we also knew that the Fascists would not willingly give up a foot of earth and that expensive street fighting lay ahead of us.

We had long since prepared our troops for this fighting. On the way from the Vistula to the Oder, during the short gaps in the fighting the theme of fighting in built-up areas had arisen. The staffs at all levels studied the experiences of street fighting in Schneidemühl and Poznan, leading to the rationalisation of the assault teams and the battalions that would play the decisive roles in the street fighting. Cooperation between the various arms was also practised.

Normally an assault team consisted of a rifle platoon, a sapper section with two or three flame-throwers, two to four guns, and sometimes also one or two tanks or self-propelled guns. An assault battalion had up to an infantry battalion, a sapper platoon, a flame-thrower team, as well as the corresponding reinforcement with artillery and tanks.

Our brigade also prepared itself for dealing with assault battalions and groups. In the technical battalion Tregub and Kuberski investigated suitable charges for blowing walls, barriers and barricades.

Within the units there was training in the demolition of various objects.

On the afternoon of the 21st April we received a radio message from Lieutenant-Colonel Golub. Laconically he told me: 'Find me at point 17–24.'

'The 3rd Shock Army is fighting in the north-eastern suburbs of Berlin,' remarked Sokolov after he had checked the coded map. 'Golub's group is already in Karow.'

The street fighting became more and more bitter from hour to hour. The nearer our troops got to the city centre, the more ferociously the enemy fought. He fired from dug-in tanks, from tank turrets and from bunkers. Machine guns fired from windows and rooftops, and machine-pistols in the streets. In the entrances of buildings and behind barricades *Panzerfausts* lay in wait. Numerous natural and artificial obstacles obstructed our movement.

The commitment of tanks and self-propelled guns in the streets was difficult, because within the city their manoeuvrability, their most important fighting asset, was limited. Thick clouds of smoke hung over the city and hindered the use of aircraft. Thus the artillery played an especially important role in the street fighting. Guns of all calibres, from the little 45mm to the heavy 203mm howitzers fired point-blank.

The significance of the sappers also grew by bounds. The sappers, ensuring the advance of the infantry, blew up everything that the gunners and tank-men could not destroy. But this had to take place in close cooperation with the other arms.

My task consisted above all of organising the cooperation and the exchange of experiences in the fighting until then. This is why I drove to the 7th Battalion fighting in Falkenburg, where Issaiev, the youngest of our battalion commanders, was still assessing his fighting experiences. We only got forward with difficulty in the vehicle. There were heaps of rubble everywhere; bomb craters and burnt-out tanks blocked the way. Twice we had to change tyres before reaching the headquarters of the 7th Battalion.

'How's it going, Michail Jakovlevitch?'

'As usual, Comrade Colonel! The sappers are dealing with the assaults by platoons, blowing up barricades and fire positions.'

'Have you come across mines?'

'None so far. It looks strongly as if the Fascists have run out of equipment. Perhaps they also no longer have the time. Apart from that, the streets are asphalted, which is not very helpful.'

I could see an unspoken question in Issaiev's eyes.

'And what else is there?'

'The commander of the 89th Rifle Division is demanding a company from me to send in. If I were to fulfil all his orders, a whole brigade would not suffice.'

Yes, that was the unfortunate problem with this cooperation. When it came to the laying or removal of mines we had, even when also under difficulties, fought for the right to decide for ourselves how and with what forces to deal with it. Here under street-fighting conditions we had to start apparently from the beginning all over again. What should I say to this battalion commander? Advice was quickly given, but Issaiev must also be able to translate it into action.

'Let yourself formulate exactly every task. Decide yourself how many men you can deploy to it. If a company is too much, send only a platoon.'

In my notebook I wrote: 'Speak to the 5th Shock Army's Chief Engineer about the proper use of sappers.'

At that moment the deputy battalion commander, Major Ogurzov, came pounding down the cellar steps. His face was beaming. He was holding a *Panzerfaust* in his hand. The enemy had placed great hopes in this weapon. Its hollow charge could penetrate 150 to 200 milli-metres of strong armour and it had a range of about 100 metres.

'A fine piece of equipment,' said the major. 'Our boys have quickly learnt how to use it.'

That morning we had captured an ammunition dump with several hundred *Panzerfausts*. Ogurzov had familiarised himself with and trained the men on the weapon. Later our sappers used the *Panzerfausts* successfully in the street fighting. One shot in a window was sufficient to silence the enemy firing point, and three *Panzerfausts* were sufficient to break through a slate or thin wooden wall.

Lieutenant-Colonel Koslov's 2nd Battalion was with the 26th Rifle Corps at this time, which was leading an obstinate fight around the Alexanderplatz and the surrounding streets.

I had to go to Koslov and asked my driver: 'How do you find your namesake?'

'Even if I don't find anyone, Comrade Colonel, I will take you there to the millimetre. My vehicle is always tanked full. That is how things are when Koslov comes to Koslov.'

Volodia wanted to calm his nerves with a joke. Since the 21st April he had had only two hours sleep per day.

We drove along Frankfurter Allee. The broad street was blocked with heaps of rubble. One came across wrecked vehicles at every turn. White flags hung out of the windows, but there was no sign of the inhabitants.

The nearer we got to Alexanderplatz, the more the guns thundered. The command post of the 2nd Battalion was located in the cellar of a five-storey building just 30 metres from Alexanderplatz.

Lieutenant-Colonel Assonov reported: 'We are fighting in Alexanderplatz, the Town Hall, the S-Bahn station and the Police Presidium. The units are working with the assault groups.'

At that moment the battalion commander entered the command post, his uniform covered in dust.

'Twice we have tried to break through this damned wall, but it is still standing and won't shake. We have only made a few blisters,' grumbled Koslov unhappily.

The enemy was conducting a bitter defence near the command post. Some *Panzerfaust* men that had occupied a shop nearby made it especially difficult for us to act. A high wall had to be breached in order to get round the enemy. Sappers from the 2nd Battalion had twice tried to blow it in vain, and were now preparing a third charge.

'What's the matter, are the loads too small or don't the calculations work out?'

'Tregub and Kuberski experimented in the village,' said Koslov, 'but the walls there were not as thick as these are here.'

A soldier entered the cellar and handed Koslov a message. 'The commander of the 2nd Company, Captain Artamonov, informs me that the wall has been blown. The storm group have forced their way in behind the shop and occupied the ground floor.'

Quite close we heard a hollow explosion and dust trickled down from the ceiling.

'Assault guns,' said Koslov unimpressed, and unfolded a map of Berlin. 'At the moment our troops are attacking the Police Presidium, an old building with strong walls. The doors and windows are barricaded with sandbags. Tuschev's company is cooperating with General Fomitshenko's 266th Rifle Division. It won't take much longer. Then they will attack the S-Bahn station and the Town Hall.'

The words 'Town Hall' gave me a jolt. That was somewhat similar to our own 'Town Executive Committee'. There must be departments of the city administration there responsible for the various branches of the city's economy.

'Boris Vassilievitch, as soon as the Town Hall has been taken, send in a smart officer. He should look for the plans of the drainage system and the U-Bahn and bring them here. We could well need them for the fighting in the city centre. We must also use the underground facilities to get behind the enemy. But don't forget that the Germans could suddenly appear behind them.'

The fighting in Berlin continued undiminished. Assault battalions and groups broke the bitter resistance of the enemy and forced their way step by step into the city centre. Our sappers played an important role as our troops surrounded the strongpoints, blowing breaches in the walls for our infantry to get behind the enemy's backs.

On the 25th April elements of the 47th Army and the 2nd Guards Tank Army of the 1st Byelorussian Front that had gone round Berlin from the north met up in the Ketzin area with the 4th Guards Tank Army attacking from the south. Berlin was surrounded!

As before, we found Lieutenant-Colonel Gassenko's battalion with the 2nd Guards Tank Army.

The many small rivers and canals going round Berlin formed a serious obstacle for our tanks. They were from 8 to 30 metres wide and most had firm banks. Numerous bridges went across these water obstacles that the enemy either blew or mined as we approached. The correct timing for the taking of a bridge depended often on the success of a whole division. Speed and dexterity were thus especially important. The allocated sapper reconnaissance units were carefully selected and well equipped, and were led by clever and decisive commanders.

On the 24th April the leading battalion of the 47th Tank Brigade reached a wood 4 kilometres east of Nauen. The scouts reported that both railway bridges over the Havel Canal had been blown. The bridges on the highway were undamaged but were strongly guarded and prepared for demolition.

We immediately sent a platoon of four tanks, submachine-gunners and a sapper platoon of the 3rd Guards Battalion. The tanks rolled forward under cover of a smokescreen and opened fire on the soldiers guarding the bridge. The German soldiers took cover, enabling the submachine-gunners and sappers to cross over the demolished railway bridge in the canal and attack the bridge guards from the rear. Sergeant-Major Sokol and Privates Demin and Varava rushed to the demolition cables. But before they could reach them they were knocked down by bullets. Immediately the commander, Captain Schimarovski, Sergeant Netschipurenko and Privates Buschuiev and

Doronin replaced them. They cut through the ignition cable and neutralised the charges there of half a ton of Trotyl and three 250 kilogram bombs as the submachine-gunners gave them firing cover.

Once the charges were neutralised, Captain Schimarovski signalled the way clear with green flares. Now the 47th Tank Brigade was able to cross the bridges and enter Nauen. The Fascists fled, leaving their weapons and equipment behind.

Next day the leading battalion of the 9th Guards Tank Corps had to stop at the Sacrow–Paretz Canal near Potsdam. The railway and road bridges over the canal had been blown, and the enemy were firing from the opposite bank with artillery and mortars. The approaches to the destroyed bridges were covered by several machine-gun nests.

The middle span of the railway bridge had been blown, but the girders still lay on both outer ones. Lieutenant-Colonel Gassenko had a good look and decided to let the tanks drive over this bridge. Piles were made out of the bridge beams lying in the water, which reinforced the planks. While the bridge was being built, the sappers removed twenty mines from the approaches. The following morning the 65th Tank Brigade crossed over the repaired bridge.

Captain Kurnossov's company also distinguished itself, ensuring the success of the 47th Tank Brigade, the sappers sitting on the tanks of the leading unit. Near the Brandenburg Gate they smashed into an artillery regiment on the march. In the pursuit of the fleeing enemy, two tanks crossed over the Silo Canal in an enemy column and opened fire on the bridge guards. Lieutenant Guryliev and his sappers got up and rushed to the bridge rails. They cut through the ignition cable and separated the explosive charge. The bridge fell undamaged into our hands. Once they had recovered from the first shock, the enemy tried to regain the bridge but were beaten back by tank-men and the sappers.

After taking Brandenburg and Potsdam, the 9th Guards Tank Corps turned and attacked Berlin from the west.

The 9th Guards Tank Corps forced its way into Charlottenburg with some heavy fighting. On the morning of the 30th April the tanks were rolling towards the Tiergarten. Once more the sappers had to clear mines, barricades and barriers, and blow breaches in walls. They formed attack teams with members of the 33rd Motorised Rifle Brigade.

The Fascists had set up a large barricade on the Charlottenburger Bridge, all the approaches being mined. On the night leading to the

2nd May some sappers slipped through to the barricade under the cover of fire from the tanks and infantry. Although the enemy were using mortars, the sappers cleared twenty-two mines. Sergeant-Major Morgov and Sappers Muravkin and Schulenin were wounded but continued working, blowing the way clear for the tanks with several charges. Then they cut the ignition cable and disarmed the five 150 kilogram bombs under the bridge.

At the end of April our headquarters were in a suburb, although our troops were already fighting in the city centre. We had to change position as soon as possible. General Joffe tasked Lieutenant-Colonel Golub and myself with finding another place for our headquarters. We selected one near the stadium in Weissensee.

The street fighting was getting ever harder. Fighting broke out for every street, every building and every barricade. Our 2nd and 4th Battalions were fighting with the 3rd Shock Army and the 5th and 7th were with the 5th Shock Army.

On the night leading to the 29th April General S.N. Perevertkin's 79th Rifle Corps crossed the Moltke Bridge under a hurricane of fire and reached the entrances to the Reichstag. When we heard this news we immediately reached for our maps. We were less than a kilometre from the Reichstag!

Also fighting in this area was Lieutenant-Colonel Eiber's 4th Battalion, which belonged to Lieutenant-Colonel Golub's operational group. I drove to his command post at Plötzensee on the morning of the 30th April. Golub had established himself in a cellar and reported that the 4th Battalion had taken part in the storming of Ministry of the Interior, where the men had had a hard time.

Suddenly anti-aircraft guns thundered nearby and bombs exploded.

'Comrade Colonel, would it not be better if we took cover?' suggested Golub. Without waiting for my assent, he ordered his radio operators: 'Forward, men!'

In the comfortable trench, covered and lined with planks, we waited in safety for the air attack to end. A machine sped low over us. At the same moment there was a crash. It was dark in front of my eyes. When I came to several seconds later I could not hear anything, but that came back very quickly. We had all come through with our skins intact, but a nasty surprise awaited us in the cellar. The ceiling had collapsed from the bomb explosion nearby. Had we remained in the cellar, it would have been bad for us.

Golub continued his interrupted talk. 'Do you know, Viktor Kondratievitch, that the storm battalion is a mixture of infantry, sappers, gunners, tank-men and flame-thrower teams working together. The men come from various units and hardly know each other. Even the commanders can hardly find time to know each other. But as we all know, only a precise cooperation guarantees success.'

I had already applied some thought to this. During the fighting for Poznan and Prague it had become clear to me that the street-fighting structures were not really suitable. Even the engineers' assault brigades that had been trained for breaching strongly fortified defensive strips and for fighting in towns had neither artillery nor tanks. In our brigade there was not even a single heavy machine-gun. The fighting in Berlin showed that street-fighting demanded assault regiments or brigades. They should consist principally of infantry units to which sufficient sappers, depending on the situation of either a company or a battalion size for every rifle battalion, should be attached. Naturally flame-throwers, its own artillery, self-propelled guns and tanks also went with it. With this composition the cooperation would be far better organised.

On the afternoon of the 30th April we heard that the fighting for the Reichstag had begun. As Golub's operation team had no exact details, I decided to sort out everything on the spot. Between Plötzensee and the Moltke Bridge were only a few kilometres in a straight line. But the attempt to get through by a direct route failed. Rubble, bomb craters and burning buildings blocked the streets. Finally we reached the Moltke Bridge.

Near the approach to the bridge stood a smoke-blackened *T-34*. A traffic controller waved us to drive on or the enemy would immediately shoot up the vehicle. We crossed the bridge at walking pace, turned right and found ourselves in front of a large building complex – the Ministry of the Interior. The windows on the Spree side were either bricked in or barricaded with sandbags.

In the inner courtyard I unexpectedly came across Major Tschernov. The deputy political adviser looked exhausted. He reported briefly to me on the state of the 4th Battalion. He had participated in the fighting for the Ministry of the Interior and blown up several barricades.

'How's the political work going?'

'Before the battle we held several meetings on the significance of the fighting in Berlin. In Captain Kanaschin's company the Communists took sponsorships of the recently joined young soldiers. This initiative was also copied in the other companies.'

While making some notes, it occurred to me that no better form of Party political work could be done than in this situation.

'Would you like to take a glimpse of the Reichstag?' Tschernov asked.

The Reichstag could be seen clearly through a hole in the wall. Behind the windows on the first floor shots flashed from time to time.

'The ground floor is already in our hands,' explained Tschernov. 'Now we are driving the Fascists out of the upper storeys. It won't be long before they are finished.'

But the fighting continued. On the morning of the 1st May the deputy battalion commander, Major Poleshtchuk, came to Lieutenant-Colonel Eiber's observation post.

'The enemy are attacking with tanks and self-propelled guns from the Tiergarten and want to break through to the Reichstag!'

Immediately the companies of Captains Kanashin and Suchanishvili were alerted. In all haste they laid a hundred mines in the Tiergarten. Shortly afterwards a self-propelled gun lost a tank track. Several shells penetrated its side. Our heavy *IS* tanks had opened fire. Then the other enemy tanks and self-propelled guns withdrew, still firing. The counterattack had been beaten back.

On the evening of the 1st May the resistance eased off. Only here and there submachine-guns let rip. Towards midnight it became quiet. The 6th Battalion had accommodated itself in a school. Lieutenant-Colonel Roshdestvenski lay with his staff in a former administrative building. Not far off was also the 1st Battalion. Late that evening Lieutenant-Colonel Frolov and Lieutenant-Colonel Roshdestvenski reported on the de-mining of the city. Finally they went off to rest.

Towards 0400 hours the sentries of the 6th Battalion heard engine noises and the rattling of tank tracks. Apparently a strong enemy group was trying to break out of the enclosed part of Berlin. The sentries opened fire and raised the alarm. The sappers took up defensive positions. Meanwhile the battalion's chief of staff, Major Rebrov, made contact with the brigade staff by radio and told them what was happening. Lieutenant-Colonel Frolov radioed his battalion for help. Behind the 6th Battalion lay an anti-aircraft gun regiment. The crews brought their guns into position and engaged the enemy with heavy fire. Now came the moment for Captain Stalev's company. His men blocked the enemy's route with mines. The sappers also successfully used *Panzerfausts* in this fighting. They destroyed one tank and a self-propelled assault gun. In this fighting the enemy lost one tank, two assault guns, several vehicles and about fifty men.

As dusk fell the 1st Battalion attacked the enemy in the flank. Almost 200 men and officers were taken prisoner.

On the morning of the 2nd May powerful loudspeakers conveyed the appeal by the commanding general of the LVIth Panzer Corps and battle commandant of Berlin, General Weidling, to surrender unconditionally. For hours afterwards short bursts of fire came from here and there, but these outbursts were quickly quelled. Peace finally came at about 1500 hours. The capital of Fascist Germany was in our hands.

Chapter 4

Battle Comrades

By Army-General Stanislav Poplavski

Born in the Ukraine of Polish parents, Poplavski was conscripted into the Soviet Army in 1923 and promoted sergeant upon completion of basic training a year later. He later graduated in the top ten from the Military School for Red Cadres, where he remained as a major and instructor in general tactics and the Polish language. In mid-1940 he was posted as chief of staff to the 720th Regiment.

When the Germans attacked and his regimental commander was wounded, Poplavski took over the command and was later awarded the Order of the Red Banner before being posted as chief of staff to the newly raised 363rd Rifle Division; shortly afterwards he was promoted lieutenant-colonel. In January 1943 Poplavski was appointed commander of the 185th Rifle Division of the 29th Army, six months later becoming commander of the 45th Rifle Corps. In October 1943 he watched the newly raised Polish Kosciuszko Division going into action for the first time near Lenino. At the end of August 1944 he was summoned to Moscow and transferred to the Polish Army.

The Polish Army raised by the Soviets consisted in fact almost entirely of Soviet citizens except for those young Poles who had reached military age during the war.

Poplavski continued to serve with the Polish Army until his retirement in 1956, when he returned to Moscow, as did several of his compatriots who had served in the Polish Army while retaining Soviet citizenship.

* * *

On the afternoon of the 5th April I was summoned to the telephone. I was still thinking about the tactical exercises that I had been going through with the 3rd Division, from which I had just returned to Greifenberg [Pomerania].

I recognised the well-known voice of Colonel-General Malinin. 'What is your army doing?' As I knew that headquarters did not like long accounts, I replied briefly. Malinin listened to me and then posed the question: 'And what do your soldiers think about Berlin?' I got up from my chair. 'All our soldiers and officers are waiting impatiently for the order to attack Berlin!'

This impatience, which was also apparent from my voice, seemed to impress the Front chief of staff. Jokingly he remarked: 'And I thought that you enjoyed doing coastal defence.' Then in a serious tone he went on: 'Orders are on their way to you. From them you will see your next task.'

I immediately summoned my staff officers and our new chief of staff, Rotkievicz. They came apprehensively, not realising that I was hiding my overwhelming delight. Eventually I said solemnly: 'Friends, I have invited you to give you some highly unpleasant news. The Polish Army will be participating in the Berlin operation!' A roar of sheer delight erupted.

On the same day I was summoned to a conference at Front headquarters. There I learned that our army would be part of a group on the right flank of the 1st Byelorussian Front that would be conducting a secondary thrust. On the premise that one could expect a three-day training course for the army commanders, the fighting tasks of the various formations were discussed. This concerned cooperation during the attack, and possible variations in the conduct of the battle.

After returning to Greifenberg, I first went to visit the Polish airmen. The 4th Mixed Air Division under Colonel Romeyko was located on the airfields in the Märkisch–Friedland area, and the preparations for the Berlin operation were already in full swing. From early until late intensive fighting training for all personnel was under way.

In the name of the government of the People's Republic of Poland, I decorated those who had conducted themselves especially well in the previous fighting. Most of them were Poles who had come from the Soviet Union. There were also younger Air Force members that had come directly from Poland, and felt themselves closely connected with the 'veterans'. The whole Polish Army already knew about these young experts who flew machines bearing the Polish national emblem. There were also those to whom I gave fighting decorations. Next to them stood their loyal companions, the Polish technicians, who set an example in air safety.

Back in Greifenberg I immediately dealt with a difficult problem: the regrouping of the Polish troops on the right flank of the 1st Byelorussian Front. To be precise, within six days (8th–13th April) we had to conduct a march of 200 kilometres and concentrate in the Königsberg area. The redeployment had to be conducted secretly, so only night marches were envisaged.

According to the operational plan, the 1st Polish Army and the 61st Army, with which we had cooperated in the liberation of Warsaw, had the task of expanding the breakthrough by the Front's main forces and simultaneously securing it against a possible counterattack from the north. The 1st Byelorussian Front had already gone on the offensive on the 16th April, while the 2nd Byelorussian Front further right would attack four days later. The enemy could use this opportunity to transfer strong reserves to strike the main body of Soviet troops in the flank.

The regiments moved in accordance with the timetable to the south-west. At night I drove along the roads where the 3rd, 4th and 6th Divisions were marching. Discipline and order were being strongly adhered to by them, as were the camouflage instructions. The columns only used the right-hand side of the roads, leaving the left-hand side available to traffic in the opposite direction.

The following night I inspected the cavalry brigade. For the first time they were conducting their move by horse, the Uhlans sitting well on their horses. Not for nothing were the Poles known as born cavalrymen. The remainder of the night I spent in Stargard so that early in the morning I could call on the 77th Rifle Corps, which was to relieve us. I was just about to leave when I saw a Soviet general in the neighbouring yard. He recognised me, and I went towards him, and in fact it was an acquaintance from the academy, Stepan Kinosian. He immediately recognised me in my Polish uniform and looked me over before opening his arms for a welcoming greeting.

Kinosian was chief of staff of the 49th Army and was awaiting the arrival of Rokossovski. As I had not seen this famous army commander since 1941, and would very much like to see him again, I stayed on for a while with Kinosian.

On the road appeared several cars. In front was a big Mercedes, out of which Rokossovski climbed. Energetic and elegantly clad, he joked and laughed. I stood to one side, waiting for a suitable moment. Rokossovski had already glanced in my direction, when I finally went up to him.

'Was that your cavalry I saw on the march?' asked the Front commander, after I had saluted him.

'Indeed. They are Uhlans of the 1st Independent Cavalry Brigade!' I answered.

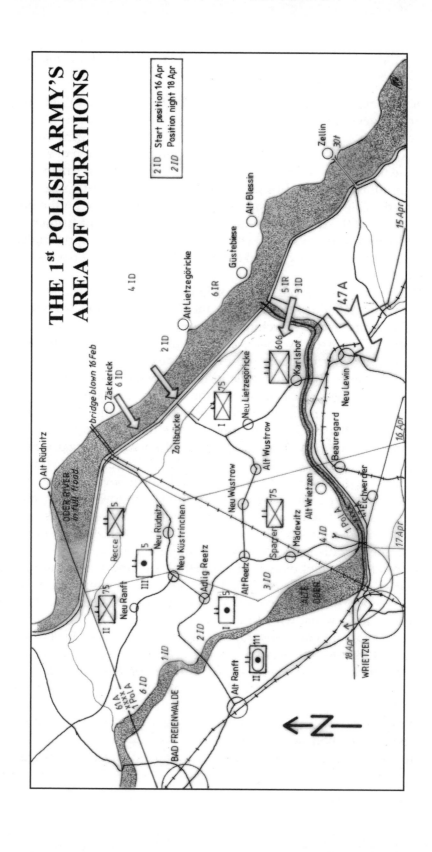

THE 1st POLISH ARMY'S AREA OF OPERATIONS

21D — Start position 16 Apr
21D — Position night 18 Apr

Zellin
30t

Alt Blessin

Güstebiese

4 ID

Alt Lietzegöricke

6 IR

3 ID
5 IR

47 A

606
Karlshof

bridge blown 16 Feb
Zäckerick
6 ID

21D

Zollbrücke

Neu Lietzegöricke

Alt Rüdnitz

I 75

Neu Wustrow

Alt Wustrow

Neu Lewin

Beauregard

ODER RIVER
In full flood

5
Recce

5
III

75
II
Neu Ranft

Neu Rüdnitz

Neu Küstrinchen

Adlig Reetz

Alt Reetz

3 ID

75
Sparrei

Mädewitz

Alt Wietzen

4 ID

Alt Eichwerder

1 Pol A

17 Apr

16 Apr

15 Apr

21D
I 5

II 111

Alt Ranft

WRIETZEN

18 Apr

1D
6 ID
61A
XXX
1 Pol A

BAD FREIENWALDE

ALTE ODER

←N—

'A fine brigade! Judging by their appearance, the cavalry men are not badly trained. Their bearing on the horses is exemplary, and the horses are magnificent.'

With this approving remark from the mouth of an experienced rider, and that was from Rokossovski himself, one could be really happy.

'The Polish soldier is a good soldier,' went on the Front commander-in-chief. 'I am Polish myself and know the bravery of my people in war. In the liberation of Gotenhafen and Danzig the tank troops fought excellently, even though that is the youngest branch of the army. The members of the Soviet tank troops have spoken very laudably of them.'

Rokossovski was in a hurry. He wished our army success and went on to a commanders' conference.

I hurried to get to the commander of the 77th Rifle Corps, General Posniak. I found the corps commander in Gross Wuhbiser. He too was an old acquaintance of mine, as we had both taught at the Frunze Academy before the war. But there was no time now to recall those days. I had to familiarise myself with the terrain in which my army had to engage.

We began on the right wing near Alt Rüdnitz and gradually approached the Oder. The east bank, being higher than the west bank, enabled us to overlook the enemy defences to a depth of almost 5 kilometres. We defined the actual lines of the rifle and communications trenches on the maps, as well as the situation of the firing points and the minefields.

The Fascists had had enough time to construct their positions, having been here for about three months. The open flat countryside extended up to the Alte Oder and was cut through by numerous high water dykes and road embankments. The enemy had arranged a strong anti-tank defence here, and the Oder itself, which had overflowed its banks for almost a kilometre, formed a serious obstacle.

Then we went to the Güstebiese area to General Pozniak's observation point. The place was especially well selected. One could see the whole of the enemy defences. Even the bridgehead that our left-hand neighbour, the 47th Soviet Army, had formed on the western bank of the Oder was visible. What interested me most was that we too had to force the river.

'What do you think?' I asked Posniak. 'Is the bridgehead adequate for the 47th, at least to take a Polish division in the northern part?'

'I think so, yes,' replied Posniak, convincingly.

I then went to see the commander-in-chief of the 47th Army, General Perchorovitch, but he was afraid that our troops would cramp his own regiments.

I was obliged to take my concern straight to Marshal Zhukov. Perchorovitch then showed himself agreeable. He said that he was ready to take not one but two Polish divisions in the bridgehead. Later other elements were also deployed there.

Hardly anyone doubted any more that approaching catastrophe awaited Fascist Germany. Even Hitler concerned himself with winning time in the hope of at least evolving a separate agreement with the Western Allies, so that the Anglo-American troops would occupy the greater part of Germany, including Berlin.

Influential Anglo-American circles did not balk at breaching the Yalta Conference agreements. Germany's unconditional surrender and the shared occupation of its territory – especially Berlin – by the Red Army did not correspond with their political views. According to the decisions of the Yalta Conference, there was a demarcation line between the Soviet and Anglo-American troops. But on the 2nd February 1945 Churchill informed Eisenhower by telegram that 'I regard it especially important that we meet as far east as possible.' The British standpoint in this matter was emphasised by the English military historian Fuller with brazen openness as follows: '... for the Americans and British lies the only possibility of saving what remains of middle Europe by occupying Berlin before the eastern Allies can get there.'

The Fascist leaders did not neglect to exploit this convenient situation. In compliance with their hints, the German high command opened the central sector of their western front and concentrated all their efforts in the east on the defence of the Oder–Neisse River line.

I will not try to describe all the positions that the enemy erected on the Oder and Neisse Rivers. I only want to point out that this line consisted of three strongly constructed lines of defence. The enemy wanted to hold up the Soviet troops here long enough for the Anglo-Americans to be able to get to the capital of the Fascist Reich and negotiate a separate peace treaty. Altogether there were more than a million men defending the approaches to Berlin. They had more than 10,000 guns and mortars, over 1,500 tanks and self-propelled guns, as well as 3,300 aircraft.

For once and for all to put an end to Fascist Germany and simultaneously finish the intrigues about Berlin, the Soviet high command decided to conduct the Berlin operation as quickly as possible.

Also participating was the 2nd Polish Army under Divisional-General Karol Swierczevski. With its five infantry divisions, an artillery division, a tank corps, two anti-tank brigades, two self-propelled artillery regiments, an independent heavy tank regiment as well as other elements, it was a powerful, well equipped operational formation. It would be superfluous to say that it was the Soviet Union that had equipped these troops with modern weapons. During the war the People's Poland had the following equipment at its disposal: 302,994 rifles and carbines, 106,531 machine-pistols, 18,799 light and heavy machine-guns, 6,768 anti-tank rifles, 4,806 mortars and 3,898 guns. 630 aircraft were handed over to the Air Force. A tank corps and two independent tank brigades were equipped for the Polish armed forces.

Up to the 9th April the 2nd Army was concentrated north of Bunzlau. It came under the 1st Ukrainian Front and took part in a thrust on Dresden.

Two German infantry divisions defended the strip to be attacked by the 1st Polish Army. One of them – the 5th Light Division – had been torn apart by us in Pomerania, but here it had been necessarily replenished. We first had to deal with the 606th Infantry Division. Apart from this, reconnaissance in the Wriezen area had established the presence of the 5th Motorised Infantry Division and a group of tanks. The gunners had discovered about eighteen enemy artillery and mortar batteries.

The 2nd and 3rd Divisions would lead the main thrust out of the bridgehead with the 47th Army. Alongside our 1st Infantry Division, which had to force the Oder in the Christiansaue area, they would drive forward via Neurüdnitz to the Alte Oder and take the river crossings.

The first reconnaissance in force was made by the 2nd Infantry Regiment in the Zäckerick area. However, it was badly prepared and ended in failure. Where the Oder had to be forced was a submerged high water dyke that the boats could not cross. Before this problem had been discovered, and a suitable position found, it was daylight. I had to reprimand the regimental commander, Sienicki, and got a deserved reproof from the Front commander-in-chief myself. But this reprimand applied to me as much as Bewziuk and Sienicki, for example. All had now understood that the crossing of the Oder had to be prepared much more carefully.

At this point the army's sappers and bridge-building elements were operating with initiative. For the beginning of the offensive they had constructed 200 boats and arranged for the necessary equipment to be taken across the river. During the forcing of the Oder the sappers twice erected a pontoon bridge under fire, the first time south of Güstebiese and then – the same bridge again – 6 kilometres downstream. Apart from that they set up several ferry crossing points and a 200 metre long 30-ton bridge on piles. This bridge was the main traffic link for the Rear Services, not only of the 1st Polish Army, but also our right-hand neighbour, the 61st Soviet Army.

Two days remained before the attack was to begin, and during this time the idea arose of also moving the 4th Infantry Division into the bridgehead to create a stronger striking force. I consulted with Karakoz and Bordzilovski. They supported me, although the undertaking was naturally risky. If there was room for another division in the bridgehead, the density of troops would result in heavy casualties in an air attack. Colonel Romeyko assured us that his pilots would dependably cover our infantry.

So Kienevice moved his regiment to the west bank of the Oder by night, inserting them between the 2nd and 3rd Divisions. That concluded our preparations for the operation.

The War Council of the 1st Byelorussian Front addressed an appeal to the soldiers and officers of the 1st Polish Army in which was said among other things: 'Through your famous victories you have won the right of participating in the attack on Berlin with your sweat and blood. Fulfil your fighting tasks, brave fighters, with your usual decisiveness and dexterity, with honour and fame. Upon you depends that with a mighty attack you will break through the last enemy defensive positions and destroy them. To Berlin!'

On the 14th and 15th April the Front's various armies carried out powerful reconnaissances. This confused the enemy. A captured officer made the following statement: 'At first one thought that the attack would begin on the 14th April, then one estimated the 15th April. Finally one was convinced that the Soviet troops had actually postponed their attack.'

The change in the weather may have contributed to this conclusion. Thick fog lay over the ground and the bed of the Oder River was completely covered. Karakoz and I did not leave the command post all night. There was already enough excitement, and now came the bitter blow played by the weather!

But finally it took pity on us. At dawn on the 16th April a fresh wind arose and the fog dispersed. Before daybreak the thunder of the guns announced that the 1st Byelorussian Front had begun the Berlin operation. Following a half-hour artillery preparation, the 1st Polish Army went into the attack at 0615 hours.

It seemed as if the enemy had never and nowhere defended themselves so bitterly as at the Oder. From the start our troops had to repel one counterattack after another. Nevertheless they still broke through the enemy defence and advanced 5 or 6 kilometres. In doing so the 1st Division remained somewhat behind the other units. It had to cross the river fighting. A small gap opened between our army and the 61st Army, and the 1st Division had to keep an eye on their right flank the whole time. Under these circumstances I placed the 6th Infantry Division in the gap during the night leading to the 17th April and ordered it to secure the Army against thrusts from the north. Communications with the divisions worked well and the reports on the progress of the fighting arrived at the command post on time.

The 3rd Infantry Division had the greatest success, its commander, Zaikovski, having been promoted brigadier-general meanwhile. Its units advanced 7 kilometres and took Altwriezen, Altmädewitz and Neukietz, the regiment on the left flank reaching the northern edge of Wriezen.

Members of the 47th Army had already penetrated the town from the south. In order to speed things up, I had the 4th Infantry Division drive into the sector between Zaikovski's division and the 47th Army. The enemy now gave up Wriezen and quickly withdrew his units, our troops hard on his heels.

Once the 5th Light Division had been driven back to the Alte Oder, our units made an advance of 15 kilometres. Then they came up against a new enemy, a training formation thrown against us, the 156th Infantry Division. Once our units had repulsed six of their counterattacks one after the other, they advanced a further 10 kilometres and reached the line Trampe–Danewitz–Schmetzdorf.

The gap between us and the 47th Army was now almost 10 kilometres, so the Front introduced the 7th Guards Cavalry Corps at this juncture. As the situation consolidated straight away, it was possible to increase the speed of attack.

Late on the evening of the 20th April our Army and the 61st Army resumed the attack. I let fresh forces – the 6th Infantry Division and the cavalry brigade – into the attack. This developed immediately. Towards noon on the 23rd April, our units, in close collaboration with the Soviet cavalry, forced the Oder–Havel Canal in the Oranienburg area and hit the 3rd Naval Division that the enemy had hastily thrown in here from other sectors of the front.

The Army headquarters crossed over to Birkenwerder, an idyllic corner. Surrounded by woods, the whole place was submerged in greenery. The first flowers of spring adorned the gardens of fine-looking villas. Everything invited rest and recuperation, but that was not for us. We soon moved the headquarters on to another place.

Immediately before leaving, three German workers approached us. I invited them inside a house and offered them Havana cigars that we had captured. Each one gratefully took a cigar, but did not light them, pocketing them instead. The visitors had come to thank us for their liberation. The oldest – he must have been well into his sixties – affirmed that they greeted the defeat of Fascist Germany with all their hearts. 'I am a Communist,' he said, 'and these two are both partyless Anti-Fascists. Threatened with death, we have had to hide ourselves. Your victory has given us the opportunity to breathe freely again.'

'And what do the other workers of Birkenwerder think?' I asked.

'The whole population is frightened by Goebbels' propaganda, but many are gradually beginning to understand that you are bringing us peace, progress and democracy, of which, General, you may be convinced.'

The words of the German workers sounded sincere and strengthened my hope that the fate of future Germany would lie in the hands of such Anti-Fascists. The German Communist gave me a tobacco pipe that I still have today.

I told Jaroszevic about the encounter with the German workers. He was also of the view that the German population would recognise the deceitfulness of the Fascist propaganda more every day.

And so it happened. Gradually the ice in the relationships between the population and our troops began to melt. The people were more communicative. They chatted with the soldiers more often, and asked questions about Poland and the Soviet Union. They offered their help in repairing the roads and crossing places. Children and old folk lined up at the field kitchens with eating utensils in their hands.

On the 24th April the units of our army, which had advanced 80 kilometres fighting, had reached the line Kremmen–Flatow–Börnicke–Nauen and had gone onto the defensive as instructed. They had to cover the right flank of the Front's main group, which was completing the encirclement of Berlin.

Already the next day it became obvious that the enemy had in no way been beaten. At daybreak elements of the 25th Motorised Infantry, the 3rd Naval and the 4th Police Divisions undertook a counterattack. Especially strong was the pressure on the junction between the 5th and 6th Polish Infantry Regiments. The regiments were unable to stand the pressure and withdrew 3 kilometres. In doing so the commander of the 2nd Infantry Division, Colonel Surzyc, made a mistake, enabling the enemy to make a small bridgehead on the south bank of the Ruppiner Canal.

The attackers were stopped thanks to the heroism and resourcefulness of the gunners of the 2nd Howitzer Brigade under Colonel Wikientiev and the anti-tank brigade of Colonel Dejniechovski firing at point-blank range.

In the end we needed two days to clear the area of the enemy. Surzyc's failure had cost us dear. Certainly he was a young commander and took the failure to heart, as also did Rotkievicz, who had commanded this division shortly before.

We established ourselves temporarily on a 40 kilometre wide sector and prepared for a thrust towards the Elbe River, the Army headquarters moving to Marwitz.

On the way to Paaren, where the operational staff were located, we came across Ribbentrop's country mansion. It lay in a thick wood of ancient oak and beech trees on a picturesque lake. A high iron fence shielded it from the outside world. Within the mansion was an underground bunker reached by a lift with upholstered walls and benches.

I visited room after room fully astounded over the unusual luxury, cut across the sports room with wall bars and rings, and looked at the treatment room with its most modern medical apparatus and the air conditioning engine room. I looked at the expensive crockery, crystal vessels, weapons and hunting trophies, and thought of the Goebbels-like pomposity that I had seen from afar as I drove past Lanke. There, rising above a lake before a background of a cloudless sky, and particularly picturesque to look at, stood a still more luxurious palace than Ribbentrop's, the summer residence of the Fascist Reichs Minister for Propaganda, with its turrets and much ornamentation.

In view of all this luxury in which the Fascists criminals lived, I had to think of the sea of blood and tears that had accompanied their rule. I instinctively thought of the many death camps that we were liberating every day.

Imprisoned in the Sachsenhausen Camp near Oranienburg were people from various European countries and German Anti-Fascists. There were many Polish girls among the prisoners. The Fascists had carried them off as forced labourers in the armaments industry, putting them behind barbed wire for the slightest offence.

In one barrack block languished a Spaniard who had been incarcerated in Fascist torture chambers for almost five years. He looked as if he was over seventy, and was so weak that he could not even speak. Fellow sufferers gave his name: Largo Caballero, former prime minister of Republican Spain. Largo Caballero was immediately taken to the medical battalion of the Kosciuszko Division, where doctors and nurses tended him day and night. When I was able to get away from my work for a little I went to see him. Caballero was already getting better and he told me about the last days of the fighting against Franco, how he had fallen into the hands of his enemies in France and how the Fascists had mocked and abused him. Once restored to health, Largo Caballero was flown to Moscow.

On the 23rd April a group of political workers who had visited Sachsenhausen Concentration Camp sent me a written report. Although this was not the first statistical report about cruelty and death that I got to read, it made my blood cold. There had been about 200,000 prisoners in the camp. They were weak from hunger and exhausted by sickness, having been forced to work fifteen hours a day, beaten with whips and kicks. Dogs were set on them, and they were shot and hanged. The army's political apparatus saw to it that these deeds, these bestial acts of Fascism, were brought to the attention of all elements of the troops.

On the 27th April the 1st Polish Army and its neighbour took part in the war for the last time along the Rhin Canal. The heavy fighting lasted until the 30th April.

The XXXXII Panzer Corps tried to assert itself against all logic and reason. Prisoners said that the losses in men and equipment in the units amounted to 70 per cent. One German officer declared despondently: 'This counterattack was the last. There are no longer sufficient forces to hold out.'

And in reality the Fascists withered away. Our divisions conquered Fehrbellin, Hern, Landin, Strohdene and many other places. The last enemy troops withdrawing towards the Elbe River in our sector were defeated.

The following episode is reported here. On their retreat the Fascists had blown the bridge west of Rhinow. Tanks and guns were jammed together [waiting to cross]. The sappers had not arrived in time on this occasion.

I climbed into my car and went to the bridge. Its metal girders had been thrown from the central pillars by the explosion, but their ends were still fast in the embankment, forming a deep saddle, whose lower part hung in the water. How could one sort this out? I looked around. Wooden beams were stacked on the river bank. The thought hit me: fill the saddle with the beams! With the help of some soldiers I carried the first beam across. The tank soldiers assembled on the bank understood me without a word. They immediately joined in and soon the crossing point was ready. The convoy of vehicles moved off.

Meanwhile the Fascist command hastened to get the remainder of their troops across the Elbe. They stuck to their intention of rather being prisoners of the Americans or British than the Russians, but we got ahead of them first and pushed them out of the way.

The 1st May had arrived with a clear, sunny morning. There were no clouds to be seen. As usual, I was up very early. Suddenly my adjutant, Captain Huszcza, entered the room. 'General Zymierski has arrived.'

Buckling my belt, I hastened to meet him.

The commander-in-chief listened attentively to my report on the fighting by the 1st Polish Army, checking with his hand on the map the situation of every formation and unit. Afterwards he summoned the divisional commanders and wished them well on the 1st May. He had them pass on to the regiments his thanks for having conducted their military duties so selflessly. Then we drove to the 4th Infantry Division, whose allocated tanks were already over the canal.

The commander-in-chief stopped at the front line in the soldiers' trenches, at the battalion command posts and the artillery's firing positions. Everywhere he spoke to the soldiers and officers about the fighting and the future of Poland. It was the 2nd May by the time we returned to army headquarters. Captain Huszcza was waiting for me on the doorstep. He gave me a radio message. I looked at him and my breath stopped. Rola-Zymierski noticed this and asked me with a concerned voice: 'Has something happened?'

'Berlin has capitulated!' I said, inwardly excited.

Officially the surrender of Berlin had yet to be confirmed, but the historically important event was already being discussed by the troops. Everyone was certain that the war could end any day. And we were proud that Polish soldiers had participated in the defeat of the enemy's Berlin group.

The 1st Infantry Division 'Tadeusz Kosciuszko' – pride and ornament of the Polish armed forces – fought in Berlin during the last days of the war. Already on the 29th April the Front commander-in-chief had called me at an unusual hour, about 1500 hours, and asked for a situation report. I usually reported to him at 1800 hours. As I reported to Zhukov what positions the troops had taken at 1300 hours, he interrupted me with the question: 'How is that, Stanislav Hilarovicz? Don't you still want to partake in the storming of Berlin?'

'We having been waiting impatiently for such an order to arrive from you, Georgi Konstantinovitch. We are ready to undertake this honourable task,' I replied, moved and hopeful.

'Which division would you deploy?'

'The 1st Infantry Division, the Kosciuszko Division!'

'I approve your choice', the Marshal said, 'See to it that a regiment of this division is moved immediately to the Reinickendorf area, where it is to be at the disposal of the commander-in-chief of the 2nd Guards Tank Army. The remaining elements must be there by 1800 hours on the 30th April. The Kosciuszko Division's sector will be taken over by the 61st Army. General Belov has already been informed.'

From these words I gathered that the participation of the Polish division in the assault on Berlin was already decided. Yes, we ourselves had already more than once disturbed the Front commander and his member of the war council, Lieutenant-General Telegin, with this matter. Thus had our request been met.

Rotkiewicz then set to preparing the appropriate orders, whilst I discussed with Jaroszewicz the significance of this event to our army. We were agreed that the participation of the Kosciuszko Division in the storming of the Fascist capital was a perfect example of the brotherhood in arms of the Polish and Soviet peoples and their armed forces that must be valued.

'Should one not prepare and distribute a pamphlet appealing to the soldiers of the 1st Division?' suggested Jaroszewicz.

'Not a bad idea,' I agreed. 'The division's political department can deal with it.'

Early next morning I drove to the 1st Infantry Division to assist with the move of the regiment and wish the soldiers and officers success in the forthcoming operation. The units were already in the trucks provided by Zukanov's soldiers, and the political department's assistants were bringing them what they had printed on freshly coloured leaflets. I still have a sample today as a valuable momento. The text read:

Kosciuszkovcy!
You are setting off to take part in the storming of the Fascist beast's cave. You have been entrusted with the great task of planting the red-white banner, your country's symbol, that has never gone under and never will go under!

The soldiers read the pamphlets several times as if they wanted to learn these impressive words. Finally the column of Kosciuszko fighters moved off towards Berlin.

Next, the 3rd Regiment took up the fight, attacking from the Charlottenburger Chaussee. To the right of it operated the division's 2nd Regiment and to its left the 12th Soviet Tank Corps. The tanks had already penetrated as far as the Englische Strasse area, but individual enemy groups remained in their rear trying to stop fuel and ammunition supplies. Now Polish troops came to the aid of the tank soldiers, battalions of Colonel Archipovicz's 3rd Regiment. They had to fight for every building and every floor. The attacking infantry were supported by gunners. With their accurate fire they opened up the way for the infantry through the city district. Finally the Soviet tanks could be seen, fighting half-surrounded.

The tanks were topped up with fuel by the tankers brought forward and the fight was resumed after a short pause. Covered by the fire from the Soviet tanks, the Polish infantry's assault groups entered the buildings and cleared them of the enemy.

Soldiers of the 2nd Regiment took part in the storming of a housing complex near the Landwehr Canal. The fighting did not ease off for a minute during the night. Enemy resistance was first broken towards morning as the Soviet tanks and Polish infantry appeared on Berliner Strasse. But there they were checked by a housing block in which the Fascists had established themselves. Frontal attacks brought no success, but a group of our soldiers managed to get in from the rear. They reached the first floor up a staircase and threw down grenades, causing panic among the Fascists. Now our shock troops made a resolute attack on the next building and then the whole block. Almost 200 prisoners were taken in the fighting.

The Technical High School, surrounded by barricades, was strongly defended. The Fascists covered them with the fire from guns that had been installed in neighbouring buildings. The soldiers of the 2nd Regiment were sent sappers to assist and explosives came on request.

The infantry stood beside the gunners. Often they dragged the guns after they had dismantled them – carriage, barrel and wheels – into the upper storeys of the buildings, thus becoming able to fire in retaliation over the heads of the Fascists.

The Technical High School could not be taken until the morning of the 2nd May. Afterwards the soldiers crossed the S-Bahn and railway lines and penetrated the Zoological Gardens. On the Budapester Strasse they met up with soldiers of the 1st Ukrainian Front who were storming Berlin from the south. It is difficult to describe the pleasure that seized the combatants at that moment. The soldiers of both brotherly connected armies clasped each other, threw their hats into the air and gave loud cheers. This was the long foreseen moment of triumph over the Fascist beast!

Nevertheless it was a little premature to celebrate victory. Soviet and Polish soldiers were still fighting in Bismarckstrasse and Schillerstrasse, where the 1st Regiment under Lieutenant-Colonel Maksymczuk was attacking. It had entered the battle later than the other elements of the division and had come under strong artillery fire. The battalions deployed east of the Schloss-Strasse, which was defended by SS and Police units.

The attack of the 1st Regiment had begun here at 0300 hours on the 1st May. The soldiers pressed forward fighting on Bismarckstrasse. The artillery fired at point-blank range, the walls of buildings collapsed noisily and there was the uninterrupted fire of machine-guns and machine-pistols. The Polish soldiers attacked the German *Panzerfaust* men, who were waiting for the Soviet tanks with hand grenades.

The enemy was firing from a cellar with machine-guns, forcing the Polish troops to the ground. But Sergeant Levczyszyn crawled, pressed to the tarmac, to the building and threw two hand grenades into the cellar. The machine-guns fell silent. Soon the building was in the hands of the Polish soldiers. On the roof they hoisted the red-white flag, the first Polish flag over Berlin's ruins!

And again a hail of bullets fell on the tarmac, this time from the first floor of a large corner building. The gunners came to the infantry's help again. The advance continued.

A U-Bahn line ran under the Bismarckstrasse. The first stations could be taken relatively easily, but then came a station that the Fascists had turned into a strongpoint. Guns, machine-guns and even a tank had to be used. Lieutenant Wassenberg's gunners assisted in the taking of this little 'fortress', firing at point-blank range. Under cover of their fire, the infantry forced their way into the strongpoint and the garrison had to surrender.

In the advance along Grolmannstrasse the mortar crews under platoon leader Bdych especially distinguished themselves. They dragged their weapons along the sewers in the rear of the Fascists. An unexpected barrage from the rear and a simultaneous attack from the front and the Fascist defenders of a large building complex were finished.

I quote these episodes as they show quite clearly how decisively and bravely the Polish soldiers behaved in the street fighting and thus helped the Soviet soldiers in destroying the enemy. In the storming of Berlin the members of the Kosciuszko Division had covered the weapons and flags of the Polish Army with glory.

Two regiments – the 1st and the 2nd – had engaged later in the battle than the 3rd, but were able to end it sooner. But finally also the 3rd Regiment pushed forward to the Brandenburg Gate riding on Soviet tanks. The enemy resistance was finally broken. Only occasional bursts of fire from machine-pistols here and there were still heard. That evening peace came to liberated Berlin.

Polish aircraft were also involved in the Berlin operation, including the 1st Mixed Air Corps that had arrived at the front in April 1945 with 300 combatant aircraft. The Polish high command had altogether four air divisions and three regiments of auxiliary aircraft at its disposal.

Two days before the beginning of the Berlin operation our 4th Air Division, including the technical air battalion, moved to airfields 30 kilometres north of Küstrin.

If I am not mistaken, it was on the 24th April that the commander-in-chief of the Polish Air Force, General F.P. Polynin, came to my command post. I knew him already from before the war. Later we met on the western front where he was then commanding an air army and organising air support for the ground forces. Polynin spoke very highly of the Polish airmen. For example, he particularly praised Lieutenant Bobrovski and Second-Lieutenant Lazar, who had participated in the air battles over Eberswalde, and also both Lieutenants Kalinovski and Chromy. During a reconnaissance flight they had attacked two *Focke-Wulfs* that were wanting to bomb our positions. Kalinovski shot one of the aircraft down, while the other one, after it had discarded its bombs, flew off.

Polynin had come with an operational team to see me in Wriezen. Among them was the chief of staff of the Polish Air Force Telnov, the chief engineer Koblikov, and other generals as well as the commander of the mixed air corps Agalzov. They occupied the command post permanently and directed the aircraft in accordance with the tasks of the infantry divisions.

From the first day on we maintained close contact with the airmen. I learned from General Polynin that an infantry division from the Steiner group had pushed forward to the Ruppiner Canal with fifty tanks with a view to making a flanking attack. Our situation on the northern bank of the canal was anyway somewhat difficult. We only had the cavalry brigade left in reserve and a redeployment of the widely spread out division would be very difficult. But we could not let the considerable forces of Steiner's group cross over to the southern bank.

'Can't you deploy the air force?' I asked General Polynin.

'They will attack immediately!' he replied.

I told him that I wanted to relocate Vikentiev's howitzer brigade and Dejniechovski's anti-tank brigade there.

The losses that the Steiner group incurred through our airmen, gunners and troops of the 2nd Infantry Division were so considerable that the planned counterstroke ended as a local counterattack.

With their attacks, the Polish airmen destroyed the enemy positions and delayed the bringing forward of his reserves into our army's attack area. On the 29th April alone there were 237 sorties by aircraft of the 4th Air Division. In the night leading to the 30th April the 2nd Bomber Regiment attacked the enemy concentration in Fehrbellin, and in the night leading to the 1st May the Night-Bombing Regiment 'Krakow' attacked troops in Neustadt and Friesack. On the 2nd May the night bombers bombed the Fascists retreating from the blows of our army to Rhinow and Spaatz.

Assemblies of troops had formed in Rhinow, where several roads met, and from where ran the shortest route to the Elbe crossing points. They were subjected to intensive air attack. On the 3rd May fighter and bomber aircraft strafed the enemy columns on the roads between the Havel and the Elbe, thus destroying a large number of vehicles, extensive amounts of equipment and hundreds of soldiers.

Early on the morning of the 3rd May Rola-Zymierski and I drove to the 6th Infantry Division on the army's right wing. Its 14th Infantry Regiment under Major Domaradzki had already crossed the Havel with improvised crossing means and reached the Elbe bank while pursuing scattered groups. The remaining regiments of the 6th Division soon followed, Colonel Szejpak being the most agile this time.

For the whole of the 4th May the commander-in-chief remained in Berlin with those elements that had participated in the storming of the city. That evening the duty officer brought us a telegram from Korczyc. The Polish Army chief of staff congratulated Rola-Zymierski on his promotion to Marshal of Poland – in other words the highest rank in the Polish Army. I was congratulated on my promotion to colonel-general.

Berlin had fallen, but the fighting at the approaches to the Elbe continued relentlessly. In the Klietz area the 4th Infantry Division encountered the resistance of strong forces defending the crossing places. A large underground explosives factory was still at work near the town. No Polish soldier was allowed in and no worker out. General Kieniewicz did not want any advice. A surprise attack could well resolve the problem, but Kieniewicz feared that the mad director could blow up the factory. It could not be excluded that the demolition would be effected with a long fuse. A solution was found unexpectedly. Two captured soldiers offered to conduct negotiations with the underground factory. 'We will deal with the workers and not the Fascist directors,' said one of them. 'I am a worker myself and will soon convince them.'

In fact it did not take long and hundreds of people left the underground factory with white flags. Only one did not come up: the director, who had shot himself.

During the morning of the 4th May the 2nd Division reached the Elbe, followed in the night leading to the 6th May by the 4th Division, which had beaten the enemy in the Klietz area. Now the whole right-hand bank of the Elbe in the army's sector was in our hands. American troops had reached the river on the other side.

Once Marshal Rola-Zymierski had left for Warsaw, I quickly went to the Elbe. Everywhere on 'our' bank fluttered the victorious flags of the Soviet and Polish units. In honour of the joint victory, the Allied armies greeted each other with gun salutes. Our representative, Colonel Stanislaw Domoracki, went to the Americans, taking with him the best wishes of the Polish soldiers on the victory over the common enemy.

Our units left Berlin. The regiments of the 1st 'Tadeusz Kosciuszko' Division with the Grunwald Cross 3rd Class and the Virtuti Militari Order 4th Class marched in parade step past the Brandenburg Gate, over which the Polish flag waved next to the Soviet one.

The army was reassembled near the Seelow Heights and the headquarters accommodated in Seelow itself.

Later I was permitted a stay in Berlin. My sight-seeing naturally took in the Reichstag, on whose walls thousands of inscriptions could be seen, among them also the signatures of Polish soldiers.

The city was breathing again little by little. Here and there were people with picks and shovels, clearing ruins and dismantling barricades. Not far from the Brandenburg Gate a queue of Berliners had formed at a Soviet field kitchen. A jolly cook filled the utensils they had brought with them with *Kascha*. The orders of the City Commandant, General Berzarin, were conveyed over loudspeakers, spoken by representatives of the new German self-administration.

The crimes of the Fascists in Buchenwald, Majdanek and Auschwitz were broadcast from a vehicle. The Berliners standing next to it listened attentively, some shaking their heads unbelievingly. The loudspeaker fell silent. From the crowd rose a voice damning Hitler. A woman cried out, 'We are all guilty for this war and now we have to pay!'

On one square the inhabitants and soldiers were watching a film in the open air. Being shown was the Soviet film *Soja*. I went nearer to observe the reactions of the audience. 'I cannot believe that the German soldiers could be guilty of such bestiality,' said a woman standing nearby. 'That is Russian propaganda!'

'Unfortunately that is all true,' a man answered her in a low voice.

To be in Berlin and not call in on General Berzarin was simply unthinkable. He commanded an army to which my corps had once also belonged. I had the friendliest feelings for this talented army commander and outstanding man. Without thinking about it long, I ordered Wladek to drive to the Soviet Kommandatura.

In Berzarin's reception room were packed many people, both civil and military. The General greeted me warmly: 'Yet another representative of a friendly army! How would you like to be greeted; strictly according to etiquette or unconstrainedly?'

'Better unconstrainedly.'

'Shall I tell you the latest lies of the Fascist underground muck-rakers?' Berzarin wanted to know. 'Here is it: yesterday about 50,000 Mongol soldiers arrived from the Elbe, plundering and murdering their way through the city. It is said even the Soviet commandant was completely powerless against them. Naturally some of the inhabitants panicked.'

'But everything is quiet in the city,' I remarked.

'Yes, the anxiety has died down again. Even the distrustful inhabitants have noticed that rumours of that kind come from Fascists who have not been uncovered yet.'

Berzarin then told me about the protocol on the interrogation of General Weidling – the commander of the Berlin defence sector – and other Wehrmacht generals being completed. They threw light on the circumstances in which the Reichs Chancellery and the headquarters had governed during the last days of the Fascist Reich: reciprocal mistrust of those who long before had quite different opinions, reciprocal threats, doubts, uncertainty, indifference about the fate of the Berlin people, suicides.

I did not want to detain Berzarin any longer from his important obligations. We parted warmly. Could I then have believed that this was our last encounter? It hit me deeply when I heard of his death.

Chapter 5

The Steel Guard

By Lieutenant-Colonel Wenjamin Borissovich Mironov

Mironov was an experienced officer, having attended the Tomsk Artillery School and the Frunze Academy before participating in the defence of Kiev, serving in a parachute battalion behind German lines near Smolensk, at Stalingrad, then on the Northwestern Front, the Kursk bend, Byelorussia and Brest. He had been wounded near Briansk.

Mironov now commanded the 347th Guards Heavy Self-Propelled Artillery Regiment of JSU-152s equipped with howitzers with a range of well over 9,000 metres. Their high explosive shells, weighing 96lb, and the armour-piercing shells, weighing 107lb, were so bulky that only twenty rounds could be carried. The vehicles had a crew of four (or five if equipped with radio).

* * *

Prelude

On the 30th January 1945 the brigades of Colonels Chotimski, Vainrub and Yeshov, as well as our regiment and a regiment of medium self-propelled guns (SPGs), thrust into Küstrin from the north and took up the fight for the town. That same day Captain Ivan Koslitin sent me a bottle of Oder water as evidence that the scouts had reached the east bank of the river in the Alt Drewitz–Küstrin sector. The Political Officer, Major Nikolai Ossadtchi, took a gulp out of the bottle and proudly reported: 'The Oder has good water.' Adjutant Michail Sacharkin added: 'Suvorov and Kutusov have already slaked their thirst from this river.'

So we had reached the Oder, the last big water obstacle to be defended by the enemy on our way to Berlin. The river had frozen over a few days before. The ice was free of snow and reflected the sun's rays like a mirror. The east bank dropped steeply.

I drove to Alt Drewitz to find our corps commander, General Krivoshein. On the way I met Koslitin, my reconnaissance officer. He briefed me on the layout of the German defences. The enemy was

The JSU-152.

making every effort to defend Küstrin in order to evacuate fighting equipment, factory equipment and transport to the west bank and win time for the construction of the Oder–Neisse line of defence. Koslitin showed me a sketch with the indicated objectives that had been compiled from lengthy observation, prisoners' statements as well as details from airmen, infantry and armoured soldiers.

In front of the Oder bridges the enemy had erected two rows of bunkers. Between Küstrin and the Oder bridges were crammed military transports and convoys. The railway station was full of trains and war material. 'This transport must certainly be destroyed. If the enemy can bring it over the Oder, he can throw it against us in battle' was Koslitin's opinion.

This comment seemed to me so important that I decided to ask General Krivoshein to be allowed to attack immediately. I came to Alt Drewitz. Suddenly someone called me. I turned round and saw Major Loslov, my former deputy in the light SPG regiment.

'Where's the corps staff?' I asked.

Koslov pointed to the neighbouring building and groaned.

'Has something happened?'

The major shrugged and said to me in a breaking voice, 'I have finished as a regimental commander. Here is the order.'

We sat down on a heap of rubble and the major recounted: 'The light SPGs were deployed east of the railway in defence as they had no more fuel. Then, when the enemy tanks attacked, they could neither manoeuvre nor withdraw. Nearly all the regiment's guns were destroyed in this action.'

'How could you let things go like this?'

Koslov took a deep breath. 'The Rear Services had not sent us any fuel and I dared not report to the regiment as not fit for action and pull them out of battle.'

We said goodbye to each other. Subdued voices came from the roomy cellar of a building. General Krivoshein was sitting at his desk and assailed me straight away with the question of how many self-propelled guns (SPGs) I had had to leave behind me on the way. 'Except for two trucks that should arrive any moment, the regiment is complete,' I answered him.

Krivoshein silently took my map and drew a cross on the Oder bridges and the Küstrin railway station. These were precisely the objectives that Koslitin had spoken about.

'Take into account', the general exhorted me, 'that the leaving of covered firing positions to fire over open sights requires especially rapid handling by the crews.' Following this remark I was dismissed and was able to return to regimental headquarters, where Sacharkin, my adjutant, and Major Shabalin were already waiting for me. I told them what the general had ordered and we discussed the details. Finally Shabalin and Koslitin worked on the plan of battle while Sacharkin and I set off to the company commanders to select the firing positions and observation posts.

Before us lay the picturesque panorama of the old town of Küstrin and its fortress, from where the German artillery was firing. Right on the edge of town, at the most prominent point, was a factory with a tall chimney.

Our SPG went through a depression. 'Stop here!' I called to the driver. 'This is the right place for our firing position!'

I ordered Lieutenant Muraviov to take up position with his submachine-gunners on the forward slope of the high position to secure the SPGs' position. A little later the first soldiers went forward, their spades flashed faintly and clods of earth flew through the air, the soldiers working without a break.

Soon the SPGs were able to roll out of the woods into their prepared positions. Startled by the noise, a wild boar decamped, its young following, grunting and squeaking. When Lieutenant-Colonel Pashitnov, our training officer, saw the boar, he was immediately overcome with hunting fever. 'To hell with the camouflage,' he swore. 'Can I shoot now? We could have a tasty roast this evening.'

I went through the positions. Our Communist Party Secretary, Captain Anatoli Postnikov, was telling the soldiers that we were standing on historical ground. The great army commander Kutusov had defeated the Napoleonic troops here 132 years ago on the 31st January 1813. Postnikov ended his explanation with an appeal for them to be worthy of their famous predecessors.

The observation posts of the regiment and companies were constructed on the same heights 2 kilometres from the enemy defences on the northern edge of the town. From there we could concentrate our fire on the railway station, the Oder bridges and Küstrin fortress. The heights on which we found ourselves were dug up in all directions, but the sappers' constructions went on and soon there was a thick net of positions in this narrow area.

As Major Shabalin saw the telephone lines being laid openly to the command post he waited furiously for the communications men to arrive. 'They seem to me to be signallers,' snarled Shabalin. 'Is it really so difficult to understand that a cable laid in the open can be torn apart by shell splinters or the tracks of an SPG? Damned incompetence!'

There were guardposts with machine-guns in front of the command posts for the regimental commander and the adjutant, and the observers had taken up their positions. Meanwhile all the queries were answered except for that of cooperation with Colonel Vainrub.

'If we haven't resolved the cooperation problem by nightfall, it looks bad,' Sacharkin said concernedly. I too was slowly becoming unsettled. The connection had to be implemented. 'Yudin! To the command post with the Jeep immediately!'

My driver climbed out of the trenches and hurried to a bush behind which the vehicle stood. At that moment an SPG appeared in the distance with my deputy on his way. Shortly afterwards it stopped at my command post. Lieutenant-Colonel Pashitnov, our training officer, climbed out slowly and came reeling towards me. He was wearing a thick bandage around his head. 'Sorry for being late, but I came under fire from the enemy artillery three times,' he announced.

We squatted in a trench and Pashitnov reported what he had learnt. The attack was due to begin at 0700 hours next morning. 'How is it with the motorised infantry?'

'As soon as the attack begins they will set off across the Oder. We have to support them with our fire.'

It was already dark when I entered the Party Secretary's dugout. Captain Postnikov was sitting at a table on which newspapers were heaped. He was preparing for a discussion with the troops, in which he would talk about the specialities of the enemy defences on the Oder. The fortifications extended for a considerable depth and were apparently thicker than those on the Vistula. Yet the Oder was the last of the Vistula–Oder defensive systems. When we broke though them our attack on Berlin would be speeded up considerably. Postnikov wanted to talk to the soldiers about this.

Anatoli Postnikov was clever and cold-blooded. These qualities were needed by a political officer as much as by a troop commander. The appeals to the combatants to accomplish heroic deeds and not to spare their lives only fell on fruitful ground if the political officer presented a good example. For Postnikov such behaviour was a matter of honour.

I said good-bye to Postnikov and went to the command post. A cold wind was coming over the Oder and whirling snowflakes in the air. The moon shone as a narrow sickle simmering through the snowflakes. On my left the outline of an SPG rose indistinctly. Someone was playing a harmonica in the vehicle. Another softly sang a melancholy song. I listened for a while and hoped that this would not be the last night for them both.

The first morning on the Oder. All around us everything was quiet. There was still fog over the river and the low-lying terrain but one could already make out the bridge across the Oder. Gradually the haze lightened over the town and the morning sun shone through.

The last preparations for battle were being made at the observation post. The adjutant made contact over the radio with the companies, while I used the telephone. Suddenly I heard General Krivoshein's voice: 'Start your work!'

A red Verey light went up from the corps command post and shone over Alt Drewitz. 'On the troop assembly before the bridges – Sector 101 – concentrated fire!' I ordered the companies.

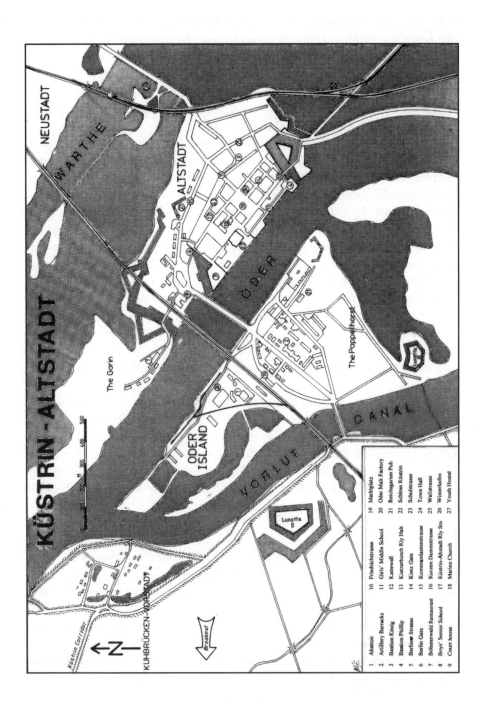

KÜSTRIN - ALTSTADT

NEUSTADT

WARTHE

ALTSTADT

ODER

The Pappelhorst

The Gorin

CANAL

ODER ISLAND

VORLUT

Lunette D

Lunette D

Küstrin Garrison

KUHBRÜCKEN-VORSTADT

Breakout

N

1   Abattoir
2   Artillery Barracks
3   Bastion König
4   Bastion Philip
5   Berliner Strasse
6   Berlin Gate
7   Böhmerwald Restaurant
8   Boys' Senior School
9   Court house

10 Friedrichstrasse
11 Girls' Middle School
12 Kattewall
13 Kietzerbusch Rly Halt
14 Kietz Gate
15 Kommandantenstrasse
16 Kurzen Dammstrasse
17 Küstrin-Altstadt Rly Stn
18 Marien Church

19 Marktplatz
20 Oder Malt Factory
21 Reichsgarten Pub
22 Schloss Küstrin
23 Schulstrasse
24 Town Hall
25 Wallstrasse
26 Winterhafen
27 Youth Hostel

Captain Sacharkin repeated the order with a series of red Verey lights. The first shots thundered, soon amalgamating into a thunderous din. The shells hissed towards their goals. Dark fountains rose in front of the bridges on which were enemy vehicles and infantry.

German soldiers hurried about confusedly here and there on the river bank, sinking in the snow. The tanks and vehicles added to the confusion as they drove for cover behind the buildings. Some were already on fire, as was Küstrin railway station, where trains were burning. Our SPGs switched their fire to the brickworks on the forward edge of the enemy defences.

I left Sacharkin in charge of the command post and drove with Yudin to the 4th Company to control its direction. As we arrived, the fighting reached its climax. The SPGs were firing uninterruptedly. Their hatches were wide open as the submachine-gunners passed shells to the crews.

Lieutenant Chorushenko was standing in an open hatch. In his right hand he held a telephone, in his left the radio microphone, immediately relaying Lieutenant Beltshikov's fire orders to the crews by radio. Now and then he set down the telephone to write down the details of the next firing task. 'The Ukrainian knows his job,' remarked Yudin.

I glanced inside Lieutenant Kiritshenko's SPG. The hot air engendered by the firing hit me in the face, and my ears thundered. The crew were functioning superbly. Kiritshenko put the earpiece of his helmet against his ear and repeated the orders he was getting from Chorushenko to the crew. Pavlov reeled from his handling of the shells. 'Dear shells, open the gates of Berlin for us,' he said laughing and wiped the sweat from his face.

Cholopov operated the gun's height and traversing machinery and aimed the gun at the town centre. The snow had thawed near the SPG and the frozen earth had turned into a swamp. The gun barrel was so hot that one could burn oneself on it. The submachine-gunners squelched through the mud, passing along the shells.

'This is just like the SPG artillery. Even in winter it can change to spring,' said Guardsman Yuri Golovatshiov laughing, and threw another shell out of the hatch. 'A hot day for us, but purgatory for the Fascists.' He had removed his fur jacket and cap and rolled up the sleeves of his tunic. His dark blond hair was shining with sweat, his eyes flashing.

The barrage came to an end. Tank engines howled into life in the woods behind our positions. A new stage of the battle was about to begin. The SPGs rolled forward. I quickly went to my vehicle. Sacharkin and Pashitnov sitting near me in the SPG looked at smoke-covered Küstrin. 'Hopefully we will not get involved in street-fighting,' groaned Sacharkin.

His fears were realised sooner than we would have wished. Enemy anti-tanks guns opened fire on our SPG. I ordered the company com-manders to engage the enemy guns immediately, the crews firing at a distance of 700 metres. At this point the tanks approached from Alt Drewitz. Without encountering earnest resistance, they went on into Küstrin at high speed and overtook us. Colonel Vainrub signalled us to follow him.

Several flashes came from the buildings next to the factory. As the first shells exploded near the tanks, Vainrub became mad with anger.

'What's holding you back? Fire whatever you have. They are knock-ing against my boxes,' he shouted. We covered the enemy with our heavy shells, and the German anti-tank guns fell silent. Vainrub's and Major Bortovski's tanks forced their way into Küstrin. Right in front was the tank of my countryman, Staff-Sergeant Ossipov.

General Krivoshein ordered me over the radio to provide two SPGs as an assault team for Bortovski.

A hurricane of fire fell in Küstrin. Gukov's vehicle left the mass of tanks and SPGs, and rolled forward. I worried about him like a favourite son and was delighted with his success. Here was a man who in front of everyone's eyes became born again, overcoming his fear and straining his willpower and nerves to overcome the densest turmoil of war.

It was not easy to control a storm troop; it demanded nerve and circumspection. Thus all the best commanders were entrusted with this task. Lieutenant Porfiri Beltshikov's company was to occupy the high street close to where Colonel Vainrub was located. We wanted to follow Beltshikov, but just then spotted a *Tiger* in a factory gateway. Its gun rocked and it seemed it was about to fire.

'Fire, Anatoli!' I ordered.

Lieutenant-Colonel Pashitnov pressed the electrical trigger. The 122mm shell hit the turret of the *Tiger* and bounced off. The tank turned and rushed off at top speed, but could not escape our second shell.

The enemy put up a bitter resistance. In a radio message to Army Group *Vistula* Hitler had ordered the Oder defences to be defended to the last man. We knew about this speech and had not reckoned on being able to thrust through to the west bank off the march, but already the first attempt was being made.

Chotimski's infantry were already across the ice, although coming up against heavy machine-gun fire from Oder Island, which, with its thick pasture, lay right in the middle of the river. Gradually the speed of the men slowed down, their bounds becoming shorter. Fighting on the ice resulted in even heavier casualties, as no one could dig in.

Lieutenant Muraviov's machine-pistol infantry joined the attack. They slid over the ice and fired with their weapons. When the enemy noticed them, he switched his fire in their direction. The machine-pistol infantry got no further.

Muraviov wanted to make direct contact with the SPGs and ask for fire support, as right nearby a burst of machine-gun fire ripped the ice and blew splinters of ice into his eyes. The radioman fell, the radio set was damaged. Muraviov put a hand over his face. He was bleeding, the ice splinters having wounded him. As he looked around, he noticed Guardsman Anikushkin lying motionless next to him and covering his head with his hands. 'Anikushkin, what is wrong? Are you wounded?'

The soldier turned to look at his company commander. 'I am still breathing!'

At this point Beltshikov's crew silenced the German machine-guns. Muraviov got up and stormed towards the island shouting 'Hurrah!' The company followed him. Anikushkin overtook his superior. Guardsman Yuri Golovatshiov moved light-footedly with the machine-pistol, Guardsman Yermolaiev running next to him. Machine-gun fire from trenches ploughed up from heavy shells came towards them. Steering with his hands, his head stretched out, Yermolaiev crashed forward. Near Muraviov someone cried out, but once the machine-pistol men's attack had got under way it was not to be stopped. Man to man fighting began in the trenches. One soldier tried to stop Anikushkin with a raised pistol but he hit him in the body with his machine-pistol and pulled the trigger.

Muraviov's company took the island. The infantry had hardly dug themselves in when German shells burst over them. Thick smoke stood over the island. Suddenly the firing ceased. Some shadowy figures appeared on the other bank.

'Company – fire!' commanded Muraviov.

Golovatshiov lay next to Anikushkin and fired. The enemy came ever closer and threw hand grenades from a distance of about 30 metres. Nevertheless they were stopped and had to turn back.

Again the island lay under heavy artillery fire. Then bombers attacked. Metal splinters scattered like specks of earth into the river. No one seemed able to survive this inferno. But as the enemy infantry went into the attack, they were met by dense machine-pistol fire.

Once our artillery had silenced the enemy guns and our fighters covered the island from air attack, I got into radio contact with General Krivoshein. 'Who's in charge of the infantry?' he asked.

'Muraviov. Do you remember him? He always speaks slowly.'

'Yes, I know who you mean. Before the war he was a Kolchos chairman.'

'That's right, Comrade General.'

'Award him in my name the Order of the Great Fatherland War 2nd Class! He fought excellently. I will sign the order immediately and send the award by courier.'

'Certainly, Comrade General.'

A little later an officer arrived from Krivoshein's staff bringing the Order. I took it and crawled to the island, where I found Muraviov after a long search. He was lying in a shell crater with some of his soldiers, holding a pair of binoculars with hands stiff from the cold. Fragments of ice hung from his felt boots and from the hem of his greatcoat. His teeth were chattering.

'Excuse me, Comrade Lieutenant-Colonel, we don't look very smart,' he greeted me.

'You can't help getting dirty in battle. The only thing that matters is that you and your company are sitting on this island in the Oder. Chotimski has praised you highly. His infantry have formed a bridge-head near Küstrin and are holding it. The gateway to Berlin is almost off its hinges. Do you realise what that means?'

'If it wasn't obvious to me, I would not be sitting here.'

'On behalf of the President of the Supreme Soviet, I hand over to you for bravery and heroism the Order of the Great Fatherland War 2nd Class!'

'I serve the Soviet Union,' replied Muraviov in a subdued voice as I placed the decoration on his chest.

After a strong handshake I returned to Küstrin. Fighting was still going on in the streets. The enemy was firing out of windows, cellars and rooftops. His mortars took us regularly under fire. Oil tanks were burning on the river bank, turning the sky black with their smoke.

Without question, we had to take one of the Oder bridges, but how could we get through this heavy fire? Apart from this, the enemy was firing at us from the fortress with artillery and with machine-guns like needle pricks from the rear. I called my company commanders on the radio. The first to respond was Nikolai Ivanov.

'How's it going, Nikolai Jegorovitch?'

'It's building up,' he answered. 'We are already running out of ammunition! I am waiting for a truck with anti-tank shells. We can get neither the bridges nor the fortress with shrapnel shells.'

'You'll get the shells, don't worry. Concentrate your fire on the fortress, give every crew an exact target and keep hammering at the fortress until the regiment has got forward to a bridge.'

'Understood.'

A little later the fortress walls vanished in a cloud of smoke and brick dust. But it still took several hours until the fortress was finally silent.

Major Bortovski's tanks of the 9th Tank Regiment and the SPGs of the 4th Company advanced towards the bridges. In the first wave of tanks were the SPGs of Mussatov, Beltshikov, Monogorov and Saiev. From time to time they stopped and long tongues of flame came from their guns. But it was much more difficult for the 19th Mechanised Brigade, as machine-gun fire kept pinning the infantry down.

The embankment at the bridge was ploughed up by shellfire. A deep anti-tank ditch barred our way. Lieutenant Beltshikov's SPG rolled to the edge, stopped briefly, then slowly disappeared into the depths.

'What on earth is he up to? He'll turn over!' cried Lieutenant-Colonel Pashitnov.

The right track had already sprung off and the SPG slid to the bottom of the anti-tank ditch. Beltshikov left his SPG and ran to another one from which to command his company.

'He knows how to look after himself,' asserted Lieutenant Vinogradov.

Suddenly Beltshikov raised his arms, swayed, fell in the snow, recovered and then collapsed again.

'He seems to have had it. Look at him, he can't get up anymore,' Major Sacharkin said.

'Forwards. Through the anti-tank ditch!' I shouted to the driver.

Meanwhile Sergeant-Major Axianov, the gun loader in Beltshikov's crew, went to his commander's aid. He went forward by leaps and bounds up to Beltshikov, loaded the wounded man on his back and crawled back to the anti-tank ditch. As he let the wounded man flop into the ditch, he was hit by a bullet.

My SPG had already crossed over the anti-tank ditch and silenced the enemy position. Once that was done, we hurried to help the wounded men. Axianov lay on his back with his arms outspread. The bullet had hit him in the temple. Beltshikov groaned. His lower jaw was shattered. We called the medical orderlies and had him taken to hospital. The attack continued.

Then from corps came the order to hand over the fighting sector to the arriving elements of General Berzarin's army, to go north to Königsberg and clear German troops from the area from the east bank of the Oder to the Baltic. The order was obvious, as we could not attack any further west without first destroying the enemy forces that were threatening our flank and rear near Stargard.

As dusk fell, the fighting died down. It began to snow in thick flakes. Soon a thick blanket of snow covered the blood-soaked battlefield. I ordered Lieutenant-Colonel Pashitnov and Major Sacharkin to get the regiment together and concentrate in Alt Drewitz. I myself went off to corps headquarters with Lieutenant Vinogradov. On the way I made contact with the company commanders. They had already received the order to assemble. Only Lieutenant Beltshikov's company found itself in a difficult situation. Following the wounding of their company commander, they were practically without leadership. The SPG was intact but the radio contact to it had been lost. Vinogradov asked for it to be sent to his company. My constant escort was often jumping into dangerous situations and mastering them, so I immediately agreed to his request.

Leaving the 4th Company without a commander was unacceptable and I decided to appoint Lieutenant Mussatov as the new company commander. His calm and his ability to deal with situations cold-bloodedly and to assess them soberly impressed me. Apart from that, he had completed the training course at the tank school in Ulianovsk and had belonged to the regiment from the start.

As General Berzarin's army's leading elements approached Küstrin, we handed over our sector and left Alt Drewitz for Königsberg-on-the-Oder.

Back in Küstrin

Many times have I watched troops getting into their ready positions. But what was played out on the roads to Küstrin exceeded all previous experience. Infantry, tanks, artillery and sappers were advancing in an unending stream. In this flood our regiment seemed no more than a drop in the ocean. And then again in the woods of Küstrin! Here the troops stood even thicker than on the roads leading in. Wherever one looked there were tanks, guns and trucks. As we came to our allocated area we passed an unusual column of three-axled trucks with mighty searchlights mounted on them. They were to blind the enemy during the night attack.

I went to the staff bus in order to snatch some sleep. Although I was dog-tired, I was unable to fall asleep for a long time. Near the bus Lieutenants Kuklin and Muraviov were talking: 'Yes, Petra, it would be great to survive the war. Woods, fresh air,' groaned Kuklin. 'How often have I ploughed on until supper time. Then when I got home I would be exhausted. My children would fly around my neck: Aniutka with her blonde plaits and my four mudlarks, Vitka, Petka, Volodka and Tolka. My fatigue would immediately be blown away. Will such happiness ever be repeated?'

After a short pause Kuklin started: 'Do you know, when the war is over you will be once more in charge of a collective farm and everything will go back to normal.'

The sound of German aircraft came nearer and the noise swelled. The air sentry, who was located high up in a pine tree, cried out: 'Aircraft alert! Everyone under cover!'

I quickly left the bus and jumped into a slit trench. The first Junkers were already diving out of the clouds. Lieutenants Ivanov and Salichov opened fire with their anti-aircraft machine-guns. The leading aircraft dived down. Several seconds later there was an explosion. But the other aircraft stayed on course and dropped their bombs. I pressed myself down on the ground and pulled a mattress over me. Ear-deafening explosions filled the air, splinters smacking against my boots.

Gradually the noise died down and I carefully climbed out of the slit trench. Dead and wounded were lying everywhere. Yudin had been killed, our regimental doctor severely wounded. Salichov too had been hit in the chest and legs. His breathing was intermittent. Gumar had already survived three wounds, but this time it did not seem he would survive.

'Sascha, where are you?' he groaned.

'Here, Saititch.' Lieutenant Boldyrev knelt next to the dying man.

'Write to my sister in Akmolinski. I have revenged the death of our brother Baka.' Salichov breathed a few times, gasping for air, and then fell silent for ever. We silently lowered his head. No one could quite grasp that this cheerful, brave man was no longer with us. The losses from this air attack forced us to be careful, to reinforce the air sentries and set up anti-aircraft weapons.

Soon afterwards I was ordered to Gorgast by General Krivoshein. I immediately drove off.

I met the general in the middle of the ruins with several other officers, including Chotimski, Vainrub and Babaian. All were wearing camouflage clothing. General Krivoshein lay on the ground observing the flat ground between the villages of Genschmar and Golzow. When he saw me, he called: 'Mironov, come here!'

I lay down next to him and unfolded my map.

'Your regiment will go with the corps reserve in the direction Buckow–north-eastern edge of Berlin behind Babaian's brigade in the breakthrough.'

I lowered my face as I did not think it right that mine should be the last regiment through the breakthrough sector. From my face the corps commander saw what was going on inside my head and went on: 'No grounds for sulking. Once we have broken through the fortifications and thrust forward to Berlin, you regiment will be involved at all stages.'

The mechanised brigades were assigned as the first echelon and Vainrub's tanks for the second. These would form an armoured group thrust in the event of quick success.

The general's information that our line of attack in Berlin went though the special 'Z' Sector in which the Reichstag lay cheered us all up. 'Imagine, it is up to us to wipe out that wasps' nest,' Vaintrub whispered to me.

Once the work on the bridgehead was over, Krivoshein ordered the brigade and regimental commanders to follow him to the corps head-quarters in Küstrin. Shortly afterwards our small convoy stopped next to a big tent. The corps commander invited us to the table. When everyone had sat down, the commander stood up and announced in a solemn tone: 'Comrade Commanders! Before the historical battle for Berlin begins I would like to have a few words with you. Not as the commander in chief, but as a fellow combatant.' We put down our maps and notebooks.

'Dear friends. We have studied our basic tasks, planned the attacks and done all the necessary paperwork. Now we have to deal calmly and decisively and not give in to difficulties and obstacles, however great they may be. Instead consider what a great honour has been allotted us in storming the Fascists' den. Let us prove ourselves worthy of the trust of the military leadership, the Party and the people.'

I returned to my regiment as dusk fell. Now I especially missed Yudin. His place had been taken by Grigori Finogenov, a younger, inexperienced man, who had difficulty finding his way in the dark and became ever more nervous. Fortunately I knew the ground and we reached our destination in good order.

Captain Koslitin was already waiting for me at headquarters with news. Between the Oder and Berlin lay several defence sectors. Lakes, rivers, canals, woods and villages offered the enemy the possibility of being able to offer resistance for a long period of time. The enemy had set up three defensive strips on the approaches to Berlin. The first, the Oder–Neisse defensive line, had a depth of up to 40 kilometres. The second ran along the Seelow Heights, and the third was formed by the suburbs with numerous strongpoints and fire nests. Then came the Berlin defences with three defensive zones: the outer perimeter zone, the outer defensive ring and the inner defensive zone. Apart from this the Berlin defences were divided into eight sectors, in the centre of which lay the special 'Z' sector.

I called Odartshuk, Kravtshenko and Sacharkin to discuss things over with them. Kravtshenko complained that he had too few soldiers in his supply platoon. Apart from this, he was lacking radio equipment for properly maintaining communication with the regimental headquarters.

Major Sacharkin and I looked for a solution. We could take no crew members from the SPGs. Equally indispensable were the submachine-gunners and scouts. Without them we could not go into battle.

'Take Minogian Yegorova's group,' suggested Sacharkin. 'You know how keen and brave the girls are. Especially Minogian. She can take the place of any man. At Königsberg she was up front with the first tracked vehicles.'

'Agreed,' said Kravtshenko, delighted. 'Next to their many-sided security tasks the girls can milk our cows. As you know we have obtained our own herd in order to improve the meat situation.'

I had Minogian called. Flushed from her fast run, she entered the headquarters bus.

'Would you like to help the Rear Services with your group?'

'As often said, I prefer being with the fighting units. But it has to be?'

'Then report to Captain Kravtshenko straight away.'

'At your orders, Comrade Lieutenant-Colonel.'

Kravtshenko really did not have it easy. He not only had to look after shells and fuel: beginning with foot bandages for the soldiers, via the regimental kitchen to the transporting away of the wounded, and the security and defence of the Rear Services, he had a multitude of problems to deal with.

Once they had all gone, Sacharkin pulled a small letter out of his map case. 'I have received more information from corps headquarters,' he said. 'Tomorrow early, the 14th April, part of the rifle units will make a reconnaissance in force supported by a strong artillery group. The attack by the rifle units begins on the night of the 15th/16th April. We have to cross the Oder on the 16th and pass through the break-through point on the 17th.'

I was quiet for several seconds trying to concentrate on the plan. 'Our superiors have sprung surprises again. Not only on the enemy, but also on us,' I remarked sarcastically.

'You are right,' Sacharkin said. 'At last the moment of surprise can decide the success of the whole operation.'

We discussed how we could best move the regiment to the bridge-head. There were about 7,000 [actually 3,000] tanks and self-propelled guns in the woods north of Küstrin that all had to be moved across the Oder. If the rifle units moved forward to the bridges the roads would soon be blocked and the enemy would know the direction of our main thrust for sure.

I therefore decided to ask General Krivoshein to allow me to get to the crossing points on the morning of the 16th April, so that we could be called forward to the bridges by companies. The general agreed.

'It seems that we have settled everything.' I said good-night to Sacharkin and turned in.

The Historic Battle Begins

The night of the 16th/17th April was dark. Not a star stood in the heavens. Shots rang from either side of the Oder. Then quiet returned. It was a night on the front line like so many others, but no one slept, for the attack on Berlin would begin in a few hours.

At the predetermined time the thunder of a gun tore through the quiet. We had all been waiting for this signal. The *Katiushas* fired, and shortly afterwards the artillery and mortar batteries. The infantry attacked the first enemy trenches even during the artillery preparation. The rattling of their machine-pistols and rifles came over to us. The infantry had engaged in the fight with the forward elements of the 9th German Army.

The beam of a searchlight bored into the sky. That was the signal to cease the artillery preparation, and tanks and infantry went into the attack.

Tanks and self-propelled artillery rolled in an unbroken stream across the Oder bridges. Our regiment followed the tanks of Babaian's brigade. I wanted to drive ahead to the bridges in my Jeep, but others overtook me. Trucks and fighting vehicles moved in a tight column and could squash my light vehicle. I climbed aboard my SPG and got through on it. The drivers were afraid of it and let it pass. Only the tank-men were unimpressed by it and drove on unperturbed in their vehicles.

On the morning of the 17th April I received the order to go through the breakthrough sector and thrust forward quickly to the Seelow Heights with the other elements of the tank armies to which the Front's mobile groups belonged.

During a short stop I mentioned to one of my machine-pistol men that his boot was torn. 'Report it to your sergeant-major, he should exchange it for you,' I called out to him.

'Unnecessary, Comrade Lieutenant-Colonel. It should last until we get to Berlin.'

On the Seelow Heights the enemy had concentrated strong artillery forces and dug in assault guns and tanks. On the slopes were several trenches whose approaches were covered by barbed wire and mine-fields. Our regiment attacked north of Seelow in the Gusow–Platkow–Batzlow direction. At Gusow the self-propelled gun crews secured the 37th Mechanised Brigade's crossing of the Alte Oder.

Staff-Sergeant Cholopov opened fire on Schloss Gusow and silenced a German machine-gun. Then with some well-aimed shots he put several armoured vehicles of the 11th SS Motorised Division *Nordland* out of action.

Near Platkow there was a more interesting episode. Goats emerged from a wood to drink in the river. Apparently Cholopov must have had tears in his eyes from shooting so long, for he thought there were enemy infantry before him and fired several shots. Major Sacharkin, watching this through his binoculars, laughed out loud: 'That can't be true! Such an experienced fighter, and unable to distinguish goats from infantry!' But Cholopov had the last laugh. Our cook praised him in the highest terms, for he could prepare a wonderful Borscht from goat-meat.

There was bitter fighting on the Seelow Heights. Under these circumstances the Front War Council decided to bring reserves into the battle. Hundreds of fighter-bombers and fighters appeared over the enemy positions. At dawn the infantry resumed the attack. I drove to the commander's conference and saw the troops on the move. On the right went Vedeniev's tanks, on the left Vainrub's. At corps headquarters I discovered that the troops of the 1st Ukrainian Front, which had been fed into the battle from the Sandomierz bridgehead, were successfully thrusting forward to the west.

*   *   *

Unlike Marshal Zhukov, Marshal Koniev had made an immediate break-through of the enemy defences in his area and had meanwhile persuaded Stalin to let him participate in the battle for Berlin. Stalin, who was jealous of Zhukov's popularity, seized this opportunity to humiliate him. Stalin's taunting then led to Zhukov attempting to force the issue by introducing his two tank armies into the battle prematurely, severely impeding the 8th Guards Army's assault on the Seelow Heights' defences.

*   *   *

The infantry climbed up the slopes of the Seelow Heights; the engines of the tanks and self-propelled guns, towing vehicles with mortars, howled agonisingly as they struggled up the slopes, with the artillery also under tow. Following a renewed artillery bombardment, the attack made considerable progress and the enemy had to abandon the Heights. Finally our troops conducted some severe fighting at the enemy strongpoints of Batzlow, Buckow and Fürstenwalde.

Our column stopped before Batzlow. The village was on fire, and the fighting continued for several hours, personally orchestrated by the corps commander.

In contrast to March, April was sunny, warm and dry. Numerous woods were on fire and thick smoke made breathing difficult. The fighting was bitter and costly, but our tanks and SPGs advanced quickly on the asphalted roads. We drove into a small village. Nothing moved. The inhabitants had left their homes. Wherever one looked one saw thrown-away weapons, destroyed equipment and dead soldiers. But the enemy was still conducting an increasingly bitter resistance.

The fighting had not abated for four days, but our regiment was still in the reserve as before. We followed the corps' first echelon, stopping, camouflaging the vehicles in a wood and rolling on again. Slowly the troops became nervous. They wanted to get involved in the fighting at long last.

Our advance battalion had liberated Zepernick and was approaching Malchow. There, towards 1000 hours on the 20th April, they were brought to a stop by the enemy. Sacharkin and I drove forward and observed the enemy.

Malchow was surrounded by rifle trenches. From further left towards Wartenburg came flashes of gunfire, and the thunder of the guns came across to us. Part of our corps had become stuck in the enemy defences and found itself under heavy fire.

General Krivoshein had decided to widen the wedge and push on further. Because of this, Yershov, the new corps chief of staff came to see me. 'Our leading elements have reached the city area,' he reported. 'The corps commander is putting everything into taking Malchow and then attacking the city with all our forces.'

'Wonderful!' I replied. 'At last there is something for us to do.'

When I reached the general, he was already talking to Bogdanov. From their talk I could make out that the army commander-in-chief was pleased with the results of the first stages of the attack and was now demanding the speedy taking of Malchow and Weissensee. Krivoshein signalled with his hand for me to wait for him at the regiment.

On the Perimeter of Berlin

A new day broke. The sun shone like a ball of fire over the fully blooming garden. Our heavy SPGs were standing in a field next to the highway. A signpost bore the inscription: 'Berlin 7km.' Our aircraft were bombing the city.

The SPG crews had made themselves comfortable next to their vehicles and were waiting for the order to attack. A little further off, next to some bushes in bloom, lay the commander of the 4th Company, Valentin Mussatov, on his spread-out waterproof coat, studying the map. He was thoughtfully chewing a grass stalk. He knew how many

dangers a big city like Berlin concealed, so was going through everything in his thoughts. That meant thinking over all future handling in
advance, not only his own, but also those of his subordinates.

The arrival of General Krivoshein interrupted Mussatov's thoughts.
The corps commander had us called together and explained the situation to us. 'The infantry cannot break through the outer defensive
ring on their own. They urgently need worthwhile support. This task
falls to you.'

Krivoshein had me hand him my map and drew a red arrow from
Birkholz to Malchow and on to the north-eastern edge of Berlin.
Smiling, he handed me the map: 'There you have your Berlin, do with
it what you want.'

As I turned round to look at him, he went on: 'The defence in
Malchow must be burst apart by the force of your heavy SPGs. Then
force your way into Berlin with your infantry.'

Lieutenant-Colonel Pashitnov had the regiment parade. All were in
the best of spirits. I looked at my men. Yes, with these men I could
fulfil my tasks should they be not too complicated. Many of them had
travelled the difficult way from Moscow to here. They would now
travel with the inexperienced men and support them.

Mussatov's company would attack in the first echelon and be the
leading company on the march as well as in the development phase.
This decision was right up Mussatov's street. His eyes flashed. 'Thank
you for your confidence, Comrade Commander.' He put his helmet on
and his company rolled off.

Ivanov's company had the task, in cooperation with Mussatov and
the tanks of Chotimski and Sokolov, who had replaced Colonel
Yershov, to break into Malchow and attack the north-eastern edge of
Berlin. A few days earlier the regiment's Communists had accepted
Ivanov as a member of the Communist Party. Major Odartshuk had
handed him his membership card today.

Mussatov came across the first obstacle before Schwanebeck. The
Buch–Birkholz road running across his line of attack was on a high
embankment and hindered the company's deployment. Although it
was dangerous, he had to drive on in column ahead. The SPGs increased speed and passed through the village of Schwanebeck without
a fight.

Through a liaison officer I informed Mussatov that he should deploy
into line as soon as he had Schwanebeck behind him. But Mussatov
replied: 'That is not possible. Another road is already running ahead of

us. It is only passable in column. There is an underpass at Point 71.3 of the road going past.'

It was obvious to me what was going to happen to us. If the regiment was unable to deploy in time, it would cost us more in losses of men and equipment, as the direction of fire would be impeded. 'You must deploy as quickly as possible. Look for a suitable spot left or right of the road,' I told him.

Mussatov called up the SPG commanders, Chorushenko, Bushuiev and Shevtshuk, by radio. They were to reconnoitre the ground. Meanwhile the companies stopped. I became worried when almost thirty minutes had passed and Lieutenant Mussatov had still not reported back. We could not stop for so long right under the nose of the enemy – the danger of air attack was much too great. I sent a messenger to Lieutenant Ivanov and ordered him to go round Mussatov's company and attack Malchow. But hardly had the 2nd Company begun overtaking than the 4th Company returned. Mussatov did not want to be removed from the lead. The vehicles of Chorushenko, Luschpa and Ivanov followed him.

Finally Malchow lay before us. Only about 400 metres separated us from the village. I left my SPG, sought a suitable position and observed the terrain. Colonel Chotimski joined me. To the right of the village an anti-tank ditch ran towards Pankow, while to the left lay meadows and fields. The entrance to the village was barred with a barricade of tree trunks and stones. Our SPGs were not equipped for such difficulties: either the tracks would come off or the engines would fail. Chotimski promised to get some *Sherman* tanks to Malchow.

But Mussatov ordered his driver, Lieutenant Kusnezov, to accelerate and cross the barricade. He asked the commanders of the other SPGs to fire at the barricade to pin down any possible *Panzerfaust* men. Stones and splinters flew all around, but the barricade remained standing. It only shrank a little.

Mussatov got closer to the barricade. The first *Panzerfaust* shots were already flying towards him from the anti-tank ditch. In reply Ivanov showered the ditch with shrapnel to protect Mussatov. I got into contact with Lieutenant Muraviov and pressed him to thrust forward faster with his machine-pistol men.

Kusnezov turned the SPG on the barricade once more. Its tracks churned like powerful shovels at the obstacle. Finally he made it, and the SPG stood on the other side of the barricade.

I immediately told Ivanov to support Mussatov effectively. Muraviov's machine-pistol men had not yet arrived. Majors Ossadtchi and Sacharkin concerned themselves with Mussatov and his crew, who were having to fight unaided. 'What do you think? Could he hold out there for thirty minutes? ' I asked. 'Reinforcements can't get there sooner.'

'He would rather die than go back one step,' replied Ossadtchi.

I was of the same opinion, but also did not want to provoke fate, so I sent Ossadtchi and Sacharkin to the companies to hurry them up. All seemed to be done, but my concern for Mussatov had not lessened. I contacted him by radio again and again.

'It's hot here in Malchow,' he reported. 'I'm hardly 300 metres from the barricade. There are Fascists everywhere. We are firing with everything we've got. Goldman and Kusnezov are keeping the enemy back with hand grenades. Should the *Panzerfaust* men come here, then its "good night!"'

'Hold on, old chap, help is coming soon.'

'We'll get through it soon.'

A few minutes later I talked with him again. 'What does it look like now?'

Mussatov coughed violently: 'It's just happened. A *Panzerfaust* got us. We can hardly breathe for smoke. My hearing has been damaged a bit. I don't know what actually happened. I was sitting in the gun aimer's place, Sergeant-Major Goldman standing behind me. Suddenly there was an almighty blow and a bright flash. The *Panzerfaust* must have hit the side right at the spot where Goldman was standing. He was killed instantly.'

'How is the SPG?'

'The engine is still running. We are driving into a building and climbing out of the emergency exit hatch. Then we will be able to defend the vehicle better.'

Thereupon the connection with Mussatov was broken. I hurried to the village. A tank whose engine had failed was blocking the SPGs. A towing vehicle was already there to pull it aside. Now the way was open for us. Among the charging submachine-gunners I discovered our Yura.

Now that reinforcements had arrived, Mussatov could leave his cover. I hardly recognised him when he stood before me. He seemed to have aged a year.

'A shame about Goldman. Although he was a German, he had no time for the Fascists.' Without another word, Mussatov climbed into his SPG and drove off. At the village exit his vehicle was hit by an anti-aircraft gun. This finally finished it. Also several tanks caught fire. But Mussatov was not to be stopped. He climbed into Lieutenant Chorushenko's SPG and rolled on with Lieutenants Schevtshuk and Bushuiev.

The enemy set about defending himself bitterly. Anti-aircraft guns and an assault gun fired from secure positions. Chorushenko lost his life in this fight. A shell hit his SPG and went through the side. Once more Mussatov had to climb into another SPG, this time Buschuiev's. Although Ivanov's company had also engaged in the fight, we did not get any further. Tank troops and SPG crews were at a loss. Nevertheless somehow they had to get on. Finally Ivanov came up with an idea. Quite close by, on a bend in the road, stood some trees and bushes. Perhaps one could overcome the enemy under cover of them? The company commander explained to his men what he had in mind. 'Now friends, who will take the risk and go first?'

Deep silence. Everyone knew this was one's life at stake.

'Who will take on the fire protection?' asked Lieutenant Luschpa timidly.

'I will,' answered Ivanov. 'You can leave that to me.'

Luschpa took a long testing look at the road as if he wanted to imprint every metre precisely on his mind. Then he decisively threw his cigarette away and went to his crew. 'Now men, are you ready? We'll go first.'

Korotov, the driver, shrugged his broad shoulders. 'What else is for us to do? One must chance it. We can't stay here in this nest for ever. Let's go, Commander!'

'Mount up!' ordered Luschpa and disappeared into the SPG. Lieutenant Korotkov, Sergeant-Major Tschorny and Sergeant Koshevnikov followed him. The vehicle slowly got moving.

Attentively I observed a trench nearby. As I moved towards it, Luschpa immediately warned me: 'Careful, the trench is occupied!'

Luschpa aimed his gun and fired several times. The shells exploded in the trench. Ossipov and Mussatov had also fired. Shortly afterwards soldiers climbed out of the trench and raised their hands.

Chotimski told me to increase the pressure on the enemy. 'If we haven't reached Berlin by nightfall, our attack will be stuck fast. I will bring infantry forward and then you attack between the first trenches. Vainrub will bring his tanks up to the anti-tank ditch.'

I observed through the periscope. Slowly the barrels sank to horizontal. *Panzerfaust* men approached us openly. Korotkov's SPG stormed ahead. The Fascists got no closer, not even to fire another *Panzerfaust*. Now Korotkov had reached the trench, threatening to crush the men in the trench with the SPG. The enemy soldiers threw their weapons away and raised their hands.

Korotkov now wheeled towards Berlin. At this moment the SPG was hit in the side by a *Panzerfaust*. When I reached the vehicle, Sergeant-Major Tschorny and Sergeant Koshevnikov were already pulling the driver out of the hatch. The shell had torn off both of Korotkov's legs. Fiodor groaned and asked for vodka, but nobody had any.

Luschpa spoke calmingly to Fiodor. 'Hold on, Fedia, grit your teeth and hold on.'

The wounded man was becoming weaker by the minute. His face was flushed, with thick beads of sweat standing on his forehead. As the doctor appeared and checked his pulse, he shook his head concernedly. We carefully lifted the wounded man on to a stretcher and carried him to an ambulance. Korotkov had lost consciousness. Shortly afterwards came the news that he had died. We buried him in Seefeld.

The attack was resumed on the morning of the 22nd April. This time we were able to break through. I covered Krivoshein's tank in the order of battle.

Major Bortovski attacked on the right with his 9th Tank Regiment. Near me drove Staff-Sergeant Jascha Ossipov's tank. He had been decorated with the Order of the Red Star immediately before the attack began. Boldyrev's and Korosteliov's men broke into the city with Ossipov. The attack got into its stride.

The tanks and SPGs rolled along Berliner Strasse like a typhoon, firing at still-resisting Fascists with their anti-aircraft machine-guns. We stopped near a big building. Shortly afterwards Boldyrev's and Korosteliov's SPGs joined us, followed by the remainder of the regiment's vehicles and their infantry. Mussatov got out and ran into a building with some infantry. A moment later a Red Flag flew from a balcony. We were in Berlin!

The men were totally exhausted. At last they had something of a rest. Stretcher-bearers carried the wounded to a collection point. Mussatov, Ivanov and Luschpa had curled themselves up and fallen

Zhukov at his Seelow Heights command post.

Soviet armour and artillery in the ruins.

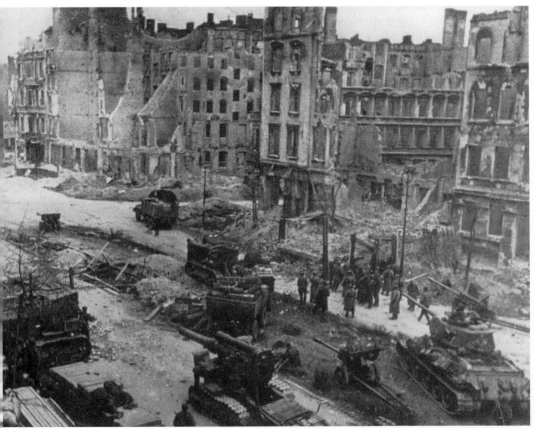

A Soviet self-propelled gun in action.

Soviet howitzers in action.

A Lend-Lease Sherman tank in action.

Carrying off the Soviet injured.

The Zoo Flak-tower with the Victory Column in the distance.

A Soviet tank and jeep at the Brandenburg Gate.

Destroyed Soviet armour outside the Technical University.

Preparing to attack the Reichstag.

The wreckage of the Reichstag after the battle.

Dead in the streets.

(*Left*) German troops surrendering from the underground railway.

(*Below*) The end of the battle: German prisoners being marched out of the city.

The Red Flag triumphantly but precariously displayed from the roof of the Reichstag.

Celebrating Soviet victory at the German Victory Column.

asleep. When Major Ossadtchi saw me he said: 'All mankind should raise their hats to you!'

A little later, in the presence of their regimental colleagues, I decorated Mussatov with the Alexander Nevski Order, Ivanov with the Order of the Red Banner, and Luschpa with the Order of the Red Star.

Colonel Vainrub reported to the corps commander that we had reached Berlin. The general replied laconically: 'I'll pass on the message to corps headquarters immediately.'

A lightning telegram sent the news of the success of the advance elements of the 1st Mechanised Corps and the 3rd Shock Army from General Kusnezov to Moscow. Our regiment received the thanks of the Supreme Commander in Chief and was later awarded the Order of Suvorov.

For heroism, bravery and leadership Semion Moisseievitch Krivoshein and I were declared 'Heroes of the Soviet Union' by decree of the Presidium of the High Soviet of the Soviet Union on the 31st May 1945.

Korosteliov, the best SPG driver, and many others received high decorations. In addition, all those who had taken part in the fighting between the Oder and Berlin were honoured with orders and medals.

In the Working Class Districts of Berlin
The fighting in Berlin demanded everything of us. We could hardly manoeuvre in the narrow streets. The enemy sat in the buildings behind thick walls, and his tanks were able to break out of the side streets at any time. *Panzerfaust* men had settled in the cellars and attacked us from there.

Mussatov and Ivanov asked for submachine-gunners to be sent to them with hand grenades to engage an enemy tank that kept rolling forward out of a side street and was preventing their advance under cover of fire from the upper storey of a corner building. Sacharkin had already deployed all the submachine-gunners. Apart from that he was doubtful that one could get a *Tiger* with hand grenades, for it had not worked on a *Panther*.

Major Ossadtchi said nothing for a long time, sitting there thoughtfully and smoking a cigarette. Then he got up and declared decisively: 'That is a job for the right men. Let's send Boldyrev and Gorodenzev. They will deal with it.'

Pashitnov nodded in agreement: 'They are the right ones. Boldyrev fought bravely at the Vistula and Gorodenzev was there in Moscow.'

Next we sent for Boldyrev. 'Have you any family?' asked Sacharkin.

'Yes, my father and mother. They live in Moscow. And then there's my fiancée. We are getting married after the war. You are most heartily invited.'

'How old are you?' I asked.

'Born in 1923.'

'And where were you trained?' Pashitnov wanted to know.

Boldyrev smiled: 'At the Tscheliabin Tank School. But I have already told you this. Don't you remember? That was in October 1943 when we arrived at the regiment with our SPG. At that time you were adjutant.'

'Correct, I had forgotten. You were constantly after me. The spare parts were insufficient for you, and then the repair mechanics did a sloppy job.'

'Next thing he was asked to join the Party. The Komsomol group was very happy with him,' reported Ossadtchi, who had kept silent until then.

'If that is so, Comrade Lieutenant, then you are our man. We want to send you and Comrade Gorodenzev forward. Take as many *Panzerfausts* as possible and put an end to that German tank there. This is especially important for the continuance of our attack.'

Gorodenzev was the same age as Boldyrev, but was already married and had two children. The two soldiers set off. Half an hour later Golovatschov reported that they had reached their goal and were going through the buildings with the assault team's infantry. Gorodenzev had been slightly wounded but was fighting on.

It was not much longer before the enemy tank was eliminated. That was Boldyrev's work. The sound of fighting ebbed in the side streets. For their courage Boldyrev was awarded the title Hero of the Soviet Union and Gorodenzev the Order of the Red Star.

Medical orderlies crept past our SPG. Liudmila and her team were on the way to the infantry. As she was attending to a badly wounded man, a German fighter flew over and shot at the nurse with his machine-guns. Liudmila collapsed. The medical orderlies Michail Maritsha and Fiodor Ailov put her carefully on a stretcher and brought her to safety in a ruined building. When an SPG arrived to take her to hospital, I called out to her: 'Liuda, what about our date in Mordvinein?'

Liudmila raised her head and looked at me: 'It's still on. As soon as I am back on my feet.'

The SPG was followed by a Jeep carrying the dead commander of the 35th Mechanised Brigade, General Babaian.

The fighting for the individual parts of the city cost a lot of blood, but the attack continued. In the middle of the confusion of battle, soldiers put up posters on the walls of the buildings. From one of them I discovered which unit they belonged to: 'We're from Berzarin's army. The Front's War Council has appointed our army commander City Commandant. That is the order for the temporary assumption of all authority by the Soviet City Kommandatura.'

'Excellent. Berlin is not yet fully taken, but Berzarin has already got the reins firmly in his hands.'

Major Ossadtchi joined us. 'Have you seen it?' I indicated the notice with my head.

'Of course! A good thing too. That will give the inhabitants new courage to carry on.'

Dusk was sinking around us. An exciting night lay ahead. German snipers kept after us. Flares briefly lit the streets with colourful light.

The most important task that night was the repair of the shot-up SPGs. The repair and recovery teams had set themselves up in the school at Malchow. I did not know how Captain Odartshuk was getting on with the work, so I got into an SPG and drove to Malchow. In the gymnasium stood lathes, jacks and defective SPGs on which several mechanics were working. 'We are trying to meet the schedules, but we lack spare parts. Apart from that the men are almost dropping with fatigue. They haven't closed their eyes for two days.'

'Send someone to the corps camp in Seelow. All the parts are available there. Sleep is unthinkable at the moment.'

Odartshuk took a deep breath. It was very difficult for the captain. His drawn face and reddened eyes clearly showed his fatigue. The workshop brigade team was led by Senior-Sergeant-Major A.D. Kiverov, who could be found wherever a hand was needed. Roman Ulanov had sent him the 9th Tank Corps' Workshop Battalion in support.

Sleep threatened to overtake the mechanics towards morning, but they put their heads under the water taps and went back to work. Once the major part of the work was completed, Odartshuk's mood improved abruptly.

Suddenly a German bomber appeared over Malchow. Seconds later we heard a penetrating whistling. We jumped into the examination pits. There were already explosions. The light went out. Flames crackled in the hall. A barrel of diesel oil had caught fire. The flames quickly took hold of the oil-smeared tarpaulin with which the SPG was covered. Should the vehicle catch fire there would be no chance of recovery as it was fully armed up.

'Quick! Everybody out!' cried Odartshuk, tearing off his coat and throwing it over the burning barrel. Although he burnt his hands, he carried on until the flames were extinguished. When the emergency lights switched on, he went checking one SPG after another. Splinters had bent the aerials and damaged the machine-gun barrels, and one SPG had its steering wheel bent.

Kiverov clapped his hands over his head. 'That nearly had us. What now?'

Odartshuk glared at him: 'Work on. Nothing else.'

As the men were returning to their tools, spare parts and a workshop truck arrived from the corps depot. Now the schedule could be maintained. Content, I left the workshop and drove back to Berlin.

The regimental headquarters were located in a cellar on Berliner Strasse. Shortly after my arrival a convoy of repaired SPGs rolled in. Odartshuk was sitting on the armour of the leading vehicle beaming. Several soldiers, including Mussatov, hurried past, hauled Odartshuk off the SPG and threw him jubilantly into the air.

The repaired SPGs were immediately shared out among the companies. Once that was done I went over the situation with Major Sacharkin. During the course of the night some important changes had taken place. The enemy defensive ring had been broken in four sectors.

Towards evening Major Shabalin brought us the corps headquarters' instructions. Our regiment was to move immediately with the motorised infantry and Chotimski's tanks to the western edge of the city, take Siemensstadt, force the Berlin–Spandau Shipping Canal and thrust towards Charlottenburg.

We set off immediately. We stopped towards morning not far from the Spandau Canal. Once we had forced it, we could attack the factories in Siemensstadt. The infantry took up positions on the southern bank of the canal under heavy fire. We took up firing positions behind the second line of infantry.

Sacharkin looked through the periscope and shouted happily: 'Comrade Lieutenant-Colonel, I can see the Reichstag!'

I turned to him: 'Where? Where? Why haven't we seen it earlier?'

'The fog has dispersed. Look, the building with the big dome on the bend in the Spree – that's the Reichstag.'

Excitedly I took over the periscope. Yes, there stood the Reichstag. Suddenly I was overwhelmed by the desire to shoot at that damned building. Sacharkin appeared to read my thoughts. His eyes flashed: 'Fire?'

'Of course! Give the Fascists one in the roof.'

I left it to Lieutenant Mussatov, as I knew how accurately he could hit at long distances. A few minutes later Mussatov came panting: 'Look through the periscope,' he said to Sacharkin.

Mussatov did not know what he wanted and went irresolutely to the apparatus.

'What have you got in the sights?' asked Sacharkin.

'A cathedral, I think.'

'That's no cathedral, that's the Reichstag. The commander orders you and your whole company to open fire!'

Mussatov turned toward me, clicked his heels together and vanished in a flash.

Happily Sacharkin recorded in the fighting log of the 347th Guards Heavy Self-Propelled Artillery Regiment: 'At 1400 hours on the 26th April the Heavy Self-Propelled Artillery opened direct fire on the Reichstag.'

From the observation post I could see how Mussatov had the drivers and commanders parade. They stood there, Shevtshuk, Sergeiev, Buschuiev and Monogarov, listening attentively to their company commander's words. Meanwhile the other crew members were preparing their vehicles. Then Mussatov's voice came through the ear pieces: 'Shrapnel! At the Reichstag, centre of target, setting 100! First SPG – one round – fire!'

A long, fiery-red flame shot from Shevtshuk's gun. The shell went howling towards the Reichstag and exploded short of its target. The second shot went too far.

'Now that you have got the range, the whole company can open fire effectively,' Sacharkin said soberly. The first salvo cracked. I looked through the periscope. The dome of the Reichstag had disappeared behind thick smoke. The company went on to fire several salvoes. Finally Mussatov had the company fall in and thanked the crews.

Machine-guns began hammering in Siemensstadt. That was our infantry. Lieutenant-Colonel Pashitnov, our training officer, ordered the company commanders to silence the enemy. The firing continued.

The infantry jumped up and worked their way closer to the canal. But before we could cross it we had to find possible crossing points.

I decided to send the scouts at nightfall. The group would be led by Staff-Sergeant Cholopov. He was experienced and clever and knew his way not only as a sapper but also with the SPGs.

'The task must be completed by 0100 hours! Understood?'

'Yes! No questions,' replied Cholopov.

The groups set off late that evening. Half an hour later the men had reached our front line. They crept into a small building and went down into the cellar, from where they had a good view over the canal. Cholopov reported: 'The canal has steep banks and is about 20 metres wide. A mortar is firing from the other side. We will now wait until it is fully dark, then we will creep up to the bridge.'

At last the time came. The scouts crept up to the canal, concealing themselves on the bush-covered bank. Someone was talking on the bridge and carefully struck a match.

'We will swim across to the bridge,' decided Cholopov. 'Pavlov will remain on this embankment and maintain communication with headquarters.'

The scouts slid carefully into the water. Cholopov in front, behind him Sergeant Gaviuchin, then Sappers Pusitchev and Babashev. The ice-cold water burnt their bodies like fire.

'They've stopped at the bridge, hardly visible above water,' reported Pavlov.

Verey lights went up lighting up the ground around the bridge. The scouts vanished under the water as if ordered. Finally they reached the bridge's piers. Above them a sentry was going to and fro. Somebody gave an order and the boots came closer. When Pavlov reported that the sappers had found two explosive charges and disarmed them, Sacharkin could hardly contain himself for joy.

Slowly the time went by but the scouts did not return. The connection with them was broken. At last footsteps were heard. Wet through and frozen, Cholopov reported: 'Task fulfilled.'

I thanked them and ordered Lieutenant Mussatov to give the men 100 grams of vodka each. Shortly afterwards, we attacked the bridge supported by the infantry, covering the land between the canal and the Spree with a hail of shells. The enemy fled back to the Spree, many of the *Volkssturm* surrendering, happy that the war was over for them.

Unfortunately this was not always the result. We had to fight hard for every foot of ground. The storm troops had great difficulty forcing their way into the cellars and ground floor of a multi-storey building. The buildings around hampered our SPGs. We had no choice but to blow up a corner building. Our scouts and some signallers could enter the adjoining building to lay telephone wires. Everything depended upon the building having been abandoned by the enemy. Then suddenly a bullet whistled past my ears. I then realised that we had fallen into a trap. The enemy had made small holes in the walls to fire through. There seemed to be no way out of the predicament. But here too Babashev wanted to help. He poured inflammable liquid over several chairs, set light to them, and the room filled with smoke. Then, as he had no *Trotyl* left, he ignited it with some dummy explosive charges. It worked wonders. The Fascists hastily abandoned the building.

Despite strong resistance, our regiment got over the Spree and took up the fight in Charlottenburg with the tanks and motorised infantry of the 1st Mechanised Corps. Here the enemy defended himself even more strongly than before. He detected his end was near and wanted to hold out as long as possible.

The narrow alleys in Charlottenburg hampered our advance to the Tiergarten and to the Reichstag. Overall an SPG, including its gun barrel, was more than 10 metres long and almost 4 metres wide. So it was no longer possible for us to break through walls and trample down fences.

Lieutenant Kuklin went first with his SPG, Ivanov's company following him. Kuklin had not forgotten his oath to be the first of our regiment to break through to the Reichstag. He wanted to exact revenge for his friends Gumar Salichov and Piotr Korotkov. Nothing seemed able to stop him. When Ivanov reported to me that Kuklin was fighting well ahead of the others, I immediately sent him Lieutenant Olitshev's submachine-gun platoon to help, but it was already too late. His SPG was hit by a *Panzerfaust* and set on fire. Kuklin lost his life in this attack. This sad news hit us like a crushing blow. We removed our helmets and thought of him in silence. Our superiors posthumously awarded Kuklin the Order of the Great Fatherland War 1st Class.

Last Efforts

From documents and the memoirs of the former Fascist General Weidling, we know what the Fascist leadership clique did during the time from the 29th April to the 2nd May to prolong their defeat, if only for a few hours. The situation for the Berlin Garrison was anything but enviable. The Fascist troops had suffered heavy losses and many of their supply depots, which were mainly located in the outer districts, were already in our hands.

The Polish 1st Division *Tadeusz Kosciusko* reached Charlottenburg on the 29th April 1945 and came to our help. Our speed of attack increased and the situation for our troops improved. The supply of ammunition, fuel and foodstuffs worked excellently and our firepower increased. As stated by captured German generals, the enemy in the fighting for Berlin alone lost 100,000 men killed or wounded.

Our army's headquarters was located in Charlottenburg with the four large staff vehicles under deep cover. I went there in the hope of meeting the staff officers of our corps to learn details of the situation in Charlottenburg. General Bogdanov sat in a wireless vehicle in front of a radio transmitting his orders to the corps commanders. 'Comrade 20, send your reserve across the Spree. Lead the attack on map square 23!'

I looked at my map. This order applied to Krivoshein. The Tiergarten lay in map square 23. Once more I was impressed by General Bogdanov's cleverness. With the advance of our troops into the Tiergarten, the enemy groups would be spread even further apart. That made it even more difficult for General of Artillery Weidling, entrusted with the defence of Berlin, to command his troops. He had already lost contact with some of his troops who had now become isolated from each other in Berlin.

The commander of the 12th Tank Corps, Major-General Salminov, reported that he had completed the 'job', together with General Berzarin. General Bogdanov ordered him to report to army head-quarters for new assignments.

From the receiver came the booming bass of the corps commander, Vedeneiev. His troops had met up with the 47th Army north of Berlin in an outflanking manoeuvre and defeated the fighting German units. The general asked for the losses of officers in his armoured elements to be filled.

'My thanks for this outstanding achievement. I cannot send you any officers at the moment. However, I will consider it,' replied Bogdanov. After this talk Bogdanov went over to a radio and had a conversation, apparently with the Front War Council. As the army's war council member, General Latyshev, climbed into the vehicle, Bogdanov went straight up to him. 'Here is the new task. We are to make a thrust with part of our forces in an easterly direction along the Spree in order to support Kusnezov in the taking of the Reichstag.'

'Right. We must not give the enemy any possibility of mustering his forces,' agreed Latyshev.

I withdrew from the radio vehicle. From a neighbouring cellar I heard the regular ticking of a teleprinter and the loud voice of Radsievski, passing on instructions to the subordinate staffs. 'Attack then, Comrade Yershov, we dare not lessen the pressure on the enemy in any way. Hitler will only give up when we finally have him by the throat.'

I made my way back to my headquarters, which were accommodated in the offices of an ammunition factory in a street nearby. The staff had set themselves up in the directors' room. Out of the window one could see the street in which our regiment was fighting. A heavy mortar battery had deployed in the factory yard, and dust was coming off the walls with every salvo.

'Is there anything new?' I asked Sacharkin.

'Leliushenko's and Rybalko's elements are advancing successfully and thrusting towards us. West of Berlin Vedeneiev's tanks have made contact with Colonel Korezki's fighting vehicles of Leliushenko's army. The first to force the canal were Colonel Shamardin's motorised rifle brigade of Vedeneiev's corps, then Colonel Korezki's infantry built a bridge. Tanks were immediately sent across. Hitler's Reichs Chancellery is now only a stone's throw from us. The communications centre in the Bendlerstrasse has already been taken. Goebbels has committed suicide. Chief of the General Staff Krebs wants to discuss surrender terms with our supreme command, but the answer from Moscow is that there is only total and unconditional surrender!' And now Sacharkin had some happy news. 'Our victorious banner is waving over the Reichstag. The fighting for the Reichstag began on the morning of the 30th April. The Fascists put up a fierce resistance. Our first attacks were beaten back, but towards 1800 hours our soldiers forced their way into the Reichstag under cover of artillery fire.'

Nevertheless bitter fighting continued within the Reichstag building. I decided to increase the fighting pressure in the Tiergarten further.

As Pashitnov received the order to concentrate fire on the Reichs Chancellery, he cheerfully declared: 'For four years I have dreamed of storming Berlin. And now I have been given the task of destroying Hitler's hideout with the fire from our SPGs, an honourable task, thank you, Comrade Commander!'

Sacharkin too received an important task. He was to select a group of submachine-gunners, under the command of an officer, and they were to track down leading members of the Fascist government and senior Party functionaries and arrest them. For the first time ever Michail Ivanovitch Sacharkin lost his proverbial calm. His eyes flashed. He happily hurried to the telephone and entrusted Major Shabalin with the running of the staff.

I went to the window. The SPGs of our regiment and Chotimski's riflemen were deploying on the station square and in the gardens. They were preparing to attack Savignyplatz S-Bahn station.

But the German troops in Berlin, though surrounded and isolated from each other, were still not giving in. Mussatov sent Pavlov to me with a report that the enemy were advancing in his rear. 'Understood. I will send machine-pistol infantry to his aid immediately.'

Muraviov's company was fighting in a parallel street. There was no communication with him. The alley by which one could get to Muraviov was under fire. But a messenger had to get there. My eyes fell on Yura. I considered whether I should send him. But before speaking to him I consulted with Ossadtchi.

'What else can you do?' he said. 'If the situation demands, then you must send him.'

I called Yura to me. 'You have complained that no one gives you a fighting role. Now the moment has arrived that we need you.

'At last! What should I do?'

'Take a letter to Muraviov. But look, the alley is under fire. You must not delay, as our SPGs are in danger. Should you encounter Germans, destroy the letter. Understood?'

'Certainly! I am already on my way.' Yura took the envelope and ran into the yard. Major Ossadtchi and I went to the window. Yura ran up to and jumped over the fence. A burst of machine-gun fire whirled up the dust near him. The youngster dived into a ditch, stood up again and ran on, shells bursting behind him.

'He has had it now,' whispered Ossadtchi.

My heart was in my throat. But as the dust from the explosions blew away, we saw Yura flitting through the alley.

'He's through,' I said, relieved.

About ten minutes passed, then machine-pistol infantry appeared firing. Ahead of them ran Muraviov, Golovatshiov and Yura. A little later the youngster stood before me, scratched and beaming. 'Comrade

Commander, order executed. Muraviov's company has gone into the attack!'

Deeply moved, I clasped Yura in my arms. 'Thank you, my boy.'

The noise of fighting from the direction of the Tiergarten increased. I drove forward with an SPG and stopped about 200 metres from the Tiergarten. Mussatov's SPG stood in front of me firing into the extensive park. Chotimski's men, deployed into a defensive line, lay in front of the SPG. Strong fire from the Tiergarten was pinning them to the ground.

Meanwhile Colonel Vainrub's tanks had arrived and deployed behind us. They fired as if they were in competition with the SPGs. Sintshenko's riflemen were covering the Tiergarten with fire from the Reichstag.

The Berlin Palace was on fire. When a white flag was fluttered out of a window, General Krivoshein ordered me to cease fire and break off the attack!

'Please repeat that once more,' I replied, completely confused. 'We cannot let the enemy get away with it!'

Krivoshein laughed and explained: 'The Berlin Garrison has capitulated. Weidling has struck his weapons. The war is over!'

This news hit us like a stroke of lightning from the heavens. We had long waited for this moment. I immediately passed on the order to all the units. I myself, however, remained for a long time on the spot, unable to grasp the situation. Joy at victory and remembering the difficult battles filled my heart. We had needed four years of an unprecedented, sacrificial war to finally bring the Fascist beast to its knees. Beaten by the Soviet Army, in whose ranks were those who had had to retreat to Moscow in the hard year of 1941 but nevertheless had sworn to take Berlin. Now they had fulfilled this oath.

Krivoshein ordered the regiment to assemble. The men fell on each other's necks, kissing each other, congratulating each other on the victory. Lieutenant Kiritshenko groaned and fell to the ground. In four years of war he had not received a scratch and now he lay at our feet!

The shot [that hit him] had come from the roof of a building. Our submachine-gunners stormed the building, caught a Fascist in civilian clothing and made short work of him. 'The war is over, but we must remain alert,' warned Ossadtchi.

I had the regiment fall in and led it to the Victory Column, where Vainrub's tank troops and those from the mechanised brigades of Chotimski, Petrov and Sokolov had already paraded. A feeling of pride in my country, my people and my army streamed through me. I was delighted with my regiment, whose heavy self-propelled guns had ended their long fighting advance in besieged Berlin.

The First Days After Victory

The first changes began in our regiment. Pashitnov, Ossadtchi and I already knew about the coming transfers to other units. Sacharkin was delegated for studies in Leningrad. The soldiers in the older age groups were preparing themselves for demobilisation. Shabalin and Postnikov were empowered with the temporary command of the regiment.

The bitter hour of farewell was getting closer. Shabalin sat in the headquarters preparing the marching orders. Cholopov stood on the steps and looked sadly at his friends jumping down off the SPGs in the yard. He had come a long way with these vehicles, hit the enemy and made some difficult journeys. Now he was to be separated from all of this. Ivan Ivanovitch breathed in deeply and drew nervously on a cigarette. Gorodenzev went up to him and gave him two cans of meat. 'Take them for the journey. I have nothing else to give you.'

'Thank-you, my friend.' Cholopov took the rucksack off his shoulders, stuffed in the cans and stammered: 'Difficult to leave you. What happiness and bitterness we have experienced together! How often did one's life hang on a thread? When will we ever see each other again?'

Gorodenzev sighed. Ivan Ivanovitch took his cigarette case from his pocket and held it out to Gorodenzev: 'Keep this as a souvenir. I have not been separated from it throughout the whole war.'

I climbed on the steps. Mussatov's company marched past me for the last time singing my favourite song, 'You fight like heroes'.

Suddenly Yura appeared. He was visibly thinner. Shabalin put a hand on his shoulder. 'Now Yura, take your document. From now on you are a Suvorov Scholar.'

The boy hid his face in his hands.

'What have we here? A soldier – and crying!'

'Off you go, youngster. Remain as you were in the regiment, brave and honourable.'

A car drove into the yard. The driver reported: 'Comrade Commander, the regiment is paraded.'

I took one last look at the SPGs. Goodbye, steel friends.

Minutes later we were driving through the Olympic Village. Then we came to the railway station. The troops were standing on the square in front. On their uniforms flashed orders and medals. Our Guard's standard waved on the right flank.

'Attention!'

The band played a march. I marched across the front of the unit, looking into the familiar faces of my comrades. The stood like simple Soviet men, but what wonderful heroes! They had not only defended their fatherland but rescued many peoples from Fascism. How proud their grandchildren and great-grandchildren would be of them.

I believe that it was only at this parting that I realised what strong bonds I had with my regimental colleagues. Now they were breaking. Previously we had all had the same fate, the same aim, but now we would go our separate ways. I slowed my pace, wanting to extend the unrepeatable moment and stopped in front of Staff-Sergeant Tartartshuk. How self-sacrificingly he had repaired our SPG under the heaviest fire. The staff-sergeant looked smart in his new tunic with its snow-white collar, but also a little sad.

I went on. There stood Lieutenant Poteiev, wearing a head bandage. Next to him stood Senior-Sergeant-Major Kossarev. He too had returned to the regiment after his recovery.

Then I went past the front of the machine-pistol infantry. I spoke to Yuri Golovatshiov. The youngster had fought with distinction and wore the Order of Fame on his tunic.

'May I have your permission to make a request?'

'I'm listening.'

'I have honourably fought right through the whole war,' he replied. 'Now that I am too young to be demobilised, I go on serving. But perhaps I could have some leave to see my mother again?'

'You can go home, ten days,' I said and beckoned to Shabilin. 'Prepare his leave pass. Liubov Vassilievna will be delighted to see such an eagle of a son again. And the girls of Kemerovo will also be delighted to see him too.'

Then I saw the smiling face of our supply officer Komar. He had survived the third war alive and well, as if that was no ground for celebration!

Beside him stood our wonderful girls Minogian Yegorova, Ania Ashurina, Fisa Motshalova. They had already changed into civilian clothes. They were wearing colourful clothing but had not set aside their berets and star insignia.

I addressed the troops for the last time:

Dear comrades! The regiment is once more in the condition in which it fought the hated enemy. Many comrades have fallen in the fighting. Eternal fame is theirs! The memories of the deeds of Salichov, Chorushenko, Korotkov, Goldman, Vinogradov, Axianov, Tsherniatiev, Babaian and other fallen heroes will always remain in our hearts. You have left behind you a hard fighting time and fulfilled your duty honourably for the motherland. My heartiest thanks for this. The regimental command has agreed that all those demobilised will voluntarily return to work exactly as they fought at the front. But you will maintain your fighting ability in case an aggressor dares to attack us.

Cholopov spoke on behalf of those being demobilised. 'For me today is more difficult than being in the most stressful battle: I must say farewell to you, my colleagues.' Ivan Ivanovitch's voice trembled. He could hold back his tears only with difficulty. 'I have driven the enemy from Moscow to Berlin. But if someone attacks our homeland again, I'll find my regiment and take my place in the SPG once more.' He looked for Gorodenzev: 'My SPG and my machine-pistol I hand over today to a younger man, my comrade Gorodenzev, who will look after them well.'

Gorodenzev left the ranks, received the machine-pistol from Ivan Ivanovitch, clasped him by the hands and formally promised: 'I will fulfil your role exactly, Ivan Ivanovitch, as I did your orders in battle.'

Then 'Hero of the Soviet Union' Boldyrev came forward with the regimental banner. Bending his knee, the warrior kissed the regiment's holy relic.

The locomotive in the station gave a shrill whistle and the order was given: 'All aboard!'

Near me were Mussatov, Boldyrev, Korosteliov, Ivanov and Postnikov. They asked me not to forget them and at least to write often.

Shura went past crying. Pavlov followed me with a bag. 'Don't cry, Shurotshka, when I have done my time, I will come and find you.'

'I'll wait for you.'

'Close the doors!'

I hugged my friends – and shook the hands of many, many soldiers and NCOs.

Chapter 6

Years in Tanks

By General David Abramovitch Dragunski

Dragunski came from the village of Achmatov near Kalinin. His military career began in the 4th Rifle Regiment. In 1933 he was sent to Saratov for a three-year course on tanks and was then assigned to the 32nd Independent Tank Battalion equipped with the T-26 tank. He first saw action as a tank company commander against the Japanese invasion of Manchuria in 1936. Dragunski, by then a senior lieutenant, started the course at the Frunze Academy in the spring of 1939 and was in his final year as a student and participating in field exercises at the Ossovez Fortress on the western frontier when the Germans invaded the Soviet Union in 1941. By the beginning of 1945 he was a not yet fully recovered thrice-wounded colonel commanding the 55th Guards Tank Brigade of the 3rd Guards Tank Army of Marshal Koniev's 1st Ukrainian Front. Shortly before the launching of Operation Berlin in April 1945 he was sent back to the Soviet Union on sick leave, taking the opportunity of having a thorough medical examination in Moscow before recuperating at a health resort.

During Dragunski's absence on sick leave, Koniev's forces had smashed their way through the German lines to the southern outskirts of Berlin. At the planning conference in Moscow in January it had been decided that Koniev's forces should meet up with Zhukov's 1st Byelorussian Front in the Brandenburg–Potsdam area, but Koniev's initial attack across the Neisse River had been so successful that he had subsequently suggested to Stalin that he be allowed to attack Berlin from the south. Stalin, who was out to enhance his own position by humiliating the nationally popular Zhukov, agreed and even ordered the air force commander for the Berlin operation not to reveal the extent of Koniev's involvement. Although Zhukov was informed of this change in plan, he was determined to have Berlin to himself and assumed that Koniev's troops would not approach closer than Potsdam, as had previously been agreed in Moscow.

* * *

The T-34/85.

The Oder lay behind us and we were approaching the Neisse. We could clearly sense the presence of the front line as we went past field hospitals, bases and field workshops. Even more often we met ammunition transports, tanks and ambulances. In a dense wood we came across the Rear Services of General Gordov's 3rd Guards Army. By morning on the 21st April we had already learned something about the general situation. We found the staff of the 13th Army and here learned the direction of attack of our armoured units. Several hours later we reached the 3rd Guards Tank Army's Rear Services. The head of the specialist detachment, the small, thin Colonel Merkuliev, wanted to give a full description of the situation. He would not let the map out of his hands, showing us the front line and the location of our corps.

'And where is the 55th Guards Tank Brigade?'

'The day before yesterday it was 30 kilometres from Wünsdorf.'

'That was the day before yesterday, and where is it today?'

Although already overtaken, Merkuliev's information was quite correct.

We stayed a few hours with the second echelon to regather ourselves, wash and shave. I could not report to my army and corps commanders in a dishevelled state.

We were lucky. After we had gone back several kilometres, we came
across our traffic regulator, Mashenka Sotnik. I jumped out of the
vehicle and gave her a hug. Happy to have met this girl, I felt like a
young boy. When Mashenka was at her post, one needed neither a
map, compass nor orientation point. She knew everything and readily
gave information. Before I could ask her, she reported to me where the
brigade had gone and where it had been the night before.

'How do you know that - you weren't there?'

'This morning I met the wounded battalion commander Fiodorov
here. He told me everything. The fighting was hard. There were men
with *panzerfausts* everywhere hunting our tanks. Battalion commander
Safronov has fallen and the deputy corps commander, General
Jakubovski, is wounded.'

I had to find out from Mascha where the army headquarters were.
Again we were lucky. Mascha had just been relieved. She got into the
vehicle with us to show us the way to the headquarters. In one breath
the girl told us all the news. Then she stopped and then said: 'How
I would love to come to Berlin too!'

'This is a promise, Maschenka. We will celebrate our victory there.'

The girl's eyes gleamed with pleasure.

An officer greeted us at the barrier and led us to the army chief of
staff in a cottage. Bachmetiev filled me in on the situation and showed
me the area where our corps was located.

'I do not know exactly where the brigade is,' said General
Bachmetiev frankly. 'I take it that it is north of Zossen, almost on
the Teltow Canal.' The chief of staff then called the army commander.
Rybalko said that he was waiting for me at his command post.

That same day we travelled over worn-out, destroyed streets and
tracks to our troops. We had to constantly overtake columns of
vehicles and artillery and got through only slowly. Coming towards us
were men and women, teenagers, children and old people. Many
could hardly stand. These people in their torn clothing and ripped
shoes looked at the troops moving towards Berlin. They raised their
arms in greeting and raised clenched fists. These former forced
labourers and concentration camp inmates had gone through the
worst. I looked at them attentively, looking for my brother and sisters.
I knew how false these hopes were, but such is mankind, ever hopeful.

How many people had the Fascists moved from their occupied territories to Germany! The march of the prisoners had begun when our attack tore down the gates of the concentration camps and prisons. At that time we were in Poland and liberated those incarcerated in Majdanek, Auschwitz and many other concentration camps. More than four months had passed and this endless stream had still not dried up. Although I had already seen much misfortune and suffering in this war, these helpless people made the saddest and strongest impression. 'Victory!', 'Vive la paix!', 'Probeda!', 'Frieden!' As I heard these shouts, and saw the happiness in their emaciated faces, I thought how much sorrow the war had brought. Every front-line soldier had gone through a lot for the liberation, for our victory over Fascism and for the lives of these tortured people.

Our Jeep crawled northwards along the blocked streets. We needed no one to show us the way – the glow of fire on the horizon and the thunder of the artillery indicated it for us. Hundreds of aircraft whizzed over us towards Berlin. The dull detonations of exploding bombs could be heard kilometres away.

With little difficulty we found our way to the headquarters. I met Rybalko in the large room of a villa. Near him stood an unknown general with dark eyes and grey hair. I saluted a bit uncertainly as I did not know who was the highest ranking, both being colonel-generals. I went to the army commander. Rybalko did not let me finish my report, but shook my hand. 'I have always said that Dragunski arrives punctually. This time too his nose has not let him down.' Then he turned to the general, who was the Front's Chief of Artillery, and said: 'This is the commander of the 55th Guards Tank Brigade. He has just come out of hospital. His greatest fear was not to come to Berlin. If he now is the first to march into Berlin he will get his second golden star; if he doesn't we will take the first one off him.'

All laughed. The army commander looked me over from head to foot. 'You look well, just as after taking a cure. Now, however, it is time to get to work.'

He led me to the table, where a city map of Berlin had been laid out. The important streets were clearly marked, squares, stadiums, underground railway stations, as well as the Reichstag and the Reichs Chancellery. The blue lines of the Teltow Canal and the Spree River snaked along the edge of the city, led into the city and lost themselves somehow in the labyrinth of the streets. I read the names of the surrounding areas and suburbs. Thick woods and lakes stretched along the western edge of the city.

'This has all to be taken. The attack is directed at the southern and western part of the city. The enemy thinks that Marshal Zhukov's troops will attack from the east. However, we will attack from the south and at the most sensitive place – in the flank.'

Thick arrows showed the line of attack of General Suchov's 9th Mechanised Corps from eastern Berlin. Two thinner arrows showed the 1st Byelorussian Front opposite – Chuikov's 8th Guards Army and Katukov's 1st Tank Army. Mitrofanov's 6th Tank Corps was to thrust with his brigades directly to the north, to the city centre and into the Tiergarten. Impatiently my eyes went over the map looking for the 7th Corps and our brigade. I had failed to notice the dotted line in the middle of the arrows and crosses. The head of the army's operational department, my old acquaintance from the academy, Sascha Jeremenko, leaned his powerful arm over my head. 'Here is your brigade,' he said, pointing to the map. 'It reached the Teltow Canal yesterday. The Fascists blew the bridge right in front of your tank troops.'

I did not know what this water obstacle looked like and asked 'Is there no ford or alternative route?'

'Fords!' drawled Kamentshuk, the chief engineer. 'The canal is about 40 to 50 metres wide and there are fortifications on the northern bank. Blocked villages and massive buildings strengthen the defences.'

When I heard this, I became somewhat less confident. Kamentshuk knew what he was talking about. His opinion was highly regarded by us commanders.

'Don't frighten him, Matvei Polikarpovitch,' said Rybalko smiling. 'What is there is still standing, we must be bold, decisive and singleminded. We have nothing to fear, finally we are not alone. The 1st Byelorussian Front is coming from the east. In the north Rokossovski is striking out. On our army's left wing Leliushenko is attacking towards Potsdam. That man there is the commander-in-chief of the 28th Army, Alexander Alexandrovitch Lutschinski.' Rybalko pointed to a tall, thin general. 'When the infantry are here, we tank soldiers need have no fear.'

On leaving, General Rybalko said to me: 'Drive straight to your brigade. Get to know the situation on the spot and everything will become clear to you. In any case drive first to the corps commander, who is expecting you. What I now want to say to you is that the corps is now under General Vassili Vassilievitch Novikov. He is an old, experienced warrior. He is strong and lets nothing get past him.'

Rybalko was in good spirits and his orders were always accompanied by a little joke. I stopped again at the door. I could not help saying, 'I will wait for you in Berlin, Comrade General.'

'I will come in any case,' answered Rybalko smiling, 'but only under special conditions. You must receive me on Wilhelmstrasse. The whole of the 7th Corps will be heading in this direction.'

Once I had obtained a city plan of Berlin from the liaison officer, I made my way to my colleagues. The reunion at the headquarters and the words that Rybalko had said to me on the way excited me. Rybalko's inexhaustible energy conveyed itself to me and I seemed to be streaming with unusual strength.

The vehicle went off to the north at speed. We came to Mahlow, turned left towards Teltow and immediately came under a barrage. The communications officer who was to escort us to the brigade had selected no particularly suitable route. He wanted to bring us to our goal by the shortest route, but had not taken into account that the main road to Teltow was under enemy fire. It was too late to turn around, apart from which it was not lacking in danger to do so. We therefore had to go through, whatever the cost, our vehicle bouncing from one crater to another.

Rykov clasped the steering wheel firmly with both hands and steered us to the edge of the town, the vehicle jumping like a goat from one side to another. Then he drove along close to the buildings. Bathed in sweat, the driver angrily sought individual sheltered places, but there were hardly any. Despite all the difficulties, we reached the city outskirts. Now we had to cross a small open area and then vanish into a wood, from where it was only a few steps to the brigade headquarters.

The fire did not ease off. Shells howled over from the far bank, and one could hear the discharge of mortars. Apart from this, machine-gun fire was spraying the open areas.

Here there were neither hills nor depressions, not even a bush. Although the vehicle had turned off the field, furrowed from shells, only a few minutes before, for us it seemed an eternity as shots hit ahead and behind us. Rykov got the last ounce of power out of the Jeep. The vehicle slipped and twisted, splinters whistling around our ears. With the bodywork riddled, we eventually reached the thick wall of an abandoned property. The communications officer had been hit by a splinter, but the remainder of us had got through with a fright. The thought of being wounded so close to one's goal, or even being killed, was like a cold shower down my back. It was not the fear of death that had filled me, for one generally got used to that in war, but the thought that one could be shot only three paces from my brigade.

Finally we had survived it. We breathed out, took a slug of water, bandaged our escort, changed a wheel and carried on. The heavy fire had died down in our sector, the shells now exploding at a distance from us. We reached our destination in another hour.

I found the brigade staff in an abandoned farm that was not shown on any map. Several of my familiar vehicles – the radio vehicle, armoured car and my 'steel horse', a T-34 with the number 200 – stood close to a wall.

The greeting was short, but hearty. First I made myself known to the new chief of staff, Lieutenant-Colonel Schalunov, and the other officers that had joined during my absence. I was very happy to see Dmitriev sound and lively. He had been in charge of the brigade's political detachment for over three years.

The new chief of staff reported the situation and the brigade's role to me. All our attempts to cross the canal in the Stahnsdorf area had so far failed. He led me to the window. From there one could see Stahnsdorf, the bridge to the right of it, and the battalions that had dug themselves in on the south bank of the canal.

'I have never before experienced such fire,' said Schalunov, shaking his head.

'What is the situation with the bridge?'

'We cannot take it. The Germans have blown it, and simply to go across makes little sense.'

'What does the corps commander think about it?'

'That is clear enough: he is complaining. We have to get over somehow.'

I telephoned General Novikov and reported myself. He asked me to go to him. We were 2 or 3 kilometres apart and, under the prevailing conditions, radio and telephone communications were not very reliable. It was not right for me to leave the brigade again so soon, but when the commander demanded it, there was no arguing.

I could not get to his observation post with a car or an armoured vehicle. The Fascists were only 300 metres away from us. So I had to go on foot, or to be precise, crawl, as the strong fire pressed us to the ground. My adjutant, the liaison officer and I scurried from building to building to reach the woods as quickly as possible. It was still more dangerous here. Shells exploded constantly. Close to the edge of the woods stood some buildings and these were our saviours. We moved by leaps and bounds from building to building. An officer from the corps staff was waiting for us on one corner.

Our situation was anything but funny, but I could not hold back my laughter. The captain crept into a building and disappeared like a cat through a narrow cellar window. A moment later a hand appeared in the cellar window and waved. We were to go the same way. Either I was more heavily built than the captain, or I had not correctly judged the size of the cellar window, but in any case I remained stuck. Only with a big effort, and to the amusement of those gathered in the cellar, could I get through.

'Don't be surprised about this entrance. Normally we prefer to use the door.' An unknown voice greeted me with these words. 'But the door lies in the enemy's line of fire. When we moved in here during the night we were not aware of this, and it was too late to change location in the morning.'

Gradually one's eyes got used to the twilight. There were several men in the long room. In one corner stood some telephone apparatus and in a side room were two radio operators with their sets. Next to Corps Commander Novikov stood the commander of the tank and mechanised troops of our front, Colonel-General N.A. Novikov, and the head of the corps' political detachment, A.V. Novikov.

Once I had brushed off the dust and brought my uniform to order, I reported to the corps commander and the colonel-general, after which Andrei Vladimirovitch clasped me in his arms. I had often met this simple, demanding, fair and courageous man on my way. He was clever, good-natured and just. Those who knew him adored him. With successes he did not break into raptures of joy, but also he did not fall into despair with failures. The political workers and brigade commanders respected him for he was considerably older and more experienced than we were. He simply understood how to influence people.

I recalled the bridgehead of Sandomierz in August 1944 when our brigade was fighting against superior forces. At that time Andrei Vladimirovitch came through to us like a marvel. He brought neither tanks nor artillery with him, just a few simple, rousing words, his sheer presence in the narrow trenches making us strong.

'We both will drink champagne in Goebbels' residence,' he said to me in a quiet moment.

'God grant that we will survive this hell in one piece. For the time being I am not in the mood for champagne,' I murmured.

'Why do you want to bury yourself already? You will see, we will get to Berlin!' That was the way he always spoke. And today he said: 'You see we have met once more, not exactly in Berlin, but shortly before it. How difficult it was too, but we have made it up till now. We have even met in a quite unusual situation.'

In order to calm down a bit, I asked jokingly: 'Are there not a few too many Novikovs in one cellar?'

Vassili Vassilievitch took off his gilded spectacles and polished the lenses. 'There are fewer Novikovs in Russia than Ivanovs, especially in the Kalinin area. That we three should all be in one place, you are responsible. Should your brigade be on the other side of the canal I would not be sitting here, and Nikolai Alexandrovitch would also not have come.' The corps commander paused a moment and went to the heart of the matter. 'Nevertheless it is unpardonable that the brigade should be held up at the canal. We took the Dnepr, were the first to force the Vistula, and you have left the Nida, Varta and Oder behind you but now you are unable to get across this unfortunate canal!'

Nervously Vassili Vassilievitch moved to and fro. I was meeting General Novikov today for the first time as previously he had been commanding another corps. Nevertheless I had already heard much good about his well-balanced attitude and his courage. It was said that it was difficult to bring the general out of his composure. Nevertheless I remained careful in this first encounter with the new corps commander.

General Novikov went to the map and I followed him.

'The Teltow Canal is the last hurdle on the way to Berlin. Once we have forced it we are at our goal.' The corps commander spoke slowly, wanting his subordinates to correctly understand the meaning of every sentence.

I learned of his immediate decision to force the canal on a width of 5 kilometres and to attack in two sectors. 'On the right sector will be the Schapovalov Brigade and the 55th will deal with the left. We will let Kostin's regiment with his light SU-76 tanks attack over the blown bridge. One has only to reinforce the bridge remains beforehand.'

I discovered that there would be an artillery division in the corps' attack area and two artillery brigades in our sector. We could pin the enemy down with this and the assigned engineer battalion would ensure the crossing.

'How much time have we at our disposal?'

'One day. Report your readiness to me at the end of the 23rd April.'

There were no further questions. The details I would have to clarify myself. For the moment everything was swimming around in front of me. Firstly I must discover why our whole army was standing still in front of this damned canal. What forces were facing us? One had to examine everything, think things through properly and prepare thoroughly.

We negotiated the ground floor of the building with the corps commander and climbed carefully out of a narrow window. We could see the terrain around us for a kilometre. To the right, left and in front of us lay shot-up villages, garden allotments, individual farms, villas and gardens. Several lakes glistened in the distance. I could not find the notorious Teltow Canal at first. Vassili Vassilievitch polished his spectacles as usual and replaced them on his nose. 'On the right is Teltow, in front of us Stahnsdorf, and there is the destroyed bridge. On the right of it is the breakthrough sector of the 23rd Rifle Brigade.'

Now I could make out the canal embankment clearly with the binoculars. It was raised well above the green fields. The surface of the water was reflected at various points.

Once we had examined the terrain we returned to the cellar. Lunch was ready on the table. I dared not refuse the invitation. Andrei Vladimirovitch Novikov poured everyone a glass of vodka. 'To our victory. We will drink champagne in Berlin.'

While we were eating, Nikolai Alexandrovitch Novikov, who had kept quiet until now, said in a low voice: 'Vassili Vassilievitch, Marshal Koniev asked me to advise him yet again on your corps' special situation. The attack is aimed at the western edge of the city. Under the pressure from the two Fronts the enemy will doubtless be forced to withdraw to the west. You must block his attempt to break out. The enemy will try to eliminate you in a fight to the death. Think about it and do everything to ensure your corps will not be overrun.'

Before the corps commander replied, he polished his spectacles once more. 'I fully understand that. But I need infantry as soon as possible, otherwise the corps will fall between the hammer and anvil.' Turning towards me, he went on: 'Until now one knew you in the 3rd Tank Army as a commander that neither looked back nor feared open flanks. This reputation has now to be defended.'

'On this you can depend,' interposed the lowest-ranking Novikov, the head of the political department, Andrei Vladimirovitch.

We had to take the same route back as we had come by. But now I already knew something about the situation and felt not so out of things. The following day we used to prepare for the battle.

With the scouts, engineers, the commander of the SU-76 regiment, the battalion commanders and the officers of the attached artillery, we crept to the positions, identified the crossing points and investigated the approaches to the canal. We moved up to the canal bank, studied the enemy's firing regime and identified his firing positions.

Although we had tried hard to conceal them, nevertheless the enemy noticed our preparations. In the second half of the day he increased his fire and until late in the night big calibre shells exploded on our bank while the enemy anti-aircraft guns fired at ground targets. This day showed us what a hard nut we had to crack. In order to conquer this vast city, there was no question but that we had to change our previous tactics. Going around, attacking off the move, thrusting in the flanks or enemy rear no longer applied under the given conditions.

We tank soldiers had become accustomed to the reinforced preparation techniques in the last two years. In many big operations the commander-in-chief of the 1st Ukrainian Front operated under conditions that enabled wide-ranging manoeuvres. We avoided tedious battles, thrusting straight into the breaches and thus widening the breakthrough. Often the tanks operated up to 100 kilometres ahead of the infantry. The taking of prepared lines of defence deep in the enemy's rear was routine for us. Especially popular methods were deep thrusts into the operational area, manoeuvring towards the flanks, the taking of important centres, then a thrust towards a big water obstacle and the formation of a bridgehead. The present situation, however, left us no room to manoeuvre. Berlin, with its numerous suburbs, water obstacles, streets and buildings, awaited us.

Although we stood immediately before the city, the Fascist leaders sought our destruction in every way. Hitler hoped as before for some miracle or other. He went on forming reserves from newly established units, from his officer corps, the officer schools, the Gestapo and the *Volkssturm* battalions. The overall head of the Fascist Reich even tried to make an arrangement with the USA and Great Britain against the Soviet Union and the Red Army. Every means, whether military or

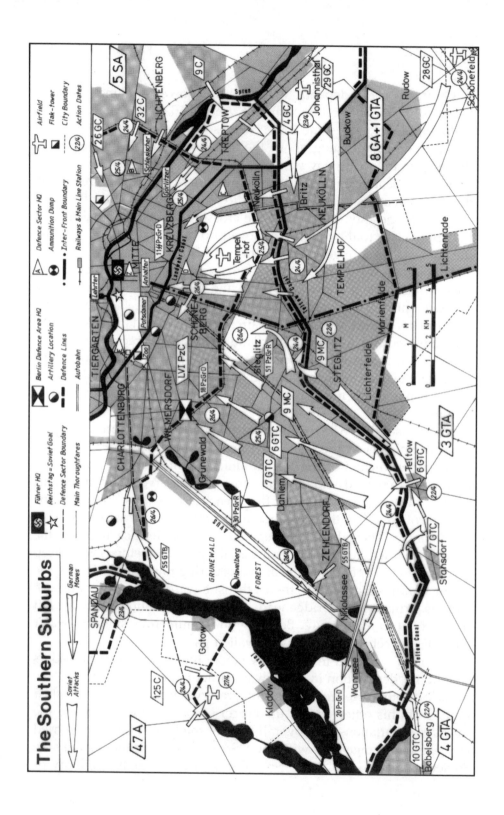

The Southern Suburbs

Legend:

- ☆ Führer HQ
- ☆ Reichstag = Soviet Goal
- Defence Sector Boundary
- Main Thoroughfares
- ⚔ Berlin Defence Area HQ
- ⚙ Artillery Location
- Defence Lines
- Autobahn
- △ Defence Sector HQ
- ☢ Ammunition Dump
- Inter-Front Boundary
- Railways & Main Line Station
- ✝ Airfield
- ▪ Flak-tower
- City Boundary
- (22/4) Action Dates

Soviet Attacks / **German Moves**

5 SA

9 C
32 C
26 GC
125 C
47 A
4 LGC
29 GC
28 GC
8 GA+1 GTA
3 GTA
4 GTA
9 MC
6 GTC
7 GTC
10 GTC

Locations:
LICHTENBERG, TREPTOW, Spree, Schlesischer, Görlitzer, KREUZBERG, NEUKÖLLN, Neukölln, Britz, Buckow, Johannisthal, Rudow, Schönefeld, Lichtenrade, TEMPELHOF, Tempel-hof, Anhalter, Lehrter, Potsdamer, TIERGARTEN, MITTE, SCHÖNE-BERG, STEGLITZ, Steglitz, Marienfelde, Lichterfelde, WILMERSDORF, CHARLOTTENBURG, Grunewald, Dahlem, ZEHLENDORF, Teltow, 9 MC, 7 GTC, Stahnsdorf, Babelsberg, Kladow, Gatow, SPANDAU, Wannsee, Nikolassee, GRUNEWALD FOREST, Havelberg, Teltow Canal

Unit labels:
114 PzGrD, 18 PzGrD, LVI PzC, 51 PzGrR, 30 PzGrR, 55 GTB, 55 GTR, 20 PzGrD

Scale: M 1 2 / KM 1 2 3 4 5

Scale: 0 1 2 3 4 5 KM

political, was acceptable if only he could hold on to life for an hour longer. Consequently there was no easy way for us.

By the end of the day the preparations for the forcing of the canal were complete. As we had been reckoning on some tedious fighting, we had distributed the infantry among the tank companies and formed storm troops out of the submachine-gun battalions, the headquarters platoon, the sapper company and the scouts. They would drive the enemy out of his hiding places in the roofs, buildings and cellars. Every tank was allocated five or six men.

However, it was also clear to me that these measures were still insufficient. As before, we lacked the infantry essential for street fighting. But where could we get more? I consulted with the head of the political section and the chief of staff. 'Could we not redeploy the tankmen that have lost their tanks in the previous fighting as infantry?'

My comrades agreed and the tank soldiers were also not against it. Assault groups were formed with machine-pistols and machine-guns taken from the destroyed tanks. The workshop specialists, clerks and soldiers from the supply units also joined them, all wanting to take part in the storming of Berlin, and I understood their desire. But the men remained just men and I feared that every inherent self-preservation instinct could be seen in them. Who would want to lose his life so shortly before imminent victory. The men might thus avoid taking risks and the momentum of the attack would falter. In such a situation conviction alone is insufficient, and the personal example of the commanders, Communists and Komsomolz was necessary.

There were no such problems in the difficult years of 1941 and 1942. In the fighting in those days everyone had little hope of survival. We plunged into the fighting, thinking of victory even though we were not convinced that we would survive. I have often seen how soldiers have gone to certain death for a small patch of earth. And it was straight from these individual small successes that the greater success of the country in deadly fighting with Fascism depended.

At this time the front-line soldiers had a saying: 'A man cannot die twice, and once does not avoid him.' There was a grain of truth in this. Next to personal bravery and hatred of the enemy, these words showed a certain doubt that one could remain alive in war.

My fears were fortunately ungrounded. I had believed I knew my men, who had grown close to me in the years of war. Now their attacking spirit overcame all expectations. The inflexible wish to win, the determination to destroy Fascism as quickly and completely as possible and the deep belief in our rightful cause brought out mass heroism. The men went into battle unhesitatingly. Whoever forced his way into the Fascist capital knew what the words 'I took Berlin' would mean to future generations.

The Teltow Canal

The attack began. The approaching dusk was submerged by the artillery preparation's sea of fire. A mighty shock wave pressed us into the earth. Dmitriev shouted into my ear: 'What a magnificent concert!'

My enthusiastic chief of staff shouted: 'Marshal Koniev has excelled himself!'

That was for certain. I had not seen firing of such intensity for a long time. The breakthrough near Kiev, the battle of Lvov, the attack on the Sandomierz bridgehead, all these vast operations could not be compared with what occurred on the Teltow Canal in the morning hours of the 24th April.

A whole artillery corps concentrated within two days on a narrow breakthrough sector, effecting a density of 600 gun barrels per kilometre of front, massing together mortars, organising the fire plan, measuring out the firing positions while on the move and finally coordinating everything, that could only be achieved by a talented army commander like Marshal Koniev and such experienced Generals of Artillery as Korolkov, Volkenschtein and many others.

Then thousands of shells roared over the heads of our tank troops. Behind us rumbled the dull thumps of the mortars. The fire trails of the *Katiushas* ripped apart the sky. General Riasanov's bombers and fighters attacked, while Pokryschkin's fighters covered them from above.

The north bank of the canal and the southern boundary of Berlin were in flames. Buildings and fortified positions fell in rubble and ashes as thick clouds of smoke rose up. The tortured and mutilated earth groaned. Thousands of enemy soldiers were killed. To confront the assault of two Army Fronts, of hundreds of regiments, of 6,000 tanks, 40,000 guns and a whole armada of aircraft was senseless.

Futilely Goebbels cried out that the Russians would never get into the city. In vain many of his believing audience put their hopes in the so-called wonder weapons. Equally fallacious were Hitler's hopes in the reserves that were supposed to be coming to Berlin from the south and west, but which were being destroyed by the troops of Generals Gordov, Shadov and Puchov in the woods near Cottbus. Those who got through the slaughter then met the blows of the armoured and mechanised brigades of Rybalko and Leliushenko. Nevertheless the Fascists, already enclosed on three sides, put up a fanatical resistance. Right until the last minute they hoped for some miracle or other, but the miracle kept them waiting. Meanwhile our troops cut off their way to the west, but even now they bit back like a wounded animal. They understood that the hour of their downfall was imminent and that we would soon be presenting them with the bill for their crimes and the millions of victims at Auschwitz and Dachau, Mauthausen and Buchenwald, the Warsaw Ghetto and Babi Jar, Lidice and Oradour. Those who had not previously been sullied with foreign blood were now driven into the trenches on the orders of their Fascist leaders. The gallows, courts-martial and firing squads awaited those who left their positions.

The world of those people poisoned by Fascist ideas collapsed. They now realised what the adventurous politics of the Führer had done to their lives. Berlin, the last bastion of the Reich, was in a fight to the death.

The watch's minute hand crept slowly forward. The murderous artillery fire moved off to the north. The bombs were already exploding somewhat to the side of us. The time for our attack came ever closer.

'Another five minutes,' Boris Saveliev, the reconnaissance commander, said near me. Schalunov looked across at me. Dmitriev looked at his watch and silently counted the minutes and seconds.

'Give the orders!' My voice seemed completely strange to me.

The chief of staff had the radio operators transmit: 'Hawk', 'Full Speed', 'Stopwatch!' 'Forward!, forward!'

A series of green Verey lights climbed into the sky. The reconnaissance parties, engineers and submachine-gunners climbed out of their trenches and cover and stormed the canal bank, the engineers dragging up the boats to cross by, and behind them came the landing troops. Major Bystrov, the commander of the engineers, was already working on the bridge with several soldiers of the landing company. These handsome lads astonished me with their resourcefulness, daring and extraordinary ability. They tried out new methods and so found a solution when others would long since have given up. One could almost say that they had a sixth sense to detect the weight capacity of a bridge or a minefield. Now a runner arrived to tell me that the light self-propelled guns would soon be able to cross the bridge.

'Everything is going according to plan,' reported Schalunov confidently.

We all knew that our brigade was only a fraction of the assault being carried out in the 3rd Guards Tank Army's area. At that same moment the combatants of the 6th and 7th Guards Tank Corps attacked.

The canal was also to be forced in the sectors of the 22nd and 23rd Guards Motorised Rifle Brigades. The riflemen had it somewhat easier than us as they did not have to get heavy tanks and self-propelled guns across, and in the worst case swim across the 40 metres.

It looked as if everyone was convinced that the result of the battle depended entirely on his personal efforts.

Once it became light we could see several dark objects on the opposite bank. These were the members of our storm groups. They were storming forwards, taking cover, getting up again and going on. The submachine-gun battalion crossed over to the other side of the canal by platoons.

I knew precisely how important it was to support the men. What could they achieve on the other bank with their light weapons. We had to help the battalion immediately or it would inevitably be destroyed.

The commanders of two brigades of the Breakthrough Artillery Division suddenly appeared near me. They had also assessed the situation and were already giving the necessary orders. Some stout-hearted gunners hastened past us on their way to establish a forward observation post on the other bank. Shortly afterwards the guns thundered, clearing the way for our battalion.

At last Bystrov reported that the bridge, which the enemy had made impassable the day before, was now usable. Nevertheless only light tanks could pass over the temporarily repaired bridge under heavy fire. The mortar battery of a submachine-gun battalion and an attached artillery battery immediately crossed over. This eased the situation for the submachine-gun troops.

Battalion commander Staruchin asked for the quickest possible support. The situation for his battalion was getting worse. The enemy had recovered from our artillery preparation and was now conducting a massive resistance. We even had to reckon with counterattacks.

The chief engineer let self-propelled guns get across the bridge. Their success could be decisive. An advance of 3 to 4 kilometres by the self-propelled artillery regiment would be helpful to us; we could then throw bridges across and get the remaining troops over.

Two artillery brigades tried to split up the enemy as our tank battalions fired from the south bank. Impatiently we waited for the crossing points to be made ready.

The artillery and tank fire fight had lasted for over an hour already. The Fascists were increasingly active. Two artillery detachments were firing on the crossing points and within half an hour the bridges no longer existed. Bystrov had only been able to get three self-propelled guns across the canal, two others having fallen into the water with the wrecked bridge. Colonel Kostin, their regimental commander, was killed in this way.

The submachine-gun battalion had to fight on in a confined area without the urgently required tanks and guns. Critical minutes began for the battalion. Then the attack came to a full stop. The three self-propelled guns had destroyed the enemy. Staruchin received effective help from only two artillery brigades, which the enemy kept under fire. On the left wing Gulevatov's battalion held down an infantry company that wanted to strike into the rear of our submachine-gunners.

This massive exchange of fire lasted several hours. We tied down the enemy's forces, but that was all that we achieved.

The same applied to our right-hand neighbour. But our action lightened the activities of other units. In the centre the 22nd Guards Motorised Rifle Brigade, followed by the 23rd, was able to force the canal, form a bridgehead and get its main forces across. Several hours later a bridge had been established here over which the tank brigades and corps rolled. The battle for the Teltow Canal was decided, the gateway to Berlin had been opened.

At dusk on the same day the brigade rolled up to its crossing point. Novikov caught us up on the bridge. The corps commander was in good spirits. 'I saw how you tried to take the bridge. But it did not work out,' he said painfully. 'In any case you have given the Fascists a proper drubbing, and that was just right for us.'

Novikov took a creased map from his boot, flattened it and spread it over the bonnet of his vehicle. With a pencil he drew a line to the north as far as Zehlendorf, from where a dotted line went on to the autobahn and then on to the western edge of the city.

'That's it. All clear?'

'Understood, Comrade General.'

'Understanding is one thing, but you must think the thing through thoroughly.' For the first time the corps commander was addressing me with the familiar 'you'. This immediately raised my spirits. 'Look right here. Wherever you turn there are buildings. Reconnoitre exactly how many and what is involved. Every building must be fought for. Our whole hopes rest with the riflemen and the assault teams.'

Novikov gave his instructions in a quiet voice. Often he had to explain his words, although for both of us much was not understandable. There were many unknowns in the task confronting me. I knew nothing about the character of the enemy defences, about the strength of the enemy and his reserves.

But we did know that we would have to bite our way slowly and carefully through the defences. Every street offered a multitude of surprises. The brigade stood on the outermost left wing of the corps and the army. There was no visual contact with General Leliushenko's troops attacking towards Potsdam. Only from the distant thunder of artillery and rumbling explosions could I guess where the 4th Guards Tank Army was.

General Novikov had his individual traits. I could observe them once more as he left. He threw his cigarette end away, then, holding his spectacles firmly with two fingers, he grasped the windscreen of his open vehicle with his other hand and jumped into his seat with an elegant swing. As he drove off he called out to me: 'Think about it, such a moment will never return. We are in Berlin!'

The vehicle turned away and drove towards the crossing point with an endless stream of tanks, guns and vehicles behind it. I had to smile over the general's last words. Who could ever forget what it was like to stand in a Berlin street for the first time?

That night the tanks, together with Serashimov's reconnaissance men, Bystrov's sappers, and Staruchin's and Chadsarakov's sub-machine-gunners reached the Berlin suburbs. We went round Schönow, leaving Kleinmachnow to one side, and pushed through the devastated woods and gardens towards Lichterfelde-West S-Bahn station. The fighting took an unusual form. The enemy was there but invisible, appearing unexpectedly and vanishing again in an inexplicable way.

Trenches, individual slit trenches, ripped up streets, barricaded cellars, firing positions in roofs, dug-in tanks at crossroads and anti-aircraft guns gave us plenty to do. We needed the whole day to clear this thickly populated area. First we took Zehlendorf S-Bahn station, then the whole city district of Lichterfelde. We reported this victory immediately to the corps commander. In reply he radioed: 'Zehlendorf has still to be taken today!'

Hastily we drove the Rear Services and repair units into Lichterfelde. They had to be in the immediate vicinity of the attacking battalions. I was afraid that they would get lost in the maze of streets and that our tanks would finally run out of ammunition, fuel, food and workshop repairs, and be stuck in the burning city. This was why I always kept my 'household' immediately behind me, and we kept a large detachment formed of members of the rear units to maintain security. My deputy for the Rear Services, the experienced and practical Major Leonov, soon found himself at home in these unusual circumstances.

At the Teltow Canal General Novikov had hinted at the significance of Zehlendorf. 'That is the key to Berlin. It opens the door to the southwestern part of the city and must be in our hands by tonight. Don't let yourself get tied up in street-fighting.'

His radio message reinforced this demand once more.

Not to let oneself get entangled in street fighting was easy to demand, but in practice it seemed somewhat different. In front of us were the Krumme Lanke and Schlachtensee lakes. To the left and right of them stretched woods, gardens and extensive villa estates. Representatives of the great bourgoisie and the Nazi Reich had once settled down in picturesque Zehlendorf. I had the battalion commanders ordered to my command post at the Lichterfelde S-Bahn station. The commanders of the artillery units as well as the scouts and sappers were also summoned.

Zehlendorf lay uniquely quiet and apparently deserted. But I knew from experience how treacherous silence can be in war.

We needed two hours to organise our attack. Then scouts under Lieutenant Serashimov drove off with two tanks towards Zehlendorf. A company of submachine-gunners marched to the edge of the woods and two artillery detachments took up firing positions. An artillery brigade near me prepared to support our 55th Guards Tank Brigade.

Two tank battalions attacked towards Zehlendorf. With the 1st Battalion was a small operations group with scouts, sappers and submachine-gunners. The 2nd Battalion followed at a distance of some kilometres. It was to support us and in case of a mishap would thrust past us on the right or left.

It was obvious to us that the enemy would not give up this important area without a fight, as his casualties showed a serious weakening of the whole defence. Roads led from the streets of Zehlendorf to the Avus autobahn and the Berlin–Potsdam railway line. If we had this area in our hands, the enemy's way to the west would be blocked. Apart from that, this was the shortest route to Charlottenburg, the Olympic Stadium and to Ruhleben, where we could meet up with troops of the 1st Byelorussian Front and close the ring within Berlin.

The quiet around us unsettled me even further. Had we already fallen into a trap? Similar thoughts also moved my staff officers with me at the railway crossing.

I quickly thought through several variations and then decided to leave behind a reserve of battalion strength. It would remain with the chief of staff at the old location. I myself would storm with the leading battalion to the dead area at the railway crossing.

Not a shot was fired in the woods. Zehlendorf was also unnaturally quiet. Eight trucks mounted with big calibre anti-aircraft machine-guns followed my tanks. The crews kept themselves ready to be able to open fire at any moment. This company had already helped us out of the mire several times, carefully protecting my command tank.

The nearer we got to Zehlendorf, the clearer the outlines of the buildings became. When we had got a little further forward, Saveliev reported: 'Serashimov has reached a square. Everything in order.'

The leading tank reduced speed, and the following tanks also applied their brakes. Immediately the engines of the anti-aircraft machine-guns were alongside my tank.

What then happened, I failed to understand immediately. A pressure wave suddenly swept off the riflemen sitting on my tank. Only when bullets pinged over my head, a column of fire rose up and the buildings rocked from the explosions did it become clear to me that, despite all our precautions, we had fallen into a trap.

Saveliev hurried to me and helped me to my feet. Instead of giving orders, I carefully brushed the dust off my uniform. This seemed unusual, but I needed these minutes to get over my fright. Fortunately no one had noticed my uncertainty, and the men already knew what to do without orders, which now came.

The gun aimers turned the turrets of their tanks towards the buildings and fired shrapnel at the upper storeys. The flak gunners fired at roofs and windows. Even the mortar men engaged. The submachine-gunners swarmed over in groups and carried out the tasks allocated to them before the fight.

I tried to assess the situation with some of my comrades, but this was not that easy in the turmoil of battle. Where was the enemy, what forces were involved? Once I was eventually sufficiently orientated, I ordered the two artillery battalions to take the streets under systematic fire. Several minutes later the large calibre shells howled over us. A little later the mortar brigade of the Breakthrough Artillery Division also opened fire.

The fighting gradually became more organised. Captain Chadsarakov's rifle company, which was going round Zehlendorf, wheeled towards the city and began with other companies to drive the enemy out of his hiding places. The 2nd Tank Battalion thrust forward to the northern edge of Zehlendorf, took the Düppel Farm and covered the brigade's main forces from the north, where a strong enemy group was preparing to counterattack from the area of Zehlendorf-West S-Bahn station [now Mexikoplatz].

Certainly we had luck that day. A *Katiusha* battalion appeared in our sector. It was under the direct command of the corps commander, but who sticks to such orders in such a situation? Quickly decided, I persuaded the battalion commander to fire a salvo. Success was soon obvious.

Resistance generally died down during the second half of the day, with exchanges of fire only breaking out here and there. The enemy defence no longer functioned as precisely as it had done at the beginning of the fighting.

Zehlendorf had to fall at any minute. We only had to clear the area around the Krumme Lanke U-Bahn station, thrust forward between the Schlachtensee and Krumme Lanke lakes to the Avus autobahn and cut off the Berlin–Potsdam railway line running parallel to it.

But unfortunately in this case the wish was as far as we got as Gulevaty reported that his battalion could not get any further forward.

It was obvious that I could achieve little by radio, and so I went with my group to Fischerhüttenstrasse. At the Krumme Lanke U-Bahn station we met up with Gulevaty's tank column.

Before listening to the battalion commander, I gave him a proper dressing-down. At last the scouts had just reported that they had reached the western edge of Zehlendorf. The submachine-gunners had also got there, and now this hold-up.

Gulevaty was angry. 'Please see for yourself, Comrade Colonel, if you don't want to believe me. Two tanks burnt. If I go right I come up against Krumme Lanke lake, and I still do not get through if I go right. Behind the railway line is the Schlachtensee lake. What should I do?'

Meanwhile I had calmed down a little and familiarised myself with the situation. The enemy was keeping the whole street under fire from a corner building. Their firing position was skilfully selected and artfully camouflaged. It was not easy for our tank troops to make out the gun and destroy it. Nevertheless they engaged – they could have lost all the tanks in this little section of roadway.

'Take the battalion and go round the Schlachtensee lake, push through to the Nikolassee lake and fulfil your task from there,' I ordered. 'This will take a few hours, but will save men and equipment.'

The first tanks tried to turn round with howling engines. As usual, it developed into a traffic jam with much noise and swearing. Suddenly we noticed that the enemy guns were silent. This had not been realised straight away in the confusion. What was up? Had the gun crews given up, or was the enemy preparing a new surprise for us?

Come what may, we seized our opportunity. The tanks thrust along the Fischerhüttenstrasse and reached the Avus motorway. We informed General Novikov by radio that Zehlendorf was in our hands.

What had happened in the corner building from which our tanks had been fired on? This question gave me no peace, and I determined to find out. I drove up closer with my tank. Several people were standing next to the building, among them Lieutenant Serashimov. I ordered the tank to stop and went up to him. 'What is happening? Why have you stayed behind Gulevaty and Staruchin?'

The lieutenant of few words pointed to the yard with his hand. We went through a little garden to the cellar entrance, in which stood the gun. On the floor lay the bodies of the gun crew, four men. On the gun hung a fighter from our brigade, the Komsomol member Vassili Lissunov. He had throttled a Fascist officer but was himself dead. We carefully loosened his hands and carried him outside.

'How did Lissunov get into the cellar?'

The lieutenant looked at me sorrowfully. 'Vassili asked my permission. He wanted to make his way through the garden to this cellar and silence the gun. What else could I do, comrade brigade commander? Two tanks had already fallen victim to these bandits, so I agreed. Lissunov crawled forward. After about ten minutes someone shouted

"Halt!" from the cellar, and then came shots and explosions. Then the gun barrel pointed upwards. We heard another pistol shot and then it was silent.' Serashimov breathed heavily and went on apologetically: 'We arrived a few minutes too late. I should have sent Tinda, Golvin and Gavrilko with him. All three were close by. Yes, I handled it badly. When I became aware, it was already too late.'

I did not reprove the lieutenant. In battle one can sometimes do something other than what one wants and not always can one think through every step and every action. Concernedly I answered him: 'Vassili Lissunov has opened the way for the brigade with his life.' With this I hoped to calm myself and the platoon leader down. I felt for the lieutenant from the bottom of my heart. The death of this 17-year-old Komsomolz, the darling of the brigade, hit us all badly.

We laid the dead boy on the tank, on which we wrote 'We will revenge Vassili Lissunov', and then went on. The fallen scout drove with us into Berlin. He found his last resting place in Berlin–Treptow, together with many other combatants who gave their lives in the fighting for the city.

The sounds of battle distanced themselves ever further from Zehlendorf. Schalunov had gone back to the staff and Leonov to the Rear Services. Once more he demonstrated what a circumspect supply officer he was. When our tank-men spoke of the 'Red Train' they meant the three or four ammunition trucks, the five petrol wagons, the vehicles with supplies and equipment and the iron ration of alcohol, which Leonov directed at the right moment to the right place. Now he wanted to know from me where he could set himself up.

I ordered him to stay exactly where he was, whereupon Leonov asked me for at least a tank and a platoon of submachine-gunners to protect him. This request was thoroughly justified, as scattered enemy groups made the surroundings unsafe and our supplies were a god-sent feast for them, but I could not strengthen the Rear Services at the expense of the fighting units. We could not afford such a luxury. Apart from this I was convinced that Leonov really wanted to be self-sufficient. He had several discreet reserves – armed truck drivers, supply clerks, the workshops personnel and other specialists – that had never let him down so far.

In Berlin

Beyond Zehlendorf, woods and lakes opened out among which stood numerous villas and tasteful one-family houses, including some weekend colonies. All this made orientation more difficult. On the map the whole area was shown as woodland, but in reality one came up against massive buildings everywhere. The Fascists had incorporated the geographical features into their defences. In our thrust to the Avus motorway we were met by shells of various calibres.

When I came up to Gulevaty on the southern bank of Krumme Lanke lake, he was already issuing orders to the infantry. The situation was unclear to him and one detected a certain lack of organisation. The enemy was firing but our troops seemed to be replying somewhat lamely. After the hard fighting in Zehlendorf the pace of the attack had slunk to a low ebb by evening.

'Trofim Jeremjevitsch, at this rate we will reach the Avus in a year's time, and we can bury our men here. Why don't you go round this villa?'

'I have tried to, but once you have one behind you, fire comes from another.'

I should really have given him a reprimand, but before me stood a man showing signs of battle and sleepless nights. To find fault with him would be hard and pointless. From my own experience I knew how important it was to extend a helping hand to people in a difficult situation, and how stimulating a kind word at the right moment could be. In any case it was not the battalion commander's fault that we were in this predicament.

The tank troops simply lacked the experience of how to fight successfully in so large a city as Berlin prepared for defence. Since 1943, and especially after the battle of Kursk, it was always: 'Don't look back!' 'Don't be afraid of open flanks!' 'Bypass the enemy!' 'Attack him boldly from behind!'

However, in Berlin things looked different. We had to take the whole city. Step by step, every building and every street had to be cleared, that being the only way to victory.

While we were discussing the situation, Schalunov arrived with the staff and two artillery brigades, and the corps' troops were streaming through the breach into the Zehlendorf area. The corps commander had sent me some direct reinforcements. I was especially pleased about two companies of the neighbouring 23rd Guards Motorised Rifle Brigade, which were like a gift from heaven for us. Gradually I had a considerably larger group assigned to me. They had to be quickly organised and sent off towards the Avus motorway.

'However, now back to work. We will now be fighting according to all the rules of the art of war,' I said to Gulevaty.

His face lit up, and Dmitriev also looked happier again. He meant that in Berlin one had to speak of either having a scrap or the art of war. I retorted that we would discuss this after we had won. One hour later we had re-established order in the companies and battalions and the brigade renewed its attack.

Seven artillery and mortar battalions, the tanks and super heavy machine-guns fired for fifteen minutes at the enemy defences in the settlements on the railway and on the Havelberg hill.

During the night we were able to break the desperate resistance of the Fascists in these areas and drive them out of the buildings. They tried to slip away through the surrounding woods, but we stopped them there too. This day the enemy lost a lot of his artillery and heavy weapons. His fighting organisation was destroyed, his physically and morally broken soldiers could not withstand our tank attacks any more. The way to the western edge of Berlin was open.

Once more we had a hard day behind us. When we counted the toll we had to admit numerous losses. However, we were in Zehlendorf and had the Avus, the woods and the Krumme Lanke lake in our hands.

Before dawn on the 26th April I drove to the 1st Battalion in my tank.

'Why are you stopped here?' I asked a lieutenant.

He waved towards a column of tanks stopped on the side of the road. I climbed out of my tank and went closer. After a long search I found Gulevaty. He was completely perplexed and studying a Berlin street map.

'Why aren't you moving?'

'I have lost my way, Comrade Colonel. Either the map is lying or the scouts have been leading me by the nose. I sent them ahead to find out where this road leads to.'

'How could this happen, Jeremjevitsch? Have you forgotten where you are? We are in Berlin. You didn't think that the Germans would send you a street directory to show the way?'

The battalion commander bent even closer over his map. To the right of us stood some individual houses from which we could hear voices. Shortly afterwards Serashimov's scout appeared. Quite out of breath, he reported: 'We were looking for Germans, but came across some Japanese, Swiss and other foreigners.'

Boris Saveliev explained the situation in detail to us. In the settle-ment were the summer residences of several embassies; when the fighting broke out in Berlin, they had taken refuge here. None of them had thought that our troops would come through these picturesque woods.

'How did the gentlemen diplomats take this?' asked Dmitriev ironically.

'Somewhat worse than a diplomatic reception,' said Saveliev in the same tone of voice. 'It seems that the gentlemen are slightly disturbed.'

'To hell with these diplomats,' I interrupted the scouts' scoffing conversation. 'Please tell us where we are. Have you found that out?'

'Yes,' replied Serashimov. 'We are near the Heerstrasse, not far from the Olympic Stadium.'

We found this orientation point on our city maps straight away. The asphalted street shown with a thick red line led to the Charlottenburg and then on to the Tiergarten Districts, and that was exactly where we had to strike.

I drove off with my operational staff to my brigade's leading bat-talion, my rifle companies, scouts and sappers, who had the difficult task of getting deeper into Berlin. The column worked its way along the Havel lake, went round the Dachsberg hill, left the individual family houses behind and turned right into the city. The brigade moved forwards slowly and carefully, ready at any time to pounce like a coiled spring.

The city gradually appeared out of the early morning mist, fires glowing in the eastern and central parts, and dark smoke rising up into the sky.

I stood up on my tank with my staff officers and looked forwards. On this morning of the 26th April 1945 our fatigue seemed to have flown. We were in Berlin's streets. I was happy about our previous success, but also filled with sadness over the fallen and wounded. How much had everyone wanted to experience this great moment.

It began to become fully light. The burning city came closer like a burning wall. On a corner a street sign read: 'Heerstrasse'. We had reached the required spot on schedule. From here we would thrust forward to Charlottenburg and the Tiergarten.

'Pass our coordinates to the corps commander straight away,' I ordered. Schalunov hurried off to the radio.

Dmitriev came up to me smiling and drew my attention to two captured *Ferdinands*. Staruchin, Ossadtchi, Gulevaty, Bystrov and

Saveliev escorted us. Somebody asked courteously 'Don't move!' and photographed us with a looted Leica camera.

Sometime we shall show these pictures to our children and grand-children, we thought, and they will quietly learn what their fathers had to go through and be proud of them.

At that hour of the morning the Heerstrasse was quiet. Fighting was going on in eastern Berlin, and troops were thrusting forward to the city centre and also pressing from the north. However, in this area we had appeared as a surprise to the enemy. We used the circumstances to attack along the Heerstrasse.

However, the unusual quiet made us mistrustful and put us on our guard. There was nothing to be seen or heard of the enemy, but we knew that this could not last much longer, so we continued slowly up the street taking every precaution. Some units wheeled right to sur-round the Eichkamp area from the north, while the others worked on from building to building.

Experience and practice played a big role. The fighting in the Berlin suburbs had taught us to work together, to maintain reliable contact as well as to conduct aimed blows at selected targets. We basically cleared every building of the enemy before moving on street by street. In front of us the scouts moved cautiously, followed closely by the submachine-gunners. The tanks drove in a column at intervals of 100 metres from each other. They were escorted by storm troops and guns. Everyone was ready to support his neighbour.

As the situation was unknown to us, the commanders had to go forward with their own units. This was the only way that they could react to every change in the situation and manoeuvre their forces and equipment. Because of this I found myself with my small com-mand team between two battalions, proceeding on foot and protected by submachine-gunners, scouts and sappers.

Schalunov ordered part of our forces to the western edge of Berlin. This consisted of tanks, the whole of the artillery and an infantry reserve that would support us in an emergency.

As we thrust into Berlin, the wood remained uncovered behind. This circumstance, as well as the districts of Spandau and Ruhleben, disquieted us, as we did not know what enemy forces lay before us. Our concern was fully justified for we had hardly left some built-up areas behind us when artillery salvoes broke the silence. A real hail of shells went over us. The whole surrounding area seemed suddenly to come alive.

From everywhere one could hear the command 'Fire!' Again the storming of sections of streets, buildings and upper storeys. Incendiary and explosive shells, tank and shrapnel shells, machine-guns, everything we had was in action. Burning houses collapsed. The light April wind carried the tongues of fire to other buildings. Soon the 1st Ukrainian Front's long-range artillery was firing on Berlin's western suburbs, and bombers and fighter aircraft appeared in the sky.

Our attack melded in with those of the regiments and divisions attacking from the east, south and north and led to the complete encirclement of the enemy. There still remained one possibility for the enemy, which was to abandon his resistance and lay down his arms, but this the Fascists feared more than anything else in the world, for their bloody crimes against humanity were too great. They defended every square metre of their capital with meaningless determination. Members of the *Volkssturm* battalions, boys and old men, had to be dragged into this fateful moment of defeat, even if only for a few moments.

But we pushed on determinedly further along the Heerstrasse and finally got the whole street under control that evening. From there our tanks and riflemen forced their way through the neighbouring streets. Towards morning on the 27th April our second battalion reached the Reichsstrasse.

I looked at the street sign as if bewitched. I had no idea that several other streets in Berlin had the same name. However, somehow it seemed to me to be the street that we had so often heard about and that it was the one in which the army commander wanted to meet me.

This was already the second day that our brigade had been fighting in Berlin. Part of the Heerstrasse and several of the neighbouring streets were in our hands and the fighting had extended to the Olympic Stadium. On the previous evening bombers, ground-attack aircraft and heavy artillery had attacked this area. We carefully made our way through the rubble, more burnt-out vehicles, destroyed trams and double-decker buses.

Although fires blazed everywhere, enemy soldiers crouched in the ruins. With every step we took we had to reckon with their resistance and that kept us on our guard. This way we lost both men and equipment. The deeper we pushed into Charlottenburg, the tougher was the resistance. Even our scouts found out no more in the chaos than their location. But, unperturbed by this, we fought fiercely to achieve our long-foreseen goal. Completely unexpectedly, the corps com-

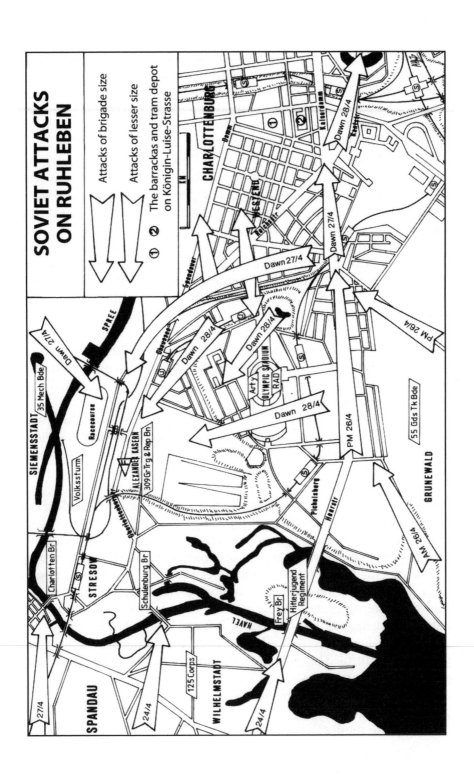

SOVIET ATTACKS ON RUHLEBEN

Attacks of brigade size

Attacks of lesser size

① ② The barrackas and tram depot on Königin-Luise-Strasse

mander ordered our 55th Guards Tank Brigade to wheel sharply to the north. Our attack was redirected at Ruhleben and Spandau, and ended on the railway line running parallel with the Spree River. According to General Novikov's orders, we should reach the Spree that same day, connect with the troops of the 1st Byelorussian Front and thus close the encirclement of Berlin's inner ring.

The corps commander allocated us his reserve in our support. I thus obtained a battalion of the 23rd Guards Rifle Brigade, a detachment of *Katyushas*, some heavy tanks and a company of self-propelled guns. An officer from the corps staff, who had accompanied these units into our area, briefed us on the situation in and around Berlin.

All three corps of the 3rd Guards Tank Army had established firm footings in Berlin and were fighting in the southern and western parts of the city, as was General A.A. Lutschinski's 28th Army. Chuikov's and Katukov's armies' wings bordered the 1st Ukrainian Front as the armies of the 1st Byelorussian Front approached the western edge of the city.

Now I understood why Rybalko and Novikov had had us wheel to the north. Once we had the Fascists surrounded, we could split them up and force them to throw down their weapons. I immediately passed on the commander's orders.

I sent off Serashimov towards Ruhleben with his scouts. Gulevaty's battalion, reinforced with submachine-gunners from Staruchin, heavy tanks and self-propelled guns, turned into the Reichsstrasse, the street by which the brigade should reach the River Spree.

Despite the haste and the pressure, we found a moment free for breakfast. A mess-tin, buckwheat and a mug of hot tea quelled our hunger and thirst and drove off our fatigue.

Dmitriev and I leant against the rear of the tank. The warm air coming from the engine radiators was pleasant on this cool morning. Schalunov was busy on the wireless near us. This restless man had a lot of work and things to worry about, having to pass on messages from the fighting units and giving the corps staff our coordinates to make the position of the 56th Tank Brigade understood.

Dmitriev silently held his hands over the radiators, looking unusually thoughtful. This was the first time that I had seen my political adviser so taciturn.

I carefully clasped him by the arms. 'Are you asleep?'

'No, I don't think so.'

'What's the matter?'

'I think I was being melancholic. I cannot explain my behaviour otherwise.' Dmitriev turned towards me, wiped a hand over his eyes, took out a tobacco pouch and quietly lit a cigarette. 'How hard have we had to fight for victory, how many men have fallen on the way so far, and how many more will still die on the threshold of victory? The bullet does not know whom it hits. It could be any one of us. A little while ago I saw Verdijev killed.'

This news hit me hard. Only a few days previously the brigade commander, Hero of the Soviet Union Ivan Kalenikov, as well as battalion commander Pjotr Fjodorov and Sergeant Major N.N. Novikov had been wounded. Also the deputy of our corps commander, the twice Hero of the Soviet Union General Jakubovski, and many, many others that I knew well had been hit. And now Hero of the Soviet Union Avas Verdijev had fallen. These losses hurt not only me, but especially my comrades in arms. But we could spare no one, and this war was demanding its victims right up to the last moment. Nevertheless, we all had to try to keep the number of dead as few as possible.

'Alexander Pavlovitch, you have again reminded all the commanders, political workers and tank-men to be careful and vigilant. The war is coming to an end, but there are still situations in which the men will take unnecessary risks.'

'Talking doesn't help, David Abramovitch. I had already agreed with the chief of staff to have the Heroes of the Soviet Union Novikov and Verdijev transferred to the commander's platoon. They were to guard the colours. But unfortunately this had not happened. Novikov has gone off with the scouts despite this, and Verdijev remained with his submachine-gun battalion. How it is with our political workers you know for yourself. They cannot be held back. Nemtschenko has fallen, and, despite being badly wounded, Malanushenko has refused to go to a field hospital.'

'So, we are not in a position to keep order in the brigade and control the hotheads?'

'That is it. We are powerless. The men want to participate in the final defeat of the enemy at any price, and then go back home.'

What Dmitriev said was true. Courage and boldness were being displayed by everyone, and they were giving evidence of this every moment of the fighting. Many misjudged the danger in the tumult of the fighting and had to pay for it with their lives. Dmitriev and I understood this fighting spirit and we also knew how difficult it was to keep things within their normal bounds. Everyone wanted to give his absolute best. Sergeant Verdijev was no exception. I knew him well, although there were about 500 men in the brigade and one could not know every face. The men come and go, new fighters replacing the fallen. Often the commanders changed, several not even getting used to their units. So, even with the best will, I could not get to know everyone. Nevertheless there were men that one saw once and could never forget.

Shells exploded near us. Artillery and mortar fire was increasing in the Spandau area. Instinctively we pressed up against the tank. As suddenly as the firing had begun, it went away again. The firing was now on another street nearby.

My small operational group had grown considerably. The staff of the artillery brigades and battalions, as well as the commanders of the attached units, had all joined us. Apart from this, Leonov had joined us with his Rear Services units.

'What are you doing here?' I started saying in my greeting. 'You are tying us down hand and foot and making it even more crowded.'

Calmly and controlled, Leonov replied: 'I could not do otherwise, Comrade Brigade Commander. My Rear Services were at the Reichssportfeld S-Bahn station, uncertain as to the situation. An enemy group attacked us from the Olympic Stadium U-Bahn station and we had to beat them back for two hours. I came here because I wanted to save the ammunition, supplies and fuel.'

I knew Leonov. He was not looking for a quiet life when he withdrew his unit. He was not looking for protection, for he was a brave and experienced officer who knew how to defend himself. I had made the error of not taking into account the special circumstances in Berlin, where the Rear Services were everywhere in danger. Once this had been clarified, I allotted a tank, a platoon of submachine-gunners and a heavy anti-aircraft machine-gun to Leonov.

For two whole hours we sought to make contact with Gulevaty but without success. I regretted having lost time through having breakfast and the talk with Leonov, and decided to follow in Gulevaty's tracks. Orientation became even more difficult. The streets were buried under rubble and with all the scrap metal lying around the compasses could not be relied upon. We had to circumvent ruins and barricades and thus lost our direction. Fortunately we soon came across wooden boards with the tactical signs of our brigade: the two circles with a '2' in the middle showing us the way. Every ten to fifteen minutes

General Novikov was demanding a situation report. His voice literally pursued me.

'I am continuing the action,' I replied laconically to all questions, although I knew that this reply would not please my superior. Finally we were not fighting alone in Berlin, but the corps commander and the army commander-in-chief were observing our 55th Guards Tank Brigade in particular, because it was at the head of the 3rd Guards Tank Army and should meet up with the troops of the 1st Byelorussian Front.

As he was unhappy with my replies, General Novikov sent a liaison officer to see me. He told me that the corps commander was unhappy with the handling of my brigade and demanded a faster rate of attack. Somewhat later the army commander ordered me categorically to close the inner ring by midday.

Once I had listened to my superiors, I and those under me remained not guilty. I sent the chief of staff to deal with the poor communications with the battalions and I reprimanded the communications officer.

The persistent questions from above and the interrupted communications with the 1st Battalion forced me to immediately climb into my tank, taking all the reserves with me, and to thrust through to Gulevaty for better or for worse.

The chief of staff tried to tell me something, but I lost my temper and interrupted him angrily: 'Enough, Comrade Schalunov, get your staff and follow me to the Spree. We will have another look at things there.'

An attack under such conditions entailed an advance of only a few dozen metres in an hour. Nevertheless there was a forward movement to the goal, which we had to reach that day at all costs.

We met wounded, a sure indication of the fighting. Next to a burning tank a lieutenant was being tended to by medical orderlies. The further we went the more often we came across evidence of the fighting.

Someone recognised me and shouted: 'Comrade Colonel, our men are there in front.'

I breathed out with relief. So Gulevaty had not been wrong. A column of prisoners of war came towards us. The dirty, tattered soldiers were moving only slowly forwards. For them the war was over. Their once so orderly Berlin now lay in dust and ashes. Stunned, the prisoners looked around them. Ruins, burning streets and blackened trees lined their route. It was already afternoon, the sun high in the sky and warming, despite the thick overhang of smoke. We removed our padded jackets.

Behind Ruhleben U-Bahn station [which is actually on a raised level] we turned off to the right, crossed a railway line and reached the Reichsstrasse–Spandauer Damm junction, where we came across an armoured car.

'Welcome your prisoners!' Boris Saveliev called out to us.

I looked at Schalunov questioningly. He too looked puzzled. 'What prisoners? What should we do with them now?' I was thinking that the scouts must have captured some important personalities, perhaps even Hitler or Goebbels. Anything was possible these days. Excitedly I walked up to the vehicle, but could see no Germans.

Two Soviet officers unknown to me jumped out of the vehicle. A large, correctly dressed major presented himself: 'Battalion commander in the 1st Krasnograd Mechanised Corps of the 1st Byelorussian Front, Major Protassov. I salute the representative of the 1st Ukrainian Front.'

The major then stepped aside to make room for his comrade. 'Captain Turoviez of the same brigade.' The slim officer sputtered out the words and ended his report with the words: 'We met up at 1200 hours on the 27th April between Siemenstadt S-Bahn station and Ruhleben.'

'Well, I'm damned!' I said. 'So you are the prisoners my scouts captured!'

Never before had soldiers so heartily clasped each other and become friends as at this moment. The order had been fulfilled, the ring closed. On the western edge of Berlin the tank-men of Colonel-General Bogdanov of the 1st Byelorussian Front had met up with the tank-men under Colonel-General Rybalko of the 1st Ukrainian Front.

Someone called out: 'This event must be celebrated!'

'Absolutely!' agreed Alexander Pavlovitch. 'This will never happen again.'

We decided to take a small drink in a half-destroyed building. While this was being arranged, Protassov, Turoviez and Saveliev reported exactly where the meeting had taken place.

'My battalion was supposed to attack towards Ruhleben,' began Protassov. 'We knew that Rybalko's troops were coming towards us from the south. We had to fight until the morning, as the Fascists had established themselves in Haselhorst. A tank platoon ran into a large enemy group in Siemensstadt. It took us two hours to smoke them out.

Then we reached the Spree. The fire had died down and our scouts crossed the river, closed up to the railway line and suddenly Soviet tanks and submachine-guns began firing. We had done it.'

'That was it! We were here between 1000 and 1100 hours,' continued Saveliev Protassov's report. 'Gulevaty was held back a bit at first. His tanks were involved in a fight and went a bit to the left. They drove a strong enemy group off Ruhleben race course and pushed them back to the Spree and Lower Spree. The Fascists lost several hundred men killed, the rest being disarmed and taken prisoner. Serashimov, myself and Chadsarakov's company pushed on further to the railway line. We met no Germans here but suddenly came under fire from the other bank. We fired back. Then we heard the familiar 'Hurrah!' Immediately afterwards we saw Soviet submachine-gunners coming towards us waving their weapons. What happened then one can hardly describe.'

'That was a pleasure, comrades,' said Turoviez. 'The sky over Berlin was almost ripped apart by our 'Hurrahs'. That was an encounter!'

The comrades from the supply platoon came and invited us to the table. Our talks now took on another direction.

As I reported the task fulfilled to the corps commander, General Novikov ordered me to send an officer from the 35th Mechanised Brigade to his staff. Captain Turoviez set off. We delegated our representative to the staff of the 1st Mechanised Corps.

The joining of the two Fronts and our involvement in it filled me with pride. But I also had a personal reason for my pleasure. The 1st Krasnograd Mechanised Corps was commanded by General Krivoshein, who was well known to me. I had served under him in 1943 and was greatly indebted to him. I regarded General Krivoshein as my teacher and was proud that his corps and my 55th Guards Tank Brigade had just closed the ring on Berlin on the 27th April 1945. Two years ago we would never have dreamt of doing this.

We cleared the enemy from the Spandauer Damm until the early hours of the morning. The brigade was to attack in the direction of Charlottenburg–Savignyplatz and on to the Zoological Gardens. The fighting died down a bit during the night but blazed up again with renewed strength in the morning. The worst was the fighting in the area west of the Tiergarten, the enemy putting up a desperate resistance. Here and there our troops had got mixed up with the enemy somehow, so that our pilots found it difficult to find targets without hitting our own troops. The artillery of the 1st Byelorussian Front had moved more densely into the city centre and their explosions were already dangerously close.

There were ten rifle and tank armies in the destroyed city, a great number of rifle, mechanised, tank and artillery corps, hundreds of regiments of all types, over 6,000 tanks and about 40,000 guns and mortars. This vast concentration of men and equipment made command extremely difficult. The boundary lines could hardly be adhered to as we lacked almost all freedom of movement. This confusion made it easier for the enemy. Despite everything, we could not withdraw any troops as the final battle had to be conducted decisively.

* * *

In the early hours of the morning of 24 April some of Chuikov's troops traversing Schönefeld airfield came across several tanks from the 3rd Guards Tank Army of Koniev's 1st Ukrainian Front. Zhukov apparently did not hear of this encounter until the evening and then acted disbelievingly, insisting that Chuikov send officers to discover what units were involved and what their objectives were.

If, as it appears, this was Zhukov's first intimation of Koniev's participation in the battle for the city itself, we can imagine the consternation this report would have caused. Apart from the blow to Zhukov's pride, this incident clearly demonstrated the lack of communication between the two marshals and their continuing mutual distrust. Having had his hand revealed, Stalin then laid down the inter-Front boundary, which was to run through Lübben via Teupitz, Mittenwalde and Mariendorf to the Anhalter railway station. When extended beyond the Anhalter railway station, it passed well to the east of the Reichstag, giving Koniev the possibility of reaching it first from the south, the Reichstag, burnt out and unused since 1933, being their symbolic goal.

Koniev was obviously aware of the GHQ order laying down these new inter-Front boundaries on the night of 22 April when he issued his orders for the attack across the Teltow Canal and for the 71st Mechanised Brigade to cover the right flank and establish contact with the 1st Byelorussian Front. Somehow this GHQ order had been withheld from Zhukov, although it was effective from 0600 hours (Moscow Time) on 23 April, and his balance of forces and reported reactions to the news of this encounter on Schönefeld airfield clearly demonstrate how unprepared he was for this eventuality.

* * *

Fascist groups streamed into the western districts, pushed back by the blows from the 1st Byelorussian and 1st Ukrainian Fronts. Fighting broke out the U-Bahn stations, in the tunnels and even in the sewers. The enemy knew his city well and manoeuvred in narrow spaces. He disappeared only to suddenly reappear in our rear, and so inflicted some blows on us.

Once more our Rear Services were attacked. For several hours Leonov and his troops fought an uneven battle against a large enemy group wanting to break through to the Havel lakes.

In these conditions our main forces were the infantry, tanks, the supporting artillery and the sappers. For the first time since the fighting for Berlin had begun we had direct contact with the brigade of my old fighting colleague, Colonel Sliussarenko.

After the link-up with the 1st Byelorussian Front, the impact of our tanks had grown enormously. Previously we had had to fear that the pressure from the retreating Fascists could not be held. Now we had General A.P. Turshinski's 55th Guards Breakthrough Division near us, the tank troops and riflemen forming a regular barrier. Nevertheless our western front sector was reinforced even more on the morning of the following day by the 3rd Guards Tank Army and the 1st Ukrainian Front.

I must admit that it was the right time. The noose tightened even more, causing critical days for the defenders of Berlin. The Fascists had finally realised that they could no longer hope for the wonder weapons so praised by Goebbels. The only salvation they saw was in a breakout to the west behind the Havel lakes. Thousands of Fascist soldiers and officers thrust in our direction. There was fighting in all the streets, and the western parts of the city were on fire.

A strong group, also comprising artillery and tanks, broke through to the Zoological Gardens, went round Savignyplatz S-Bahn station and thrust towards the Charlottenburg and Westkreuz S-Bahn stations. This group was joined by smaller groups emerging from the U-Bahn stations.

The bitter fighting lasted until morning. Our tanks and the whole of the artillery were engaged in this small sector of the front. Our riflemen fought with much sacrifice, earning the highest praise from our tank-men. They were like guardian angels in the narrow streets.

The Fascists could no longer get out of Berlin, and were caught in the trap. Now General Leliushenko's 4th Guards Tank Army from the south and General Perchorovitch's 47th Army of the 1st Byelorussian

Front from the north both reached the Potsdam area and reinforced the rear.

Together with our own submachine-gunners, scouts and staff officers, I went carefully to my battalions. On our way we came across a gallows from which three German soldiers were hanging. A placard read: 'Court-martialled for cowardice. This punishment awaits all who do not protect the Fatherland. 25th April 1945.' One of my escorts wanted to cut the ropes, but I forbade him. The Germans should see for themselves where their Fascist Führer and their so-called People's Community had led them.

We worked our way further forward. A heavy pregnant darkness full of smoke and the smell of burning was sinking over the Fascist capital.

Another day of war was coming to an end. Towards evening we received two contradictory orders. The corps chief of staff, Colonel G.S. Pusankov, ordered the attack towards the Zoological Gardens to be abandoned; the corps commander General Novikov decisively ordered an attack in this direction.

Fortunately darkness shrouded the city. We decided to use the night to pull the Rear Services in closer, reassemble the dispersed battalions and redeploy the artillery.

A liaison officer from the corps staff reached us in the early hours of the morning. He had wandered all night through Berlin to deliver a written order from General Novikov. In it I was ordered to withdraw the brigade from Savignyplatz, whereby both the line of attack and boundaries were also altered. The move was to take place in the first half of the night. What should I do now? Night was already coming to an end and we could hardly fulfil the order.

I could actually have punished the liaison officer for his lateness, but was he really responsible? He had tried despite everything to find us, had been lost for hours in the destroyed city and had thus come to within a hair's breadth of the enemy. A punishment would not have made the fulfilment of the order any quicker. At least to make up a little time, precise orders and decisive handling were required. Already within a few minutes every member of the staff knew his task and I made off to the battalions. I first drove in the car, then climbed in my tank, and finally had to go by leaps and bounds on foot from building to building.

According to the map, the distance between the staff and the leading units was over a kilometre, but two hours passed before I reached my goal. Now I could really understand what the liaison officer had gone through and was happy that I had not taken any action against him.

In the dawning light I made out tanks, artillery and numerous soldiers next to a bright two-storey building. I went up to them, entered the building and reached a large room upstairs. Sitting there were all those I was looking for: Ossadtchi, Gulevaty, Staruchin, the commanders of the artillery battalions, the sappers and the scouts. They rose as I entered.

'What are you up to, comrades?'

'We are waiting for you,' said Staruchin immediately.

'How did you know I was on my way?'

'From the chief of staff,' said Gulevaty and pulled a creased map out of his boot.

I explained the corps commander's requirements to the officers, gave each unit its battle task and laid down the timetable.

Following a short snack – there was porridge and tea – I wanted to go over to the 2nd Battalion. Suddenly an unusual silence fell over the big, almost overfilled room. Even the usually constantly talking Ossadtchi was quiet.

'What's the matter?' I asked Gulevaty.

'The deputy political adviser of the 1st Battalion, Andrei Malanuschenko, died last evening.'

For a moment I stood as if numbed, but then followed my comrades into a room nearby in which the fallen man lay. Silently I saluted him and took my farewell from him. Again it had happened to someone immediately before victory. I slowly turned round and left the room.

As we were going down the stairs I heard a German voice. Immediately afterwards a door opened on the ground floor and men, women and two girls entered the hall.

'Who are these people?'

'The occupants of the house,' explained Ossadtchi. 'They had been hiding in the cellar.'

The owner timidly reported about himself and his family. He was a professor of theology. With him were his wife, his younger brother (a scientist), his daughter and a niece. Distractedly I listened to the professor's muddled report, looking at his family and suddenly saw before me the ghosts of my parents and sisters murdered by the Fascists in 1942. On the first floor of this building lay our dead comrade. How the Fascists would have dealt with this in our place was known not only by us but certainly also by the professor.

'What are you going to do with us?' he asked timidly.

'Nothing. In any case, go back down with all your family, it is safer there.'

However, for the whole day I had to think about Andrei Malanus-chenko. I simply could not imagine that I would never see him again.

The corps commander's order to go to the Westkreuz area was not completely fulfilled. We could not make up for the time lost by the liaison officer, and my trip to the battalions made no difference. Then came the news that the 2nd Battalion was without communications. Murderous fire drove us into a cellar.

The dawning spring day finally brought our plans to nothing. Already during the night the boundary between the Fronts had been changed. Our corps was to leave the area we had occupied until now and withdraw to the area of the Westkreuz and Witzleben stations, west of Charlottenburg station.

The companies and battalions had been fighting again. Although the brigade had begun its relocation, the thick red line separating the two Fronts in Berlin remained only an indicated one. To the right of us the 1st Byelorussian Front was conducting a bitter fight. Our submachine-gunners and tank troops had got mixed up with Turshinski's infantry in our old area.

The resistance of the Fascists, who now found themselves caught between two Fronts, increased by the hour. Although the Berlin group was almost completely split apart, it continued its desperate resistance. The Fascists were streaming to the western parts of the city from everywhere. They attacked our troops like madmen, seeking to find a way out of the ring of fire.

The Berlin garrison consisted of troops loyal to Hitler. In order to maintain the establishment of the Fascist Reich for as long as possible, the Fascist leaders in the city concentrated various security battalions and SS units, as well as members of military training establishments. Apart from this, the enemy also still counted on getting help from the outside, everything that gave him the strength to continue resisting.

For the whole day until night fell artillery and tank fire thundered in the streets around the railway stations of Savignyplatz and Charlottenburg. Every metre of ground was fired on by the troops. The fate of the Berlin garrison was nevertheless already decided, our troops having formed a firm ring around the city. Nevertheless the Fascists did not give up their resistance but even conducted counterattacks in individual sectors, completely indifferent to the number of victims.

Not until night time did the exhausted and demoralised Fascists take a breath and we could eliminate the confusion in our ranks. In my sector could be found tanks from General Bogdanov's 2nd Guards Tank Army and members of the 55th Guards Rifle Division of General Lutschinski's 28th Army. Our tanks had found themselves in the 1st Byelorussian Front's area and we had to look everywhere for our submachine-gunners. Only the artillery brigades and the corps units attached as reinforcements were still in our area, Lieutenant-Colonel Schalunov keeping a firm grip on them.

All night long staff officers, political advisers and rear area services sought our units. Towards morning we had everyone brought together and had them occupy positions between the Reichssportfeld S-Bahn station and the Reichsstrasse. Here we were able to refuel the vehicles and tanks and resupply them with ammunition, and the troops found time to eat and drink.

Schalunov and Sassimenko were happy as cable communications had been established with the staff, entailing less anger with the radios. Apart from this we could maintain personal contact with General Novikov.

No one had thought that the last day of April should be the hardest. On the contrary, we thought that the fighting would die down. The evening before we had given the Fascists a good drubbing and during the night our scouts had located no big enemy groupings.

The day was warm and sunny. In our sector there were a few exchanges of fire, seldom artillery fire, and the tanks were silent. But in the city centre and in the Unter den Linden–Tiergarten–Reichstag area bitter fighting was still going on. There was even heavy artillery in action. Our air forces ruled the air. We could also hear artillery fire coming from the direction of Wannsee and Potsdam. Anti-aircraft gunfire bellowed on the southern and northern edges of the city, and tank guns thundered. Only in our corps was it relatively quiet.

The silence did not last for long, however. Towards midday scouts reported enemy forces in the Spandauer Damm–Westend area. By radio Serashimov reported a large grouping in Bismarckstrasse. We therefore had to reckon on a counterattack at any moment.

During the second half of the day the enemy moved in individual units, small groups or columns towards Witzleben–Heerstrasse–Reichssportfeld, opening unorganised fire with all kinds of weapons. Rockets soared into the sky. A column came loudly near us, led by SS officers. It was accompanied by several tanks and self-propelled guns.

Twenty years later I discovered from archive material that it involved SS units, members of the Hitler Youth and 'Totenkopf' units that wanted to break through to the west and surrender to our allies.

Our artillery battalion fired concentrated fire. That was also the signal for the others. Shortly afterwards all of our artillery joined in. The mortar batteries that had taken up firing positions in the Olympic Stadium were equally active, the tank troops and submachine-gunners also joining in the fight. I watched from the roof of a two-storey house. Hundreds of dead and wounded lay in the streets. Our fire barred the Fascists' route to the Havel lakes, but they did not give up. The fighting went on until late in the evening, by which time we had finally succeeded. On this day both the 56th Guards Tank Brigade and the 23rd Guards Motor Rifle Brigade, as well as the whole of the 7th Guards Tank Corps and elements of the 28th Army's 55th Guards Rifle Division had been involved.

That evening I discussed the events of the day with my deputies and staff officers and simultaneously prepared the next tasks with them.

'The Germans are going back along Bismarckstrasse towards northern Charlottenburg,' reported Schalunov tiredly.

'They should retreat quietly. They'll not get far, General Bogdanov's people will get them.'

The head of the medical services, Boguslavski, came up to me.

'Where shall we take the wounded?'

'To the medical battalion, to the hospital. Don't you know where you must take them?'

'You have not understood me correctly, Comrade Colonel. I am talking about the Germans. Hundreds of German wounded need medical help.'

I looked at Boguslavski, at his face grey with fatigue, his red eyes. During the war I had become accustomed not to wonder about it any more, but the medics impressed me again and again. Many had lost their relatives in this war, constantly seeing human pain, seeing the crimes of the Fascists, everything that would really leave people hardened. But this was not so as one saw time and time again. Our soldiers went mercilessly against the armed enemy, but were charitable towards civilians, prisoners and the wounded. This was not so only in the days of our victorious thrust to the west, but also in the difficult time when we had had to withdraw.

This was also the reason why Boguslavski's question surprised me. I was strongly convinced that he had long since given his instructions and that the question was merely a formality to inform me. On the 26th April a field hospital on the western edge of the city had fallen into our hands. Some three hundred badly wounded German officers were lying in a large school building. Until then they had seen no Soviet soldiers. Boguslavski now wanted to accommodate more wounded there.

Shortly after he had left me, several German doctors appeared before me. Excitably, a female doctor made it clear to me that she feared for her patients.

'You have no need to worry,' Dmitriev answered her. 'We are Soviet men, Communists, do you understand? We will look after the captured humanely and especially the wounded.'

That night all the wounded Germans in our sector we collected and accommodated in a hospital. When Boguslavski discovered that there was neither water nor electricity in the building and that the food supplies were almost exhausted, we immediately put a hundred loaves of bread, sugar and conserves from our supplies at their disposal.

During the night of the 1st May the fighting died down, although we were prepared for any surprise. As the corps headquarters was silent, I decided to call the corps commander. General Novikov did not lift the receiver for a long time, but then said his name. After I had greeted him I asked him: 'Comrade General, I urgently need riflemen. Our tanks are burning, the officer numbers are melting away. Please help us, at least with a battalion.'

The general was silent. After a few minutes I timidly asked him whether he had heard me.

'Yes, I heard you well,' answered Novikov. 'But I cannot help you. I have no riflemen.' Again there was silence. I heard the general breathing heavily. Suddenly he said: 'David Abramovitch, I have a big concern. My Jura fell in Berlin yesterday. He had led a self-propelled-gun regiment in action and ...' the voice of the general trembled. 'Jura is lying here beside me.'

'Vassili Vassilievitch, what can I say? What words can console a father's heart? Be strong! We will avenge your son and all those who have given their lives in the protection of their country!'

In these last days death still took many men, including comrades with whom I had set out on the difficult road to war. Every loss hit us hard.

After the bloody fighting on the 30th April, and the desperate attempt to break out to the west at any price, the enemy had quietened down. The artillery was silent, tanks did not appear, even the *panzer-fausts* had disappeared. The enemy soldiers had gone into hiding. We chased them out of their hiding places and liberated district after district. In the morning we had sent off a submachine-gun company under young Captain Chadsarakov on reconnaissance. In the northern section of the Reichsstrasse he fell into an ambush and suffered severe casualties. The young, black-eyed Ossete Chadsarakov was killed. Sacha Tinda, the last of the three Charkov Komsomols, also failed to return. Fortunately it transpired that he was only wounded and our neighbours had taken him with them.

In the morning there were rumours of Hitler's suicide and the capitulation of the Fascist troops in Berlin. No one knew for sure, but everyone sensed that capitulation was imminent.

Towards midday the guns fell silent. We pushed on without coming across resistance. Berlin was burning sky high, buildings collapsing, the thick smarting smoke burning our eyes.

Unexpectedly came the order to strengthen the bombardment. At 1830 hours the whole of our artillery opened a terrific fire, including the *Katyushas* and the six battalions of the breakthrough artillery division. This mighty blow was largely symbolic. We wanted to force the enemy into capitulating more quickly and unconditionally.

The whole night we moved around the area north of Pichelsberg S-Bahn station. Towards morning the German soldiers began individually or in groups to leave their hiding holes and surrender. We discovered from them that the Berlin garrison had capitulated.

During the course of the day the stream of prisoners increased. Apathetically the soldiers trotted through the destroyed city to the collecting points. They wanted only one thing: to eat and sleep. Whatever came afterwards was of no consequence to them.

Our riflemen brought a large group of prisoners to me. 'Where shall we take them?' asked a sergeant. I pointed to a sign with an arrow pointing the way to the collection point. 'How are the prisoners behaving?'

'Normally, Comrade Colonel, they are disciplined.'

I then saw that many of the prisoners were wearing neither shoulder straps nor headgear. 'On the way they are ripping off their shoulder straps and throwing their caps and badges away,' said the sergeant. 'They are apparently afraid.'

'Don't let them do so, Comrade Sergeant.'

'One cannot see to everything, Comrade Colonel, they are many and we are only five.'

I went closer to a prisoner whose uniform was incomplete. The way he carried himself indicated he was an officer. 'Why have you torn off your badges of rank? You are an officer. Are you not ashamed to do so in front of soldiers whose lives you were responsible for only a short time ago? Where is your honour, officer?'

The prisoner looked silently at his boots.

'That is no officer,' somebody called out suddenly from the column. 'He is an *Unterstormführer*.'

An SS man? That was why he had torn off his badges of rank. He was afraid of having to account for his crimes. There were still many more such as him in the crowd. They wanted to disappear in the mass and now felt conspicuous.

Suddenly the desire to talk with this mob had left me. With a wave of my hand I had the sergeant lead the prisoners away.

We connected all our thoughts about the end of the war and the defeat of Fascism with the victory in Berlin.

The soldiers found it difficult to get away from the customary war-time routine. The tanks drove along close to the buildings and the riflemen crossed the street in bounds. Although no one was firing anymore and no bombs were dropping, the years of being accustomed to it remained in every one of us. It was not only difficult to get away from the war, re-adapting was also not any easier. The war had ended, it had finished! Although we had waited almost 1,500 days for this moment, we had first to get slowly accustomed to it.

We stood in a large room of an undamaged family home. What could we say at this moment? Our faces spoke for us. Dmitriev had tears running down his cheeks. Even the strong-willed Schalunov was weeping. Like a child I wiped my face with my fist and murmured something incomprehensible to him. Serashimov called out loud: 'We have forced the beast to its knees,' and damned the Fascists with some choice swearwords. From the street came a thunderous 'Hurrah!'

I got hold of the chief of staff first: 'What happens now?'

Yes, what did await us now? For the first time since the beginning of the war I did not know anything further. At random I said: 'Vassili Matvejevitch, order everyone to remain where they are. The battalions must assemble. The other units must close up to the staff.'

We had heard nothing from the corps staff for several hours.

'We are superfluous now,' Dmitriev said pointedly. 'But that is not bad, no messages, no situation reports, no reprimands, as things progress slowly. All in all an almost paradisiacal life.'

However, the paradise did not last long. The corps staff demanded exact data over the fighting strength of our brigade. Then we received the order to get ready for further tasks.

'That looks as if we will have to go on fighting,' said Schalunov uncomfortably.

Once more the staff mechanism got moving. Towards evening the leader of the corps' political department, Andrei Vladimirovitch Novikov, sought out the brigade. We put our arms around each other, drove to one of the battalions, congratulated the fighters on their victory and returned happily to the command post.

Meanwhile the adjutant and the cook had decorated and set out the table, having found table cloths and crystal glasses in the house. Dmitriev switched on the radio and Levitan's solemn voice filled the whole building. He read out an order from the commander-in-chief. As the talk was about Rybalko's tank-men who had particularly distinguished themselves in the storming of Berlin, we jumped up from our seats and a thunderous 'Hurrah' drowned out the voice of the speaker.

Tensely we waited for the salute from Moscow, as suddenly the whole building shook and the glasses on the table trembled. We rushed out of the house and could hardly believe our eyes. Shots of all calibres made their way into the sky, including rockets bursting like fireworks. Our brave soldiers were firing their salutes in honour of Moscow, the Party, our homeland and the great Soviet people.

For the first time in ages I was able to sleep undisturbed, in a real soft bed and without my uniform. It was like a gift.

'Get up! Get up!' It was Dmitriev's voice.

In an old soldier's way I jumped out of my bed and grasped my things. 'What's up? A breakthrough?'

'Nothing's happened,' responded Dmitriev laughing. 'Have you forgotten that we wanted to look around the city today?'

The battalion commanders and staff officers had already assembled in the adjacent room. Pjotr Koshemjakov allocated us to the individual vehicles and gave the drivers their instructions.

We drove through a few neighbouring streets and then turned into Bismarckstrasse, where one saw the same picture everywhere: burning buildings, rubble, destroyed vehicles and a whole sea of white flags.

Like on a big washday, bedsheets, hand- and table-cloths and pillow-cases fluttered in the wind.

We crossed the Landwehr Canal and reached the Tiergarten. This once splendid piece of earth had changed into a rubbish heap, into a cemetery for tanks, guns and vehicles. Torn up trees, water channels, destroyed bridges and bomb craters completed the chaos. The fire of war had not improved the wide Siegesallee. The statues of the illustrious Wilhelms, Friedrichs and former Prussian military leaders had been toppled from their bases.

Until his cowardly suicide, Goebbels had prophesied that life would cease as soon as the Red Army appeared. Like so many things, it was also a lie. The firing was hardly over when life in the destroyed city stirred once more. The first thing was the children leaving the cellars. At first they came timidly closer and then ever more boldly to our field kitchens and looked at the cooks with big, hungry eyes. Pity stirred our soldiers and soon the children were squatting round our gulash cannons. But not only did they satisfy their hunger, but they also took some soup for their relatives.

Then we stood in the Reichstag, which looked grey, dusty and bombed-out. The heavy fighting had left its traces here, as elsewhere in Berlin and in Germany overall.

As we were about to go in, it seemed to me as if the building was swaying. It reminded me instinctively of a pirate ship. The interior of the building was murky, damp and cold. On the floors lay heaps of rubble, and through a gaping wall one could see the Brandenburg Gate.

We were not the only ones to come here. Hundreds of vehicles stood nearby and thousands of Soviet soldiers examined and touched the damaged pillars and walls. Wherever one looked one saw inscriptions everywhere. 'We made it!' 'We are from Moscow' 'We are from Leningrad', 'My way led from Stalingrad to Berlin'. Everyone regarded it as their right to record their name on the walls of the Reichstag. It seems as if this would confirm our victory.

The brigade staff were impatiently awaiting my return. An unusual amount of activity reigned in the building. Schalunov received me with the news. 'An order arrived during your absence. The brigade is to drive out of Berlin during the night and concentrate near the Teufelsee lake south of Eichkamp.'

On the table lay a map. My chief of staff had already established the route and informed me about the already issued orders. Why would this be good, I thought. Schalunov also had no answer. We went through various alternatives and soon lost ourselves in conjecture.

I had not spoken to General Novikov again since the death of his son. Now that the order had come to prepare to march, I dared to call him. Some questions needed an urgent reply, and above all we needed refuelling. The corps commander spoke quietly and assuredly. 'I understand your concern. It is no different with Sliussarenko and Tschugunkov. However, the enemy is no longer the same. The beast has been badly hit and your forces are sufficient for the final blow. Naturally we will help you.'

'Nevertheless, please allow me the question, Comrade General, what should we be ready for?'

'Tomorrow we will set off for the new area.'

'Where to?'

'I still have no orders, but before us is a march of several hundred kilometres.'

'To the Rhine?'

'What would we do there? Our allies have occupied this area long since. Don't pester me any more, I cannot tell you any more. We will get the order tomorrow.'

About an hour later we received maps of the areas Wittenberg, Dresden, Sudety and Prague. Then petrol tankers arrived. 'Take note, lads,' said the garrulous tanker driver informatively. 'There is no more fuel until Prague.'

We left Berlin during the night, the column creeping slowly down the Heerstrasse. Eight days previously we had come in over this road.

*   *   *

The German edition of Dragunski's book does not mention that he and his brigade holed up in the big tram sheds and adjacent apartments on Saarstrasse, a block north of the Kaiserdam, for their last two days in Berlin, as was mentioned in his A Soldier's Life, *published by Progress Publishers in Moscow in 1977.*

Dragunski's brigade formed part of Marshal Koniev's forces that liberated Prague a few days later but was not actually involved in the fighting. He then commanded the contingent of one hundred selected representative tank soldiers at the victory parade in Moscow, continuing to serve until retiring with the rank of general.

*   *   *

Forward to Prague!

Towards morning we reached the woods south of Berlin and settled down for a rest. The soldiers slept wherever they could find a place. They disregarded food and drink in order to catch up on more than twenty nights of lost sleep. Since the 16th April, the beginning of the Berlin operation, they had had no rest.

At midday our encampment was still deep in slumber. Only on the headquarters bus had several officers gathered to wait for instructions. The chief of staff and I studied the corps commander's orders. We marked the given points on the map and confirmed the route as well as the provisional plan for further action. Our 7th Tank Corps belonged to a strong armoured force being formed on Marshal Koniev's orders from the 3rd and 4th Guards Tank Armies as well as several independent tank and mechanised corps. This powerful force was to destroy the million-strong army of the Fascist Field Marshal Schörner, whose Army Group *Mitte* was the last card in the Fascists' hands, and on which they now were concentrating their last hopes.

Apparently the fate of this army group was already decided. The capitulation of the Berlin garrison was a sure indication that our troops had broken the back of the Fascist beast. But we also knew very well how the vastly strong enemy group in Czechoslovakia could prepare, what the tightly squeezed Fascists were still capable of. This was why the Front commander-in-chief demanded single-minded handling. We would attack the enemy in the flank, split him up, forcing him to be destroyed or to capitulate. In no circumstances would Prague be destroyed.

General Novikov had ordered us to march off at nightfall. A penetrating signal tore through the quiet of the woods. Several hours' sleep had strengthened the men and now they made the last preparations for the march. The commanders and political workers explained the fighting roles and talked about Czechoslovakia and its people.

As nightfall sank, we headed south. Before us lay a march of some 200 kilometres. I climbed out of my Jeep into a car. Dmitriev and Ossadtchi came with me.

The traffic regulators showed us the route through Luckenwalde, Jüterbog and Dahme, and towards morning the brigade reached the woods north of the Elbe. It was only later that we learnt that we were marching parallel to the front line and that Dresden and the surrounding area were still in the hands of the enemy. The 344th German Infantry Division and the 2nd Panzer Division with reserve and security units were defending south of Riesa and on the line Heyda–Dörschnitz–Nieschütz–Niegeroda.

In the evening, before reaching the deployment area, the corps commander and head of the political department sought us out. We were very happy to see General Novikov in good form again. I reported on the condition of the brigade and on our chances in the anticipated fighting, and complained about the weak infantry and big losses of tanks. 'I am afraid that our tanks will not make it over the mountains. Many are smoking a lot, the engines need replacing. Their running times are well over-exceeded.'

The general looked at me in astonishment. 'I don't recognise you. You are talking like a technical equipment assistant. Even if only half of your tanks reach Prague, that's no tragedy. The war is coming to an end and you start to complain. There is no cause to panic. You will get your infantry. I have already given the instructions. You will get a rifle battalion from Schapovalov's brigade.'

I thanked the corps commander and invited him to supper. However, he declined as he had to get to Sliussarenko, whose brigade was to be in the first echelon. We escorted the general to the edge of the woods. Before he got into his vehicle he pulled out a folded newspaper from a side pocket of his uniform jacket.

'Do you still remember how depressed the tank soldiers were that there was no mention of the brigade in the order of the commander-in-chief on the defeat of the Berlin group? Shortly afterwards I was convinced that the comrades had made a mistake, so I sent a telegram to Comrade Stalin. Here is his reply.'

I took the sheet and skimmed over the text. Then I went over it again to commit every word to memory.

'Andrei Vladimirovitch' said the corps commander in it to the head of the political section, 'you are still in the brigade. Tell the men what has happened and of Comrade Stalin's order.'

Then General Novikov said good-bye and jumped into his vehicle. 'See you in Prague!'

We went back to the staff bus and had our supper. There 'Political' Novikov related how hard the whole business had hit our corps commander. 'General Novikov is an old soldier and knows exactly what such an order from the highest commander does for a mechanised force. When our corps commander turned to Comrade Stalin he was not thinking of himself.' The best thing would be for me to simply read the text of the telegram. 'Justice demands that the handling of the

7th Guards Tank Corps be praised that I led in Berlin. Thus was the memory honoured of those that have fallen in this city, and the living receive the thanks due to them. I write to you as a general and the father of a son lost in the storming of Berlin!' The head of the political section paused and then continued: 'I am happy to inform you that our 7th Kiev Guards Corps has been awarded the honourable name "Berlin". Please inform all the soldiers.'

'Who was responsible for the mistake?' I wanted to know.

'With us the Novikovs', answered Andrei Vladimirovitch, smiling. 'Too many with the same name gathered at the one Front, all belonging to the tank troops. That was what was responsible for such a muddle.'

In the morning we could discover nothing of our neighbours far and wide. The brigades of Sliussarenko and Tschugunkov had crossed the Elbe to the west bank during the night and occupied their dispersal areas. As soon as Gordov's army had smashed a breach in the enemy defences, both brigades would be in the first echelon.

Our brigade remained as the corps commander's reserve in the allocated area. Once Dresden had been taken, we would thrust towards Sudty, cross the mountains and reach Teplice as the vanguard, going round Terezin to the west to Kralupy and penetrating Prague off the move.

With this decision, the Front commander-in-chief and the corps commander went for continuous, targeted handling and massive blows by the tank troops into the flanks of Army Group *Mitte.*

In the morning I was informed that we would not get across the crossing point in Riesa. On the approaches to the town there was confusion with the Rear Services of two armies and our tanks wedged together. Each one of them wanted to move forward as quickly as possible. Command under these circumstances was extremely difficult. The time dragged, however. The corps staff had already by evening broken through and the main forces followed through. We had contact with neither them nor army headquarters. A powerful voice came over the radio, often giving instructions and orders.

Suddenly an excited voice broke through this confusion. Someone reported in the Czech language the beginning of an uprising in Prague. The rebels had occupied the radio station and were asking the Soviet troops for help. Every five minutes came over the air the call: 'Listen! Listen! Help!' Every word went straight to the heart. Burning, driving us forwards. We still recalled the tragedy in Warsaw. The Prague people's alarming call for help did not leave our soldiers indifferent. The tank-men impatiently waited for the signal to march on.

On the roads leading to Czechoslovakia stood strong forces, tank and infantry divisions as well as independent elements that firmly blocked off southern Germany. Our attempts to split up this mass off the march remained futile. At 1400 hours our artillery opened up. Dresden, Radebeul and Wilsdruff came under heavy fire. There was no sparing of ammunition: the stronger the fire, the less blood would be shed.

In the second half of the day the Front commander sent the armies of Generals Gordov and Puchov, as well as the tank armies of Rybalko and Leliushenko into the battle. The whole night and the whole of the 7th May the fighting raged in Dresden and the Erzgebirge Mountains. The thrust of the 1st Ukrainian Front merged with the attack of the 5th Ukrainian Front coming over the Carpathian Mountains and accelerated the attack of the remaining troops to the west.

On the 7th May the tank brigades of the 6th Guards Tank Army under General Kravtshenko and the 7th Guards Army under General Schumilov belonging to the 2nd Ukrainian Front arrived from Austria. The combined assault by the three Fronts shattered Field Marshal Schörner's Army Group *Mitte*. To ensure its final defeat, we had to push into the centre of Czechoslovakia and securely lock the way to the west.

Another day had gone by and we were still sitting fast in the wood. We had received no orders from the corps commander. The radio connection with his headquarters had been broken during the course of the day. A cold, unpleasant rain fell.

What would happen if they needed us up ahead? We had been ordered to remain where we were until specific orders arrived. Laying the blame on the corps staff was not in my character. I carefully examined pros and cons and decided to move on in an hour, and sent out scouts and sappers to the crossing points.

The columns crept forward all night long. It was raining heavily. The rain forced its way into the tanks and the drivers' cabs of the trucks. Neither capes nor tarpaulins saved us from the soaking. Vehicles slipped into ditches, the field kitchen turned over. We had to use tanks to drag them out. But the men overcame the elements. After 50 kilometres we reached the main forces of our corps towards morning.

The rain had stopped, the sun was shining. When the field kitchen appeared the night's qualms were forgotten. Hot tea, barley soup with meat and the obligatory 100 grams of bread had the men smiling again. The general praised our initiative.

The brigade went into action that same morning. Together with other corps' units we supported the 5th Guards Army west of Dresden and our Polish brothers in arms.

Afterwards our way led over the Erzgebirge Mountains. We approached the Czech border. It took an hour to get the brigade together again. The infantry also joined us. General Novikov kept his word and sent us the rifle battalion of the Hero of the Soviet Union Davydenko. Now we had to scale the heights of the Erzgebirge, destroy security detachments and individual nests of resistance, and hurry to Prague, from where calls for help were still coming.

As we were getting rid of numerous barricades, the 56th Tank Brigade caught up with us. With long energetic steps Sacha Sliussarenko came up to me. 'Dima, you must help me out of a jam.'

'Why, what has happened?'

'My tanks are standing still, I have no more diesel. Give me at least three or four fuel trucks so that I can reach Prague.'

I asked our Rear Services and discovered that we ourselves only had five truck-loads of diesel left. That would hardly be enough for us, as Prague was still 150 kilometres away. So, even with the best of intentions, I could not help my friend.

'That is not comradely,' Sliussarenko began to complain.

'Sacha, I can't help you. If we share out the fuel now, there will be insufficient for any of us to reach Prague. And what help would that be to the uprising?'

'You must give me at least two tankers.'

Now Dmitriev tried to convince him, but his arguments too had no effect. Sliussarenko would not give up. Finally friendship won. I could well understand my colleague's frame of mind. I wrote a chit ordering the head of the technical services, Milin, to provide the fuel. Sliussarenko left me smiling. Nevertheless he did not get a drop of diesel, for I did not know that our fuel trucks had got lost during the night and would only catch up with us again just before Prague.

Our route to Prague was difficult. On the narrow, twisting mountain tracks the enemy had erected and mined numerous tree barriers. Anyone leaving the track was in danger of toppling over. We had to clear away the barriers, defuse the mines and subdue the security units.

The sappers smoothing the way for us were heroic. The tanks climbed the slopes with difficulty, the engines running at full speed, and the overheated vehicles often had to stop. Tanks towed guns and the self-propelled guns had motorcycles hanging from them as the infantry climbed the slopes with difficulty.

The radio communications with corps were functioning again and General Novikov demanded more speed from us. Rybalko was also active. 'Don't mark time! Quicker! Forwards! Forwards!' The people of Prague were still sending appeals for help. We understood the rebels. Their impatience had already been transferred to us. Nevertheless it was only with a great effort that we were able to get over the last kilometres of the mountains.

But our efforts were worth it, for we had reached the crest of the Erzgebirge. In front of us lay picturesque valleys and wooded mountain slopes. Here and there red tiled roofs peeped through the greenery.

Suddenly I heard the command: 'Brigade commander to the head of the column!' On the way I asked myself what it could be. Everything necessary had already been arranged.

Soon I saw in the distance some cars and an armoured car. Nearby stood Rybalko with several generals and staff officers. I jumped out of the vehicle. The army commander-in-chief received me with the words: 'Why are you stopping here? Kalinin and Popov are already just short of Prague.'

'We will be moving on in a few minutes.'

'Good. You must enter Prague tonight. Don't let yourself be held up. The fate of the enemy is already sealed but we must save Prague from destruction.'

The army commander-in-chief questioned me on the state of the brigade and about our reserves of supplies and fuel.

'We'll get there, Comrade General,' I assured him.

'"We'll get there" is not the right impression,' Rybalko rebuked me. 'We are going to our friends, our brothers, and as Guardsmen you should be fresh, accurate and fully prepared for battle.'

While we were talking several soldiers and officers had gathered round. It was always like that when Rybalko appeared.

'We thank you for Berlin,' the army commander-in-chief said to the men. 'You are great lads and have fought bravely. Many of you will get decorations.'

'Remember, Comrade General, you promised to come to us in Wilhelmstrasse. We have unfortunately given up waiting for you.'

'How can I make up for it?' Rybalko parried smiling. 'How could I make my way through to you? The streets were blocked. I will certainly honour my word in Prague, God willing, if I get there before you.'

'We will make every effort,' said Dmitriev, who had been silent until then.

My brigade began mounting up and shortly afterwards we reached Teplice.

The town was decorated with banners, and Soviet and Czech flags flew from the town hall. The inhabitants had left their homes and celebrated around us. Everywhere one heard 'Hurrah! Victory!' and 'I love the Soviet Union!' Women and girls threw flowers at us. We experienced the same thing in every town and every village in Czechoslovakia.

The nearer we got to Prague, the more nervous the enemy became. He knew that he was now in the steel fangs of our tank armies. The demoralised soldiers abandoned guns, tanks and vehicles, and fled into the woods and mountains to break through to Karlovy Vary, Plzen and Ceske Budejovice. But wherever he went he came across our troops.

I climbed out of my tank into my Jeep, directed the headquarters vehicles to the head of the column and led the brigade into Prague at high speed.

We reached Chynow, a small village near Prague. The Fascists had accommodated themselves there like vandals, so we were most heartily greeted by the inhabitants. They climbed on our tanks, threw flowers down the hatches and put their arms round our tank troops. A young woman came up to me with a little girl in her arms. The youngster handed me a large bunch of flowers. I took the little girl in my arms, kissed her and gave her the star from my cap as I left. Some of the village inhabitants and soldiers photographed the scene. Especially enthusiastic that day was our cook, who also happened to be the brigade's photographer. Several days later a soldier brought me a picture of the occasion – I still have it.

The last night of the war passed slowly. We spent it on the march. When the morning dawned we had already been standing on the edge of Prague. As we had received no further orders from the corps commander, I unfolded a map of Prague and looked for the city centre and castle, and on my own responsibility pushed through to Wenzelplatz Square.

From the city one could hear the dull rumbling of the artillery and the whipping of machine-pistol shots in the vicinity. Although fighting was still going on in the city centre, many of the city's inhabitants were on the streets.

As we had to reckon with *panzerfausts*, I formed a column. Davydenko's riflemen now marched at the head followed by the tanks, the headquarters and the Rear Services. Staruchin's battalion formed the rearguard. We rolled on towards the Wenzelplatz. As some of the streets were blocked by barricades, we had to make our way through some narrow lanes. Suddenly we were unable to go any further, our route being blocked by a jubilant crowd.

Rybalko's and Leliushenko's armies marched into the city from all sides, each wanting to be first to reach the city centre, liberate Prague and put a final full stop to the end of the Great Patriotic War.

My 55th Guards Tank Brigade had put hundreds of kilometres behind it within the last days but nevertheless the army commander-in-chief had promised that we would meet in the city. With horror I thought what would happen if Rybalko discovered how long it had taken us to go the few kilometres from the city boundary to the centre.

We caught the high spirits of the Prague citizens. We were happy to have got there in time so that the Fascists had been unable to destroy it more.

The streets and squares filled with people. It was particularly noisy in the city centre. The people of Prague surrounded our tanks; hats and tank helmets whirled in the air. The tank soldiers and riflemen hugged each other. Again and again came the Czech 'Nasdar' and our 'Hurrah'. With difficulty I escaped from the hugging and leant against the tank to get a bit of air. I was as if numbed.

Bright red and very excited, the chief of signals came up to me.

'Sassimenko, what's happened?' asked the chief of staff impatiently.

'Radio! Over the radio Moscow has announced that the war is over! Unconditional capitulation. Hurrah!'

We stood there deeply impressed, the smiles vanishing from our faces, everyone looking earnestly at each other. We had the feeling that we had all grown older at this moment. Then suddenly the tension eased off and we fell into each other's arms. It had finally happened! The war was over, all torments had an end.

Tired and hoarse, I stood on Wenzelplatz Square next to my true friend, the tank bearing the number 200 that had not only taken me the long way through fire, but also had protected me from death many times with its strong armour. Next to me stood its commander, Yevgeni Belov. One could understand how the men hung on to their tanks and often spoke of them like a living thing.

The engine of my tank was hardly warm, as if it wanted to give the fighting vehicle a rest after its efforts. I climbed on to the rear, sat on the vents over the engine, leant against the rolled-up tarpaulin and let my thoughts run free.

A blue spring sky hung over Prague. From now on it would ever remain cloudless and the people would never have to look around anxiously.

Rybalko kept his word. Escorted by two generals, by two Novikovs, he had worked his way through the crowded streets to Wenzelplatz. He greeted me heartily and clasped me paternally. 'I congratulate you on victory, dear fighting colleagues. We are among the lucky ones to experience this. But let us on such a day not forget those who paid for this victory with their blood.'

Rybalko's eyes glistened moistly. Vassili Vassilievitch Novikov took his spectacles off from time to time and polished them with a trembling hand. I felt a cramp in my throat.

The army commander-in-chief and the corps commander were thinking of their sons at this moment, who had fallen in this war. Rybalko lost his only son in 1942 and the corps commander his Yura only a short while ago. The war had brought great personal sorrow to both of them. The first day of peace was thus both cheerful and sad.

Prague did not quieten down the whole night long. People crowded everywhere. The windows from which the black-out had been removed streamed with bright light. That night the 55th Guards Tank Brigade would pull out of the city centre and be stationed not far from the Satalice airport. Previously the small quiet street on the edge of town had been a favourite place for lovers. Now all was jubilation and hurly burly. The sound of accordions, mouth-organs and guitars had attracted the boys and girls and all were dancing together.

The morning brought a new concern. The war was over and our superiors smothered us with paperwork. They demanded reports on the fighting, reports on the state of the tanks and lists of losses.

In the Rear Services the inventories did not tally with the records. I recorded the names of those who should receive a decoration. We all had our hands full. Only the soldiers found time to celebrate the victory and the end of the war.

Music came from everywhere. Boys and girls from Prague sang and danced with our tank-men.

The news of a football match that was to take place between a Soviet team and a Czech team quickly made the rounds of the brigade. On the 12th May many football fans assembled in a large stadium in a Prague suburb. We had carefully selected and trained our team. Among them were the platoon leader Uskov, the chief artillery quartermaster Sokoliuk, and the tank-men Schtschedin and Schischkin.

Boris Saveliev was appointed as referee. The brigade staff and the representative of the Prague administration had taken places in the tribune. The whistle blew to start the game. Everyone played with the utmost commitment. Every goal, most of which were against us, raised the atmosphere. My neighbours, the Czechs, became unsettled and slid around and whispered.

Our lads rushed all over the pitch, shot inaccurately and lacked teamwork. But all gave of their best and played fair. The game ended 5:2 for the hosts. I was a little disturbed but was startled to see our friends: the spectators streamed on to the pitch from all sides, hugged our players and threw them into the air. The sympathy of the football fans was obviously with the losers.

After the game there was a spontaneous meeting. The Prague citizens thanked the members of the Red Army. Then I spoke.

'Our team lost decisively,' I said, 'but to lose against you is no defeat. Our game today was one among friends, which is why the lost game does not depress us.'

Finally we sat down with our friends for a cup of coffee and had an animated discussion. As we were leaving, our host, an elderly engineer, said: 'I must apologise for our footballers, they behaved very tactlessly.'

'In what way?'

'Before the game we had agreed everything with you, then the devil took over.'

We had a good laugh over that.

Next day Alexander Besymenski visited our tank troops. For several years he had accompanied the 1st Ukrainian Front on the roads to war. In the Ukraine and in Poland, in Berlin and in Prague – he was with us everywhere and delighted the soldiers with his optimism and humour. Whoever met him was electrified by his youthful spirit, although he was by no means young.

Besymenski had come to us to congratulate us on our victory: 'I wanted to catch up with you in Berlin but you were off like the devil. Friends, let us go out into the open, I have commemorated a poem to you and would like to read to you now.'

We went out into the street. Someone brought out a table and Besymenski climbed on and began reciting his poem:

> The war has ended with victory,
> The hard painful years.
> Unusually long and difficult
> Was my fighting way ...
> Storming forward I hit the Germans,
> Not retreating one step ...
> I stormed Berlin and I was in Dresden,
> And came to Prague as victor.
> Under the vault of victory, under the holy banner,
> Triumphed my soldier's heart.
> My beloved fatherland and its children
> I say often and proudly,
> That with all my strength I have fulfilled
> My holy oath.
> I have stormed Berlin and I was in Dresden,
> As victor I came to Prague.

As if bewitched, we listened to his simple, heartfelt words as they emphasised what moved us all.

The rest of the day I strolled around Prague with him. He had visited Czechoslovakia many times in the 1930s and spoken at conferences. I could not have wished for a better guide to the city. He talked about the Charles Bridge, the Hradschin, the Golden Gitter and the Alchemist. We visited the theatre and walked along the bank of the Modlau. Suddenly a vehicle with starved people dressed in rags came towards us. They all looked the same – shaven-headed, emaciated and tattered. We could not even distinguish men from women. This is what the Fascists had done to the people in Theresienstadt concentration camp.

As our troops were attacking Prague, about 20,000 Jews were released from this camp. As I saw these unfortunates before me, I reluctantly thought of my sisters.

This frightful experience had so angered me that I was unable to sleep. The whole night long my thoughts were of the Fascist beasts, about the danger that had been suspended over the world only a short time ago. What luck for mankind that we had won and put paid to Fascism for ever. All we front-line soldiers earnestly believed this.

Several days later Soviet and Czech soldiers received the Order of the Czech Republic. After the award ceremony in Prague Castle those of us who had been decorated went over to the Hradschin and then over Wenzelplatz Square. Prague was still celebrating. In the meantime the city had changed: the barricades and piles of debris had vanished and the buildings looked clean.

We met members of the army everywhere. The Russian language mixed with the melodious sound of Czech. Many Czechoslovakian officers and men wore the Order of Lenin and the Red Banner. Members of our army had Czech decorations.

I don't believe it a wonder, but a coincidence. During this war I was several times witness to the most incredible encounters. On this day too I was going through Prague with a happy presentiment.

Many years after the May of 1945 I returned to Prague with a group of veterans. All day long I sauntered through the streets and hardly recognised it, the city having changed so much. Our time was nearly up and I would gladly have stayed on. In the breast pocket of my suit was stuck a somewhat faded photograph that had been taken long ago in the village of Chynov. What could have happened to those people in the meantime.

A Czech general heard of my wish to findout and promised to organise a trip to that village. Next morning a handsome officer appeared in the hotel.

'Colonel Petras reporting at your disposal.'

The colonel's unusual pronunciation, as well as his decorations – the Order of Lenin, the Red Banner and the Red Star – immediately appealed to me.

We introduced ourselves and spoke about this and that. Finally I could not hold back any longer and asked him what had been on the tip of my tongue since the beginning: 'Are you Russian?'

'I am Czech, but my children are Russian.' The colonel noticed my lack of comprehension and explained: 'My wife is Russian and as the mother is the most important member of the family, we decided that the children should have her nationality.'

I showed the colonel the photograph, explained its history and asked him to find the girl in the photograph.

'I will try.'

Next day Petras came to me in high spirits. 'Let's drive to Chynov, Comrade General, we are expected there!'

'Have you found the girl?'

'Of course!'

Then we were in Chynov. I looked around and did not recognise the village again. But what hadn't changed since the war? In this village too time had not stood still.

The village inhabitants streamed to the community office. The chairman greeted us. I showed him the photograph. Several minutes later a girl with pitch black hair came up to me. The farmers were sure that this was the girl in the photograph.

'But this one here is blonde,' I pointed to my picture.

'Yes, yes, when my daughter was still small she had flax-blonde hair,' said the girl's father.

The neighbours confirmed this.

We sat down at a big table and I had to answer many questions about the Soviet Union. Again and again toasts were drunk to the unbreakable friendship between our peoples. The girl and her husband did not move from my side.

Suddenly the telephone rang. Colonel Petras was asked for. The call came from Chynov, where they were waiting for the Soviet guest.

I looked at Petras unbelievingly. He was red-faced and scratching the back of his head.

'It is a mistake. How could I forget that we have two Chynovs,' he murmured. Then he laughed mischievously and said loudly into the telephone: 'Good, we are coming straight away!'

A whole hour later a large village appeared on a hill. My heart began to beat faster. No, time had *not* changed it. This was the correct village. Our vehicle stopped on a small square surrounded by tall trees. Between the trees hung a banner with the slogan 'Welcome!' Festively clothed people appeared from everywhere on the square. All brought flowers, just as they had done twenty years ago.

Colonel Petras presented me to the inhabitants. I thanked them for their warm welcome, conveyed greetings from my country and told them about my life since the war. And suddenly a blonde girl about two years old appeared with a bundle of roses in her arms. I could have sworn that this was the girl I had seen before – the same smile and the same somewhat creased eyes. I drew the photograph from my pocket: no doubt, it was her!

All were quiet and watching me. I was unable to speak. At this moment a corpulent woman handed me a photograph. I looked at myself.

'This is my daughter Slavka,' said the woman. 'That little girl on her arm is my niece Alenka. Look, here comes my daughter.' A blonde woman hurried across the square to us.

We went into Slavka's house together, where she showed me the five-pointed star that I had given her in the spring of 1945.

A little later we were invited to a friendly reunion in the town hall. Until late in the night we talked about the war, the reconstruction and the changes in people's lives. Near us sat Slavka, her husband, her mother and Petras. Alenka nestled on my knees. Abruptly Slavka turned to Petras, touched his Order of Lenin and asked: 'What did you get that for?'

'For the liberation of Kiev.'

Slavka nodded contentedly. For her and the others this was sufficient.

The whole village escorted us to our vehicle. The parting was hard.

Our Tatra drove through the darkness towards Prague. Petras sat next to me at the front of the vehicle. 'And to return to the subject once more, Colonel, what did you get the Order of Lenin for?'

'For Kiev and for the Dnepr.'

'Were you in Novopetroviez at General Vatutin's command post on the 30th October 1943?'

'Of course. I escorted our then brigade commander, General Svoboda.'

'Do you remember the village well?'

'From which I drank the water.'

Now I had no doubts. I clasped Petras. He could not understand and looked at me in astonishment. A few additional words were sufficient to bring back to him the memory of our talk at that time.

There are experiences that one does not forget all one's life. The photographs in my album are already faded, but the memories of that time will always remain fresh in my mind.

The Victors are Coming

May 1945 was coming to an end. The fighting in Berlin was already history and the surge of happiness had died down. In the European countries freed from Fascism the people began to take on new lives. Likewise our 55th Guards Tank Brigade, which was located north of

Prague, began a peaceful kind of existence, if this term can be applied to military life. The men worked with saws and axes to erect a camp in the woods.

We undertook political instruction and exercise training, and the soldiers occupied themselves with official duties and putting their equipment in order. In the evenings youngsters came from the surrounding villages to us. One danced and sang, or saw a film.

One Saturday evening, as I was preparing to go to the opera, the telephone rang. The corps commander was on the phone. 'You are to come to Rybalko,' he said.

'In what connection?' I asked him, somewhat disturbed.

'I don't know the details,' replied General Novikov. 'But you are to hand over the brigade and go to Moscow.'

'I must leave my brigade? Please, don't let this happen.'

'It is only a short separation,' the general tried to calm me. 'Such a duty journey I would even make on foot. So don't forget, 1000 hours at the army commander-in-chief.'

The morning that I drove to army headquarters was like a fairy tale – beautiful green, blue sky and sunshine. We drove through an avenue of blooming fruit trees. Silence reigned around us. The vehicle followed obediently every one of my hand movements.

As we approached Melnik, where the army headquarters were located, I handed over the driving back to the regular driver, as Rybalko would not tolerate any officer doing it. A traffic regulator pointed the way to a villa that almost disappeared in a sea of greenery and flowers. The army commander-in-chief greeted me in good humour and led me into a room. There I found Melnikov, Bachmetiev, Kapnik, Nikolski and many others.

I was awarded the Order of Suvorov. I was so astounded that, instead of saying 'I serve the Soviet Union,' I said 'Next time I will fight even better!' The member of the war council, Semion Ivanovitch Melnikov, burst out laughing at these words. 'Dragunski apparently wants to go on fighting,' he said. 'This war was not long enough for him.'

With the Order the army commander-in-chief handed me a letter from M.I. Kalinin. (It was during the war that the bestowing of orders bearing the name of field commanders was customary.)

'That is not all,' said Rybalko, as he congratulated me. 'The Council of War has decided to send you to the victory parade in Moscow. You will lead the tank-men of our army. What do you make of that?'

Conclusion

The Soviet medal for the capture of Berlin was awarded to 1,082,000 persons, which gives some indication of the number of troops involved, including Rear Area personnel, in the actual taking of the city. Over 600 officers and men were awarded the gold star of 'Hero of the Soviet Union', and a further thirteen received their second gold star. The Soviet military cemeteries at Treptow, Pankow and in the Tiergarten hold the bodies of approximately 20,000 of their dead.

What none of the Soviet writers here refer to is the subject and extent of rape committed by their troops within the city. It was later estimated that some 95,000 to 130,000 women were raped by Soviet troops after the fall of the city.